Gallant Sport

The Authentic History of Liverpool Races and the Grand National

John Pinfold

First published in 1999
by Portway Press Limited
Halifax West Yorkshire HX1 1XE
Tel: 01422 330330 Fax: 01422 358645
E-mail timeform@timeform.com
Internet: www.timeform.com

ISBN 1 901570 11 8

Printed and bound by
the Charlesworth Group,
Huddersfield, UK. 01484 517077

Contents

Author's Acknowledgements

I should like to express my thanks to the staffs of the following libraries and record offices where I have carried out the research for this book: Bodleian Library, Oxford; British Library Newspaper Library, Colindale; British Library of Political and Economic Science, London School of Economics; Crosby Public Library; Croxteth Hall, Merseyside; East Sussex County Record Office, Lewes; Lancashire County Record Office, Preston; Liverpool Central Libraries and Record Office; Principal Registry (Family Division), London. I owe a particular debt of thanks to Martin Walker, formerly of Liverpool Central Libraries, for locating some of the more obscure references for me and for his help in establishing the location of the Crosby race course, and to Lisa Murray at Croxteth Hall for drawing my attention to and making available to me the Molyneux papers held there rather than at Preston.

I should also like to thank James Bidwell-Topham, Julie-Ann Lambert, Tom French, Joan Harkins, Colonel Charles Lane, Sid Lawley, Professor J.A. Mangan, Nick Millea, Sir Mark Prescott, Bt., and Derek Thompson for their help and assistance. The *Liverpool Echo* kindly allowed me to use their pages to appeal for recollections of the race course during both world wars, and I am grateful to Margaret Brazendale, G. Crozier, George Gardiner, John Harrison, Harry Lloyd, J. Jones, S. McCormick and Brian and Helen Scorgie for sharing their memories of Aintree during wartime with me.

Philip Waller read through a draft of the text at an advanced stage and made a number of valuable comments and suggestions which I have tried to incorporate. And last, but not least, I wish to mention the team at Portway Press which has made the production of *Gallant Sport* a reality: Geoff Greetham and Nigel Townsend for all their helpful suggestions and support throughout the project, Wendy Muncaster and David Holdsworth for work on the typesetting and layout, and John Ingles for painstakingly checking the finished product and for compiling the index. However, all responsibility for the text, including any errors or omissions, remains my own.

JOHN PINFOLD, MARCH 1999

The Grand National of 1853

Ye lads who love a steeple chace and danger
freely court, Sir,

Hark forward all to Liverpool to join the
gallant sport, Sir,

The English and the Irish nags are ready
for the fray, Sir,

And which may lose and which may win, 'tis
very hard to say, Sir.

(Old song)

'The Duke' by Abraham Cooper R.A. (1787-1868)

Introduction

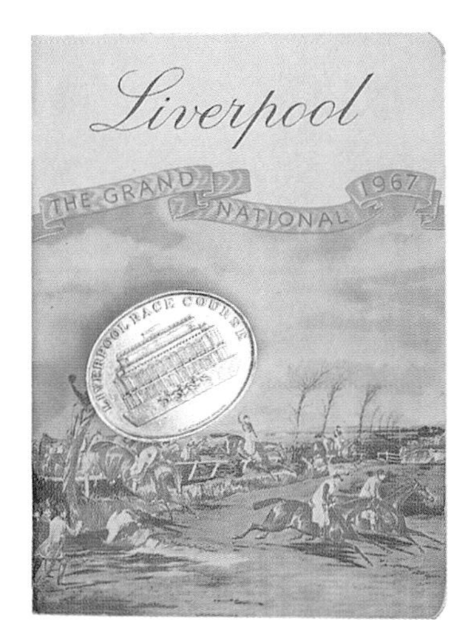

The race card for Foinavon's year and an 1840 proprietor's badge

I first went to Aintree in 1967, when I stood at the Canal Turn and witnessed at close quarters the chaos which occurred at the fence now named after Foinavon, the only horse to negotiate it successfully that year, and one of the unlikeliest winners in the whole history of the Grand National. It was one of the most sensational Nationals on record, and it fired in me an enthusiasm for the race that I have never lost; I have missed only two runnings of the race since.

During that time there have been many memorable Grand Nationals and some outstanding winners, but there can be little doubt that the greatest of all is Red Rum, whose record of three victories and two seconds in five attempts is unlikely ever to be bettered. His first victory, in 1973, when he caught the great Australian chaser Crisp on the line, was probably the finest race for the Grand National in modern times, but his third victory in 1977 was the most emotional and in many ways the most memorable. Hunted round for most of the first circuit, he was still several lengths behind the leaders as they approached Becher's for the second time. However, there the whole complexion of the race changed as the leader, Andy Pandy, overbalanced and fell after jumping the fence. Nereo also fell there, and suddenly Red Rum was in the lead, ahead of the tiring What a Buck. From the Canal Turn on, despite a brave challenge by Churchtown Boy, the race became a triumphal procession as the crowd, sensing history in the making, urged Red Rum home. He was given perhaps the most rapturous reception any horse has ever received at Aintree, and such was the enthusiasm of a section of the crowd that they pushed the railings in front of the stands over and surged onto the course almost before he had crossed the line. So great was the emotion that people wept openly, and there was even the somewhat bizarre spectacle of a representative of

Red Rum jumping Becher's in the 1977 Grand National by Mervyn Jude

Ladbrokes announcing that his firm had lost £1 million on the race and he didn't care!

Sometimes forgotten is the margin of Red Rum's victory that day. At twenty-five lengths, this had only been bettered twice in the previous half century. It should also be remembered that he carried top weight and beat a field that included that year's Cheltenham Gold Cup winner, Davy Lad, to whom he was conceding 9 lbs. It was without question one of the great events of steeplechasing history, and rightly was the lead story on the evening news bulletins and in the national press the next day.

In recent years the National has also made headlines for the wrong reasons. The most notorious of these was the 1993 race which had to be declared void after a number of the runners completed a circuit or more of the course after failing to be recalled following two false starts. On a bitterly

Red Rum's statue and the plaque erected to him outside the weighing room (Red Rum is buried near the finishing line)

cold and wet afternoon, with a strong east wind blowing straight onto the stands, the field of thirty-nine runners was allowed to go to the start ten minutes early, and was then further delayed whilst under starter's orders for another ten minutes whilst some protesters were removed from the course near the first fence. As the horses eventually lined up for the start it was obvious even from the stands that some of them were too close to the tape. The tape broke after catching New Mill House and Direct, and the field was successfully recalled. Lining up for the second time it was again obvious that some of the horses were too close to the tape. It also seemed as if the tape itself was sagging more than usual (possibly because it was so wet) and the starting mechanism itself seemed slower in working than usual. In hindsight, given the delays that had already occurred, it would have made sense to start the race by flag,

The first false start in 1993, the year the race was void

but this was not the course of action the starter chose to take. Instead, once again the tape became caught, this time under the neck of Formula One and around the body of Richard Dunwoody on Won't Be Gone Long. This disaster was compounded when the starter failed to unfurl his flag, the flagman down the course also failed to unfurl his, and a large number of the runners set out believing the race to be in progress. Nine of the jockeys pulled up before the first fence, but the rest continued. As they ended the first circuit there was an attempt by some of the officials to stop them again, but this was a failure, most of the jockeys apparently believing they were protesters running on to the course. Many of the runners took part in this unreal race, but, under the rules, once the field had completed a circuit, the stewards had no alternative but to declare the race void.

This whole affair was rightly castigated as a shameful fiasco, which fully deserved headlines such as "National Disgrace", "The Grand Farcical" and "The Grand Shambles" on the front pages of the national press. The recriminations had already begun, and the report of the Jockey Club's committee of inquiry did little to resolve matters, being widely perceived as a whitewash. Nevertheless, lessons were learned, and by the time of the next Grand National a more foolproof system of starting the race had been established.

Four years later the Grand National again hit the headlines for the wrong reasons when, just minutes before the race was due to start, the course had to be evacuated following a bomb warning. As police and bomb disposal experts searched the course, racegoers were not allowed to retrieve their belongings or cars, and many of them faced difficult journeys home or the prospect of finding temporary accommodation nearby. Many local people opened their doors to these unexpected refugees, and church halls, schools and sports centres were pressed into service to provide extra accommodation, producing scenes reminiscent of the Blitz. Perhaps slightly self-conciously, people began to evoke the "Dunkirk spirit", and nowhere was this more evident than in the authorities' commendable determination that the National itself should not be abandoned but rearranged for the earliest possible occasion, in the event the following Monday. This was the first time the National had been postponed since 1858, when the race was delayed because of snow. It was undoubtedly a gamble, but it was a gamble that paid off as around 20,000 people, many of them local residents who had never set foot on the course before, turned up to see the front-running victory of Lord Gyllene. At first there was a slightly strange atmosphere on

The second false start in 1993

The honours boards in the County Stand at Aintree

the course that day, with very tight security and people perhaps almost too determined to make a success of the occasion, but once the pre-race preliminaries had begun it was little different to normal, although one certainly noticed the absence of the crowd out on the course. The wider public interest in the race was shown by the television audience, which was estimated at 12 million, a remarkable figure for 5 o'clock on a Monday afternoon, and 1 million more than had watched the regular broadcast the previous year.

Curiously, in the long term neither of these events seem to have done the National's reputation any harm. They have come to be seen as yet further examples of the race's unpredictability, and have joined the ranks of the many strange stories the event has thrown up in its hundred and fifty year history, and the most remarkable thing about these stories is that, implausible as many of them seem, the great majority of them are true. For the race is not just the oldest steeplechase in the world, it is the one with by far and away the most colourful past.

When I started going to Aintree the stands contained many mementos of the early history of the Grand National: there was the jacket Jem Mason was said to have worn when riding Lottery to victory in 1839, there was the head of Wild Man of Borneo, winner in 1895, there were faded prints and old photographs of long-forgotten races, and above all there were, and still are, the massive honours boards, which list every winner of the Grand National back to 1837. These aroused my interest in the history of the race, but they also posed a number of questions; why was the race moved from Maghull to Aintree after the first two runnings; where exactly was this course at Maghull; what was William Lynn's role in establishing the races, and why did he withdraw from their organization so suddenly in 1839? None of the standard histories of the Grand National answered these questions satisfactorily, and it became clear that most of them were based

Lottery, but he wasn't the first National winner

The Aintree Stands in 1982...

on sources which dated from long after the events they described. I resolved to go back to contemporary sources to try and establish what the true story was, and this book is, in part, the result.

What emerges is that many commonly held views are untrue: the Grand National was never run at Maghull, the race course there having been forced to close some years earlier; 1839 was not the first time the race was held at Aintree and Lottery was not the first winner; Lynn did not retire from active involvement in Aintree's affairs in 1839; "Wizard" Topham was not responsible for changing the National into a handicap; and Captain Becher rode in the race not once but three times, and should be remembered as much for winning the inaugural running as for falling in the brook that bears his name in the fourth. For what the contemporary accounts show is that the first Grand National took place not in 1839, nor in 1837, but in 1836, and that that race, and all the subsequent ones, took place over a course which was in all essentials the same as the one in use today. The winner of that race was The Duke, owned by Mr. Sirdefield and ridden by Captain

...and as they are now

Becher, and he should properly take his place at the head of Aintree's role of honour. I believe that the evidence I put forward in this book provides the definitive answer to the question of when the Grand National began, and I hope that as a consequence the present authorities at Aintree will amend the official record accordingly.

But the story of racing at Liverpool is not just the story of the Grand National, nor even of the course at Aintree, for there were other courses in the area too, whose history has largely been forgotten. Crosby served as the venue for the Liverpool races for over one hundred years, whilst Maghull, which lasted less than ten, had pretensions to greatness which the original promoters of Aintree were determined to usurp, as much for their own personal profit as for any reasons of altruism. Indeed, had William Lynn succeeded in his original aim of gaining control of the Maghull races, there would almost certainly never have been a race course at Aintree at all.

Nor should the history of racing, whether at Liverpool or elsewhere, be presented as if it was taking place in a vacuum. Over the last twenty years sporting history has come to be seen as an important part of this country's social history, and books such as Wray Vamplew's *The Turf* (1976) and Roger Munting's *Hedges and hurdles* (1987) have done much to place horse racing in its more general social and economic context. However, most of the books devoted to the Grand National have concentrated almost exclusively on the race itself, and have generally ignored the broader social history which surrounds it. I have, quite deliberately, tried to redress this

The weighing room, one of the oldest buildings left at Aintree

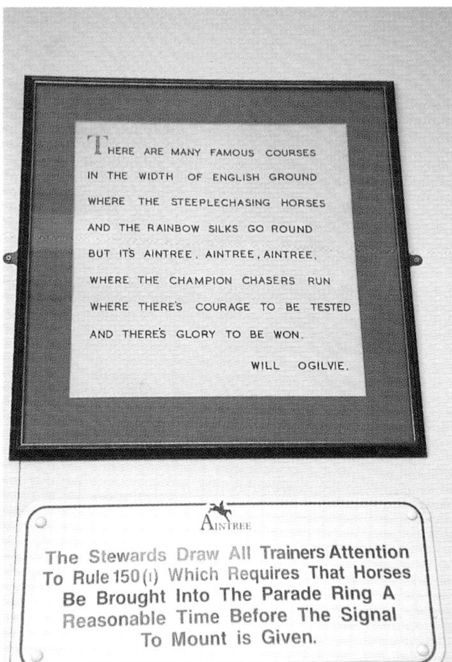

The plaque in the runner's up spot marks the performances of Macmoffat and Wyndburgh

balance by placing the development of racing at Liverpool in the context of the city's history, and giving an impression of what it was like to go racing there in the days when both racing's administration and the crowds were much less well-ordered than they are today. Racing has always attracted its fair share of colourful characters, but these were to be found not just amongst the ranks of the owners, trainers and jockeys, but also amongst the crowds of gamblers, tricksters, prostitutes and other members of the Victorian underworld who flocked to the races as to a gold mine. Their story also needs to be added to the rich folklore of Grand National history.

The unique qualities of the Grand National stem in large part from the course itself. Despite the changes that have been made to the fences over

One of the stable blocks and some of the buckets still in use from the Topham era

the years, it is still recognisably the same as that over which The Duke and Lottery raced in the 1830s, and it is a tribute both to Tophams and the present-day authorities at Aintree that the course itself has always been so well maintained. The buildings, however, have been another story. By the end of the Topham era the stands, which largely dated from the 1890s, were becoming not only shabby and neglected but also unsound. All this has now changed, the result of a major programme of refurbishment and rebuilding which has made the facilities amongst the best and the most modern in the country. The change has been dramatic, so that whereas in 1985 none of the stands were less than ninety years old, now only a part of the old County Stand remains, all the rest having been replaced with totally new buildings. Traditionalists may mourn the loss of some of the old atmosphere, but there can be little doubt that the facilities have been greatly improved and that going racing at Aintree has become a much more pleasurable experience than it was twenty years ago.

With most of the stands having been rebuilt, the oldest buildings left at Aintree are the weighing room and the stables. They are also unquestionably the most atmospheric. It is quite possible that Paddock Yard dates back to the very beginning of racing at Aintree, as a stable yard is shown there on early plans, whilst up in the New Yard the graffiti carved by American GIs during the Second World War are still clearly visible. Over the stable doors are plaques recording the names of the Grand National winners who occupied each box, whilst the water buckets still bear the name "Tophams", over a quarter of a century after Mrs. Topham sold the course to Bill Davies. To take a tour of this area in the company of Aintree's knowledgeable and enthusiastic stable manager, Derek Thompson, is to take a walk through Grand National history.

The great nineteenth century jockey Arthur Nightingall, who rode to victory in the Grand National three times, on Ilex, Why Not and Grudon, wrote in his memoirs "I love to hear the word 'Aintree' pronounced, even in a hushed whisper, for it gives me a few joyous thrills". Those are sentiments that anyone who has felt the special magic of the Grand National can share; long may they continue to do so.

John Pinfold
Oxford, 1999

1.

Early Days: Crosby, 1577-1786

Tudor Liverpool was a small seaport, whose principal trade was, as it had been for centuries, with Ireland. In November 1565 a census was taken which shows that there were then only seven streets and 138 inhabited houses in the town, giving a total population of between 700 and 800 [1]. This was probably less than the number of inhabitants a century before, a decline for which the frequent visitations of the plague, mostly recently in 1540, 1548 and 1558, was largely responsible.

Nevertheless, the town was also a parliamentary borough, which in 1547 had sent two members to parliament for the first time since 1306. The income the Council was receiving from the Town Dues was rising, and some of that money was used to provide public amusements; in 1567 a cock pit was erected at public expenses, and ten years later the Town Book provides the first evidence of horse racing taking place in the vicinity of the town. This records that in 1577 Edward Tarbock of Tarbock, near Prescot, presented to the Mayor, Thomas Bavand, a silver bell worth £6.13s.4d. which was to be run for on Ascension day each year "for ever". The course was about four and a half miles and ran along the shore from "iuxta Crosbie" to the "Banckhowse" (Bank Hall). Four horses were entered for the inaugural running, one being owned by Mr. Tarbock himself, one by William Davenport of Bramhall, and one by a Mr. Sutton; the name of the fourth horse's owner was not recorded. The race was won by William Davenport's horse and he "caryed awaye" the silver bell after promising the Mayor that he would return it to be run for again the following Ascension Day [2].

This inaugural Liverpool race meeting followed a similar pattern to other 16th century meetings, such as those at York (1530), Chester (1540), Doncaster (1595) and Carlisle (1599), where in each case the Town Council was responsible for establishing the races, and the prizes were silver or golden bells. These are the earliest race meetings in England for which there is documentary evidence. In Scotland, the race for the Lanark Silver Bell is traditionally said to have been instituted during the reign of William the Lion (1165-1214), but the old trophy, which still exists, has been dated to between 1608 and 1610. Silver bells were made in 1608 and 1617 for use as racing trophies at Paisley, but the first record of races actually taking place there dates from 1620. Racing at Newcastle, Newmarket and Epsom also began in the 17th century, whilst Royal Ascot was founded by Queen Anne in 1711.

Whether William Davenport returned the bell to be competed for the following year cannot now be established. There are no further records of racing at Liverpool for over seventy years, but racing along the shore almost certainly continued for at least part of that time, for when William Blundell of Crosby "stooped out" a new course at Crosby in 1654 he ordered his servant to "pace over the first mile of the old course of Liverpoole (which standeth partly even with a part of the Crosby course)" [3].

It is interesting that Blundell should have established a new race course during the Commonwealth when it is known that sporting events were often frowned on; but the area around Crosby was strongly Catholic and Blundell had the support of the powerful Molyneux family, so perhaps the risk did not seem very great. Blundell was, however, well-known to the authorities as a committed Royalist (he had been badly wounded in the thigh fighting for the king during the Civil War), and in 1657 he was arrested and imprisoned in Liverpool for a time. After this he went into exile abroad and only returned to Crosby at the Restoration in 1660 [4]. Presumably during this period racing at Crosby lapsed. In any case both then, and for many years after, the races took place only intermittently, and were generally matches between two horses, often ridden by their sporting owners for a wager between the two of them. Blundell's account of a trial and subsequent match at Crosby gives an idea of the kind of sport which was on offer:

"December 18, 1663 – Jack Hesketh, starting at the usual place of Crosby course, and running by Lightheeles stubb (left on the left hand) to Crosby pole, and turning back the very same way, came to the start again in twelve minutes and two-thirds of a minute, as near as I could hit it by the help of a half-quarter and half-minute glass. The horse was the Earl of Derby's, matched to run for 100l. January 11 following, with a gray gelding to carry 15 stone 9 lbs, and the horse 12 stone 9 lbs. The rider aforesaid weighed, when he gave the heat 12 stone 10 and a half lbs.; he was shamefully beaten" [5].

After the Restoration a determined effort was made to establish horse racing on a more regular basis, and the following notice appeared in the *London Gazette* for 12-15 February, 1672:

"...that Charles, Earl of Derby, with many gentlemen of quality within the two counties of Lancaster and Chester, together with the Mayor, Aldermen and Burgesses of Liverpoole, have set forth near the said town a 5 mile course for a Horse Race, which is intended to be run upon the 18th day of March next, and so for ever yearly at the same time; and as it is one of the finest grounds for the length in England, so it will be for one of the most considerable plates in the nation; and whosoever intends to put a Horse in for the same (Horses of all sizes being allowed) must have them kept within the Liberties of Liverpoole 3 weeks before the day, and if he be no contributor, must pay £5 towards the next plate" [6].

This apparently straightforward announcement immediately poses a number of problems. First, there does not appear to be any surviving record of such a race actually taking place near Liverpool at that time; secondly, and more importantly, it does not give any indication of where this ground was located. The traditional view is that it must refer to the race course that was situated on The Leasowes at Wallasey. But whilst it is true that the course at Wallasey was one of the most important in the whole country in the late 17th and early 18th centuries and always received strong support from the Stanley family, it seems much less likely that the Town Council of Liverpool would have supported racing there. The condition of entry that horses should be kept at Liverpool for three weeks before the race is also a strong argument against it having been run at Wallasey, for this would have meant the horses having to cross the Mersey at a time when the ferries were uncertain and infrequent, and when the crossing could still be a hazardous undertaking. It seems more probable, therefore, that these races took place on the Lancashire side of the river, and most modern writers have suggested Ormskirk as the most likely venue. There is, however, a possibility that the course was that at Crosby, not least because this is the only location at which it is known that the Liverpool Council actively promoted horse racing, both before and after this date. Ormskirk may have been too far afield for them to have become involved. It is also known from Blundell's notes that Lord Derby was already a supporter of racing at Crosby, and it may have made sense to him to join forces with the Town Council to promote a higher class of sport there.

In any event, this meeting in March never seems to have become a regular fixture, for in 1682 Blundell, at the request of William Molyneux drew up a set of rules for the races at Crosby, which were to be run each year on the first Monday in August. These rules also show that the course had fallen into disuse during the previous years, and indicate that, as with most other flat races at this time, the race was only won if one horse reached the winning post before any of the others had reached the distance post, which was situated about 240 yards back along the course. (This is the origin of the modern phrase "to win by a distance".) If this did not happen, a further two heats between the same horses could be run, and the winner of the most heats was adjudged the winner of the race; if no horse won more than one heat then the winner of the last heat was awarded the race, presumably on grounds of having displayed the greatest stamina. The prize was generally a silver plate.

Blundell's rules also laid down the conditions for entry. Horses were to be brought to the ground ten days before the race, aired and trained there, and housed and fed within a mile and a half of the course. The name of the horse and the person who intended to enter him were to be given two days before the horse came to the ground to a "qualified person or subscriber of 20s". Anyone entering a horse was to deposit a 40 shilling stake which was put towards the prize money of the second horse, the prize for the winner being provided by the subscribers.

There were also rules governing the weights the horses had to carry, and Blundell sensibly insisted that "riders and horses... be weighed afresh after each heat", no doubt to prevent any cheating. More curious, however, was the stipulation that "a flagon of beer be given to each rider if he require it" before he weighed out; perhaps this was a quick way of increasing a rider's weight if it was needed [7].

The races in 1682 must have been a success for the following year saw Blundell making further improvements to the course. He recorded that in or about that year he "procured a great change in this course, viz. that the starting place (which was also the end of the course) having been formerly on the Morehouse marsh, it was then changed to that pole or corner of the said course which stands on Great Crosby marsh, about 30 yards from the sandy fence or doles which separate the marsh from the holme. This is now (1686-7) both the beginning and the end of the course" [8]. Blundell does not give the reason for the change, but possibly it was to make conditions for the spectators, and the judges, easier.

In 1695 he measured the course exactly and discovered that the total distance right round was 403 roods and 4 yards, or, in modern parlance, 1 mile, 6 furlongs and 148 yards [9]. As each race consisted of two circuits, this meant races were run over a distance of 3 miles, 5 furlongs and 76 yards. To run in three heats over this distance, with only half an hour between them, was definitely a test of stamina rather than speed, and very different from the kind of racing we see on the flat today.

William Blundell, as a Catholic, remained under suspicion for most of this period. In 1689 he was imprisoned at Manchester for a short time, and in 1694 he was accused of complicity in the "Lancashire Plot". He died in 1698, his estates passing first to his son, William, and then, about eight years later to his grandson, Nicholas.

Nicholas Blundell kept a diary from 1702 to 1728, and this provides a mine of information about horse racing, not just at Crosby, but also at other venues in the locality; these included Ormskirk, Aughton Moss, Knowsley

Park and Childwall. The majority of the races continued to be matches as the following entries [10] from Blundell's diary show:

4 January 1703 – "I was at Great Crosby Race where Mr. Masseys Gelding Limber hamm wone a Plate from Pedler."

3 July 1704 – "I was at Great Crosby Race between Mr. Silv. Richmonds Bay Mair and Mr. Athertons Gray."

15 May 1706 – "I was at the Great Plate at Leverpoole where Lord Molineux his Hors beat Mr. Silvester Richmonds Maor."

On some occasions, however, the fields were slightly larger:
16 May 1706 – "I was at the little Plate at Leverpoole where five Horses run for it, a Chestnut Horse belonging to one Robinson in Wales wan it."

1 January 1709 – "...went in the Coach to see a Rase on the Sands between one Hors of Sir Frances Andertons one of old Mr. Harringtons and two of Mr. Charles Harrington; it was Cheefly for diversion and for some few shillings which was layed out in a Treat..."

During these years the Town Council in Liverpool appears to have continued supporting the races, albeit intermittently. Thus an audit taken during the mayoralty of Thomas Bickersteth in 1701 shows that money had been voted by the Council to promote the races [11]. And in November 1705 the Council voted that 10 guineas be given to the Mayor to encourage a horse race "to be held at the water side" [12]. Although it is not specifically stated that this money was to go to the races at Crosby, it seems highly likely, especially as there are no records of any other race meetings in the locality.

At some point the old course at Crosby laid out by his grandfather became disused, possibly during the period when Nicholas Blundell, also a Catholic, had to flee abroad to avoid arrest after the Jacobite Rebellion of 1715. In any case, in the summer of 1718 we find him laying out a new course:

8 August 1718 – "Thomas Syer and I went to Crosby Marsh to see where was proper to set out ground for a Hors Race."

16 August 1718 – "Mr. Carroll Molineux dined here and then I went with him to Crosby Marsh and helped to set out the Cours."

26 August 1718 – "I went to Crosby Marsh and ordered where the Distance Post should stand and saw them fixing the Chear." (This was the Judges's chair which stood next to the Distance post; the Chair fence at Aintree gets its name from this practice.)

It evidently did not take long to lay out a race course in those days, for the inaugural meeting on the new course took place on 1 September 1718, when Blundell recorded that he "was at the Gallaway Race on Crosby Marsh and was in the Chear with my Lord Darby and my Lord Molineux &c; four Horses ran and Mr. Bosloms wan the Plate".

From then on racing at Crosby took place on a much more regular basis. The main meeting was held towards the end of August each year, but there were also occasional meetings in May, July and October, the last to coincide with the annual Great Crosby Goose Fair. Both the prize money on offer and the size of the fields continued to be small, and it is no surprise that most of the horses and owners were local. This was not always the case, however, for Blundell also notes races having been won by horses from as far away as Yorkshire and Derbyshire. The local aristocracy, represented by Lords Derby and Molyneux, were strong supporters of the Crosby races, setting a trend which their descendants have continued to follow with regard to Aintree up to the present time.

Nicholas Blundell the diarist

Blundell does not make clear exactly where his new course was, but, being on Crosby Marsh, in all likelihood it occupied much the same position as the course which is shown on Yates's map of 1786, and which was the one in use between 1774 and 1786. The exact location of this is discussed in more detail later, but at this point it is worth remembering that College Road, which was originally known as Marsh Lane, cuts across the site of the Marsh [13], and that therefore all the courses in use at different times during the 18th century lay in this general area.

Blundell's failing eyesight forced him to stop writing his diary in 1728, and references to racing at Crosby are sparse for many years after that, although that, of course, does not mean that racing did not continue, merely that no-one saw fit to record the fact. Picton, writing in the 19th century and without naming his source, states that "During the Crosby Marsh meeting of 1733 a sudden darkness came on, accompanied with violent wind, so sudden and extreme that the people could not find their way and had to take refuge in any shelter they could find. Many had to remain out all night" [14]. Picton goes on to say that after this the races were discontinued for forty-three years, but this is now known to be untrue, although admittedly racing on Crosby Marsh does appear to have become much more intermittent at this time.

Nicholas Blundell died in 1737, and two years later we find the Crosby races being established on a new course, as the following document in the Sefton Muniments makes clear:

"Articles for a plate to be run for on the *new* course in Great Crosby near Liverpoole in the County Palatine of Lancaster on the 25th day of September 1739 value 30 guineas by any Horse Mare or Gelding carrying Ten Stone saddle and Bridle included.

"Every Horse Mare or Gelding that runs for this plate shall be ready to start at the Starting post of the said Course between the hours of two and three of the clock in the afternoon of the same day (when called upon) and on the Starting word (St. George) being pronounced by the Clerk of the race shall start and run in three heats on the said Course in Great Crosby aforesaid twice round at each heat turning round the furthest post at the further end of the said course or the starting post on their leaving the same on the right hand and running on the usual sides of the other posts. Every Rider shall be obliged to alight at the starting post and be weighed at the end of every heat and if any Rider wants more than one pound he shall run no more nor have any benefit of the Plates Stakes or Betts and half an hour shall be allowed for rubbing betwixt each heat. Any Horse Mare or Gelding that runs for this Plate *and wins two of the three heats and stays his or her distance in the third heat shall win the Plate* but if three several Horse Mares or Geldings win each one heat, then those three and no more shall run for the said Plate or fourth heat.

"Every Horse Mare or Gelding that runs for this Plate and does not come within distance of the first Horse Mare or Gelding at the end of any heat shall run no more.

"Any Horse Mare or Gelding as shall distance all the rest shall win this Plate and Stakes and every Horse Mare or Gelding or his her or their Rider or Riders which shall cross jostle or play any foul play shall lose the benefit of the said Plate and Stakes and pay the Betts. Every Subscriber to this Plate shall pay his and their Subscription money to the Clerk of the said race or his order on Demand and no one shall have the benefit of starting or running his or their horse (mare or gelding) as a Subscriber unless his or their Subscription be one Guinea. Every horse etc that runs for this Plate shall be entered with the Clerk of the said race at the house of Edward Duckworth in great Crosby on the Tenth day of September 1739 between the hours of twelve and six o'clock in the afternoon on the same day. And every Non Subscriber shall pay two Guineas entrance but a Subscriber as aforesaid shall pay entrance only half as much which entrance money shall go to the second best horse etc and every horse etc which shall be entered shall pay unto the Clerk of the said race the sum of *five shillings* and for entering and weighing. *The winning horse* seven and sixpence.

"And this Plate shall not be run for unless three or more horses etc start and run for the same none of which being hired or in any wise procured to start or run, and no person to start or run any more than one horse etc (which shall be bona fide his or their own at least *one* months [*sic*] before the day of starting) upon forfeiture of his or their right to the said Plate. *If but one horse to start he shall have 1/- for his trouble.*

"If any difference arise about the Plate stakes or bets *which is not herein expressed* the same shall be determined by a Majority of the Subscribers there present and the Charges of the person or persons going about to collect the subscriptions shall be deducted or paid thereout before the said race or start to Barnard Stuttard of Much Woolton.

"The charges for removing the chair and posts and colouring to be paid out of the Subscription Money. Charges to be allowed for collecting the subscription money for the plate together with the charges of advertising." [15]

A deep one and a knowing one *18th century racegoers*

For how long racing on Crosby Marsh continued under these arrangements is not known. There may well have been a lengthy period of inactivity, for the next reference to racing at Crosby dates from 1774, when the traditional summer meeting was re-established in some style. On 22 July that year the following notice appeared in *Gore's General Advertiser*:

"LIVERPOOL RACES, 1774

"To be run for on Crosby Marsh (which is a very fine turf near Liverpool) on Tuesday the 2d day of August, fifty pounds in specie, by any five, six year old and aged horse, &c., carrying weight for age and qualifications, viz five years old to carry 8st 7lb, six years old 9st and aged 9st 5lb. A winner of other £50 plates in the present season to carry 3lb extra and a winner of two to carry 5lb.

"On Wednesday the 3d will be run for on the same course, £50 by any four, five, six years old or aged horses, &c. that never won the value of £50 (matches and sweepstakes excepted) viz four years old to carry 7st, Five years old 8st, Six years old 8st 8lb and aged horses 9st.

"And on Thursday the 4th, £50 give and take, viz 14 hands, aged to carry 8st 9lb, higher or lower weight in proportion, allowing seven pounds for every year under. A winner of one £50 plate in the present season to carry 3lb extra, and a winner of two to carry 5lb.

"To run the best of three four mile heats each day and the second best horse to be entitled to £50."

The races were to start at 12 noon each day, and Lord Stanley and Sir Thomas Egerton were named as the stewards [16].

The re-establishment of the races can be seen as part of the general pattern of Liverpool's growth and development during the late 18th century. In 1773, the town's population was 34,407, having approximately doubled during the previous twenty five years [17]; and by 1790 it had reached 53,853 [18]. It was a period of rapid commercial expansion, partly fuelled by privateering and the slave trade, which made some of the leading merchants very wealthy, but was also a period of increasing pauperism. Although the town experienced something of a building boom and expanded into much previously open land, housing conditions for the poor were often unhygenic and overcrowded. In many cases there were as many as eighteen or twenty people living in one house, and cellar dwellings, for which Liverpool was to become notorious during the 19th century, were already common, with 6,780 people (12.5% of the population) inhabiting 1,728 cellars by 1790 [19].

Despite the fine new Town Hall, designed in classical style by John Wood of Bath, the opening of the Theatre Royal in 1772, and the establishment of a library, which by 1770 had 1,547 books [20], the town lacked much elegance or culture. One contemporary writer observed that

"Liverpool is the only town in England of any pre-eminence that has not one single erection or endowment, for the advancement of science, the cultivation of the arts, or promotion of useful knowledge", adding that all attempts to establish such bodies had "produced no other effects on the minds of the inhabitants than a torpid vacuity" [21].

Drunkenness and rioting were common, and it was not uncommon to see "a great number of girls, and many of the inferior inhabitants of the town, assembled in the evenings at various diversions, in the narrow streets and outlets of the town, to the great annoyance of such of the inhabitants as are disposed to a peaceable and quiet residence" [22].

Archery, tennis, skittles and bowls are amongst the sports which are known to have been played in Liverpool at this time, but dog fighting, bull baiting and cock fighting also remained common pastimes. Liverpool even had its own local version of cock fighting, in which, each Shrove Tuesday, a number of boys had their arms tied and then had to catch and kill the cocks with their teeth [23]. This kind of sport appealed primarily to the "inferior inhabitants". Horse racing, however, appealed equally to the gentry and the aristocracy, and perhaps it is not too fanciful to see the re-establishment of the Liverpool races as an attempt to improve the standing of the town and give it a more genteel appearance. The association with the race meeting of a number of other social events, such as balls and assemblies tends to support this view, and it can also be seen as analogous to the attempts which were made during the 1770s to establish Liverpool as a spa town, following the discovery of a chalybeate spring in the quarry below St. James's Walk (now St. James's cemetery).

The location of the new race course can be determined with some degree of certainty, as it is clearly marked on Yates's map of 1786 [24]. This shows that it lay slightly to the west of Great Crosby village, with a stand on the seaward side, backing onto a lane which led along the sands to Hightown and Formby. (This lane would appear to follow the same line as Warren Road, Mersey View and Oxford Road do today.) A comparison with a modern street map of Crosby suggests that the northern end of the course may well have been roughly where Alexandra Park is now, with the west side of the course following the line of the Liverpool-Southport railway perhaps as far as Brooke Road East. Charles L. Lamb [25] records a tradition

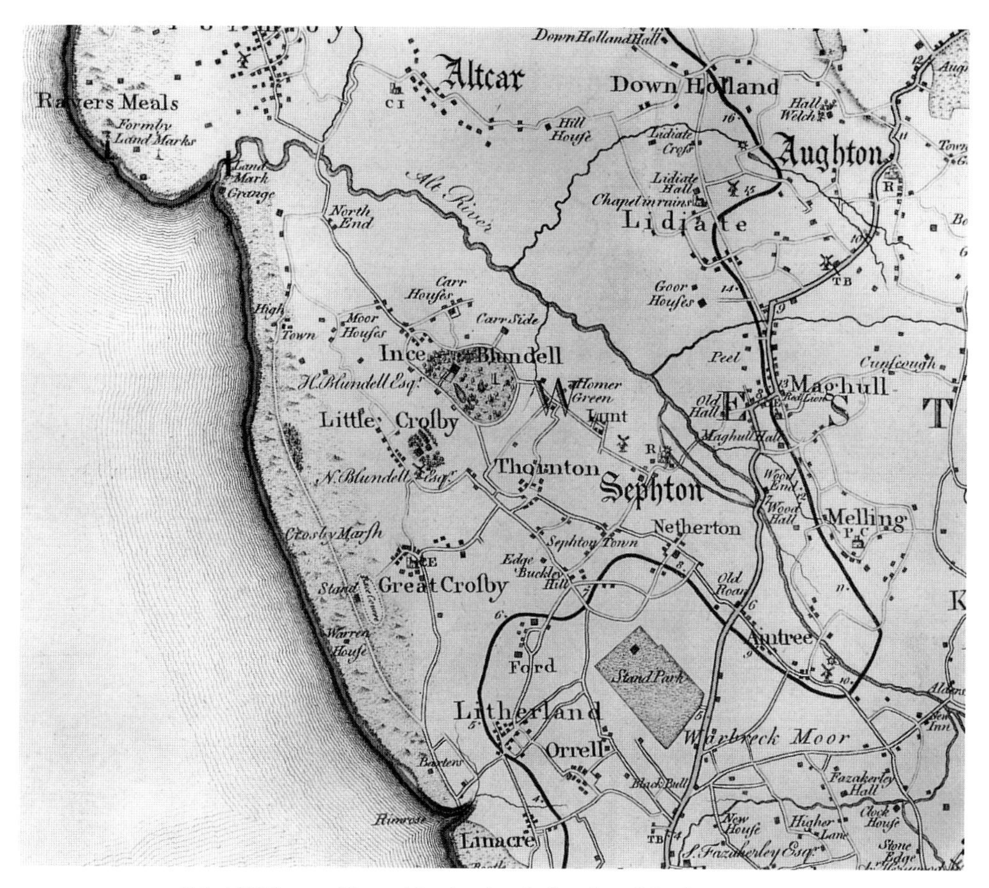

Yates' 1786 map of Lancashire showing the location of Crosby race course

that a large house named "Standfield", situated on the west side of Liverpool Road, marks the site of the stand, and this has been repeated since [26]; but this contradicts the evidence of the maps and now seems less probable, although it is at least feasible that at some point there was a stand on the eastern side of the course as well as or instead of the one so clearly marked on Yates's map as being on the western side.

No picture of this stand appears to exist, but it seems likely that it was not dissimilar to the small stand which survives at Wothorpe, near Stamford in Lincolnshire, and which is known to have been built in 1766. This is a box-like two storey building with a handsome arcade at ground level and a flat roof. The only other similar building still in existence is the small classical grand stand at Sherborne in Gloucestershire, now in the care of the National Trust, which was built in 1634 and used for watching deer coursing.

This part of Crosby is so wholly urbanised today that it is hard to visualise the area as it would have appeared in the late 18th century, but a contemporary description of the new race course makes it plain what an attractive setting it must have been: "Besides the spectacle of sport and splendour common to all races and race grounds, were many advantages peculiar to Crosby Marsh. In sight of the stands and theatrical booths which covered one side of the race ground with colours, streamers, and standards flying, lay the open sea, extending to the Ormeshead, Carnarvon-hill, and Snowdon on the west, unbounded on the north-west, and towards the Isle of Man; the sea was covered with sails, sloops, wherries, and boats, loaded with passengers, discharged at the foot of the race ground; to the east the villages and the Leeds Canal with sloops and boats, and colours flying, with people from all parts of the country and inland" [27]

The re-established Crosby meeting appears to have been a great success: "The multitudes on the ground, and the coming and returning, was a spectacle of wonder. From the winning chair to the port of Liverpool, seven miles extent over the wide smooth sandy level, was continued a train of carriages, horse, and foot, as far as the eye could carry: a nimble harlequin might have stepped from one carriage to the other, and walked on the heads of the multitude over the wide extended shore. The turf is judged by the jockeys to be the finest, and the regulations of the course, the best in England. The horses are in view every foot of the way from every stand, and into every carriage, and both horse and foot, by moving a few hundred yards into the centre, saw every contested push, and the last great struggle and combat for the prize" [28]. The newly-built Theatre Royal in Liverpool was open every night during the race week, and a grand race ball was held at the Exchange at which over 350 people were present [29].

In the following year, 1775, the date of the races was moved back from August to July, and a number of improvements were made to the course. An advertisement for the races stated that "The Turf upon Crosby Marsh is naturally fine, the Situation exceedingly pleasant, and the Marsh is now very much improved, and the course will be corded all round both inside and out" [30]. New directions were also issued regarding the use of racing colours, which it was hoped would make things easier for the spectators, and no doubt the judges as well: "For the greater certainty of distinguishing the horses, &c. and also to prevent disputes arising from not knowing the colours, each rider is desired to declare at the time of entering, the colour he will ride in, that it may be inserted in the list for each day, and it is hoped that the Gentlemen will give directions to their riders, strictly to observe this regulation, and not to mention one colour and afterwards ride in another" [31]. There is a pretty clear hint here that the previous year's races had seen some less than gentlemanly practices, and this was perhaps the first recorded occasion on which the authorities made some attempt to stamp out the corruption and shady dealing which was only too common in racing both then and for many years afterwards.

As in the previous year, the races were accompanied by a series of supporting events. "Ordinaries" (public dinners with fixed price menus) were held at Wrigley's on the Monday, Banner's on Tuesday and George's Coffee House on Wednesday, and on the Thursday morning after the final race day there was a farewell public breakfast at John Bridge's, St. James's Coffee House. Assemblies were held in the evenings, and "Macbeth" was performed at the Theatre Royal [32].

The racing seems to have taken the same form as in previous years. On the first day Sir H. Harpur's grey, Pilot, was the winner of a race run in two heats; the following day Sir James Lowther's Pleader won a race run in three heats; and on the final day Sir Pierce Mostyn's May Duke won a race run in two heats. Fields for all the races were small, and the final day's card concluded with a match between two horses over a four mile course [33].

Sir James Lowther, later 1st Earl of Lonsdale (1736-1802), was perhaps the most notable owner to enter his horses at Crosby in the 1770s. "Wicked Jimmy", the "Bad Earl", "Tyrant of the North", and "Jimmy Grasp-all, Earl of Toadstool" were some of the names given to him in his lifetime, and later he was to be memorably described by Alexander Carlyle in his *Autobiography* as "more detested than any man alive, as a shameless political sharper, a domestic bashaw, and an intolerable tyrant over his tenants and dependents". He was an avid collector of rotten boroughs in the unreformed Parliament and an unscrupulous manipulator of parliamentary elections.

His most notorious exploit in this area was in 1774 when, in the so-called "mushroom" election at Carlisle, he created no fewer than 1,447 freemen of the city in two days, all of whom were either miners from his collieries at Whitehaven or tenants from his estates in Westmorland, and could therefore be drilled to vote for the candidate of his choice. Through means such as this, he was said to control no fewer than nine seats in the House of Commons. The members for these constituencies were known as "Sir James's Ninepins" and had to vote as he ordered them. It was through his patronage that William Pitt the Younger first entered Parliament as the M.P. for Appleby, and Lowther's other M.P.s were generally instructed to follow Pitt's line. In return for this support, Pitt raised Lowther to the peerage, but this was as far as his gratitude went; he was careful to avoid giving such a deeply unpopular man a place in the government itself [34].

Lowther was active as both an owner and a breeder, and he was one of the eighteen members of the Jockey Club who registered their colours for the first time in 1762. Many of his horses were based at Newmarket,

Sir James Lowther's racing stables at Newmarket

where they were trained by William Cowl; and there is still in existence, at the National Horseracing Museum, Lowther's "Matchbook" which details those of his horses that were due to run there between 1760 and 1764.

From 1774 Liverpool Races seem to have settled into a regular pattern, with one three-day meeting in June or July. Exceptionally, and for reasons that are not clear, the meeting was moved, for one year only, to September in 1784. The bill of fare continued to be modest with most races being worth £50 and being run in two or three heats over a two or four mile course. Nevertheless, the meeting achieved a certain status, and the results were chronicled in the *Racing Calendar* published each year by Weatherby and Sons. These show that it was rare for races at Crosby to attract fields of more than three or four horses, and occasionally races were not run "for want of horses" [35]. Amongst the local aristocracy only Lord Derby and Lord Grosvenor regularly entered their horses, most of the owners appearing to be local farmers or tradespeople. Interestingly in view of their earlier leading role in establishing racing at Crosby, neither the Blundell nor the Molyneux families are represented in the list of owners during this period.

Amongst the horses that ran at Crosby in those years, one name stands out. On 27 June 1780 a four-year-old chestnut colt called Tommy won both heats of a two mile race; two years later he again won both heats of his race, over an unspecified distance; and on his final appearance on 16 June 1785 in a four mile race he finished third in the first heat but was distanced in the second, a creditable performance by a nine-year-

Returns from Liverpool Races, 1777

AT LIVERPOOL.

ON Tueſday the 1ſt of July, 50l. for 5 yr olds, 8ſt. 7lb. 6 yr olds, 9ſt. and aged, 9ſt. 5lb. A winner of one 50l. plate this year carrying 3lb. and of two, 5lb. extra.

Sir James Lowther's ch. h. Sloven, 6 yrs old	2	1	1
Ld Eglingtoune's ch. h. Blemiſh, aged, (1 plate)	1	2	2
Mr. Barnes's b. m. Venus, aged	dif		

At ſtarting, 5 to 4 on Blemiſh; after the 1ſt heat, 3 and 4 to 1 he won; after the 2d heat, Sloven the favourite; and in running the laſt heat, 8 to 1 he won.

On Wedneſday the 2d, 50l. for 4 yr olds; colts, 8ſt. 3lb. fillies, 8ſt. A winner of one 50l. this year carrying 3lb. and of two, 5lb. extra. Two mile heats.

Mr. Strode's gr. c. Aurelius, by Herod	1	1
Mr. Bell's b. f. Mary Ann, by Priam, (1 plate)	2	2

At ſtarting, 5 and 6 to 1 on Aurelius.

On Thurſday the 3d, 50l. for horſes, &c. that never won the value of 50l. (matches and ſweepſtakes excepted,) 4 yr olds carrying 7ſt. 5 yr olds, 8ſt. 6 yr olds, 8ſt. 8lb. and aged, 9ſt.

Mr. Atkinſon's b. g. Sparerib, by Hazard, aged	1	1
Sir James Lowther's b. h. 6 yrs old	3	2

old horse running against much younger opponents [36]. Perhaps he deserves to be recorded as the first Liverpool specialist.

It is hard to know how popular these race meetings at Crosby were. The newspaper reports make clear that the first meetings in 1774 and 1775, accompanied as they were by a range of other social events, were received with enthusiasm, but thereafter support seems to have waned. No doubt they attracted their fair share of the drunkenness, disorder and petty crime which always attended such events; indeed at a time when every seventh house in Liverpool had a liquor licence, when there were thirty seven breweries in the town, and when "the lower order of people" were noted for their devotion to "Bacchanalian orgia" [37], it would be surprising had they not. But there is some evidence to suggest that they were unusually riotous, since over forty years later they were still remembered as "so grievous a nuisance that the magistrates... considered the putting down of them as an act by which they conferred a benefit upon the community at large" [38]. A more popular view of the races can be found in a contemporary ballad, which was almost certainly written as a reaction to these attempts to suppress them:

"A NEW SONG ON THE LIVERPOOL RACES

Come attend me, ye Muses, and lend me a Strain,
And I hope your Assistance will not be in Vain;
Then do not be Bashful, but strike up a Lay,
That will Frighten both Vicars and Parsons away.
Oh, old Liverpool, good old Liverpool,
Not such a Big Fool as some People say.

To the Races I give you a willing Invite,
I'm sure you'll be fill'd both with Glee and Delight.
They have Races at Ascot, patronis'd by our King,
So in praise of old Liverpool's Races I'll sing.
Oh, old Liverpool, good old Liverpool,
He would be a Fool, not her Praises to Sing.

But the Horses Start what a Row and a Bother,
Pushing and Shoveing along one above another;
There are Girls on the Course with their Fine Rings and Lockets,

And when the Horses start I'd have you mind your Pockets.
Oh, old Liverpool, good old Liverpool,
May there be Business plenty to cause us to Sing.

We don't care for the Young or the Old besides,
They can't stop our Mersey, they can't stop our Tides.
They can't stop our Races, they can't stop our Fun,
And in spite of them all the Horses shall Run.
Oh, old Liverpool, good old Liverpool,
Not such a Great Fool as yet to be done.

Then let's away to the Races, and ne'er mind the Fools,
That would lay down the Law and teach us new Rules;
And Confusion to those that our Mirth would destroy.
They are worse than ourselves but I dare not say why!
Oh, old Liverpool, good old Liverpool,
Opposition to Dicky Sam is all my Eye.

And when each Race is o'er into the Booths they Toddle,
With Drinking Gin and Ale it gets into their Noddle.
And while your Money lasts they'll use you very Civil,
But when your Money's done you may go to the Devil.
Oh, old Liverpool, good old Liverpool,
He who Spends his last shilling, I call him a Fool." [39]

By the 1780s, however, the meeting was definitely in decline. In 1781 a violent thunderstorm occurred during the races which, it was thought, "contributed its share to increase the indifference or distaste" with which they had come to be regarded [40]. Three years later, in 1784, a lack of entries reduced the customary three day meeting to one [41], and in 1786 racing took place on only two of the three days [42]; thereafter the meeting was abandoned.

Any possibility of racing being resumed on the old course was ended by the enclosure of Crosby Marsh in 1816. It is usually assumed that there was no further racing at Crosby after 1786 [43]. This is not, however, the case, because there are scanty records of horse racing taking place along the foreshore after that date; the sands, of course, provided a sound racing surface, as Ginger McCain was to find when training Red Rum up the coast at Southport nearly two centuries later. Racing took place there as late as

April 1838, when a two-day meeting took place on the sands at Waterloo. All the races were run over a mile on a course which consisted of "a straight run out on the North Shore of Waterloo, the length and breadth of which was marked out by flags, and at the extreme extent allowed for the course a bathing machine was stationed, round which the horses had to make a circuit and return to the winning post". On each day there were two races, run in two heats, but the races "were not so well contested as at the former meeting, from the horse and ponies not being such "good-uns to go", although no pains had been spared to get together a superior bunch" [44]. These events attracted a large crowd, but they were essentially local, amateurish affairs, and by then the main focus of interest had moved inland. It is to these developments that we must now turn.

Notes and references

1. Picton. Memorials of Liverpool. 2nd ed. Vol. 1, p.55.
2. Liverpool Town Books. Vol. 2, 1571-1603, pp.247-249.
3. Blundell. A cavalier's notebook, p.223.
4. Lamb. The story of Crosby, p.27.
5. Blundell. A cavalier's notebook, p.281.
6. Quoted in Thompson. On the turf, p.13.
7. Blundell. A cavalier's notebook, pp.267-270.
8. Blundell. A cavalier's notebook, p.223.
9. Blundell. A cavalier's notebook, p.253.
10. This and subsequent references from Blundell. The great diurnall of Nicholas Blundell.
11. *Liverpool Town Books*, February 1704/05, quoted in Chandler. Liverpool, p.197.
12. Touzeau. The rise and progress of Liverpool from 1551 to 1835. Vol. 1, p.372.
13. Lamb. The story of Crosby, p.40.
14. Picton. Memorials of Liverpool. 2nd ed. Vol. 1, p.175.
15. Quoted in Blair. Some notes on the history of Crosby Races in the 16th 17th and 18th centuries.
16. *Gore's General Advertiser*, 22 July 1774.
17. Enfield. An essay towards the history of Liverpool, p.25.
18. Wallace. A general and descriptive history of... Liverpool, p.69.
19. Wallace. A general and descriptive history of... Liverpool, pp.69-70.
20. Brooke. Liverpool as it was during the last quarter of the eighteenth century, p.90.
21. Wallace. A general and descriptive history of... Liverpool, pp.283-284.
22. Wallace. A general and descriptive history of... Liverpool, p.272.
23. Brooke. Liverpool as it was during the last quarter of the eighteenth century, p.266.
24. The county palatine of Lancaster, surveyed by W. Yates, 1786. (Copy in Bodleian Library: Gough maps, Lancashire 13)
25. Lamb. The story of Crosby, p.34.

26. Thompson. On the turf, p.46.
27. *Williamson's Liverpool Advertiser*, 5 August 1774.
28. *Williamson's Liverpool Advertiser*, 5 August 1774.
29. Brooke. Liverpool as it was during the last quarter of the eighteenth century, pp.268-269.
30. *Gore's General Advertiser*, 7 July 1775.
31. *Gore's General Advertiser*, 7 July 1775.
32. *Gore's General Advertiser*, 7 July 1775.
33. *Gore's General Advertiser*, 14 July 1775.
34. Owen. The Lowther family, pp.280-305.
35. See, for example, the *Racing Calendar*, 1781, p.42; 1784, p.100; 1786, p.42.
36. *Racing Calendar*, 1780, p.56; 1782, p.46; 1785, p.47.
37. Wallace. A general and descriptive history of... Liverpool, pp.184-185.
38. *Liverpool Mercury*, 27 July 1827.
39. Bodleian Library Ballad Collection, item 2806 c.17 (230).
40. Brooke. Liverpool as it was during the last quarter of the eighteenth century, p.269.
41. *Racing Calendar*, 1784, p.100.
42. *Racing Calendar*, 1786, p.42.
43. Thompson. On the turf, p.46.
44. *Liverpool Chronicle*, 28 April 1838.

2.

John Formby and Maghull

Writing in 1852, the Rev. James Aspinall marvelled at the changes which had taken place in Liverpool since the days of his boyhood, fifty years before: "Then we counted her inhabitants by tens, now by hundreds of thousands. Then we talked of her acres, now of her miles of docks. New channels of commerce sprang up, new fields of adventure and enterprise were discovered in the East and the West, and the far off South. Steam gave an additional impulse to the gigantic energies of trade, the manufacturing districts soared to the miraculous point of prosperity which they have attained, and Liverpool was the main artery through which all the imports and exports of the busy lines of industry unceasingly flowed. What a different place the town is from what it was when we old stagers knew it and were acquainted with every face that flitted through its streets! Old streets and old buildings gone, and new ones occupying their places; streets where once were fields; docks where of old were strand, and shore, and forts, and baths; retired villages swallowed up by the insatiable and still growing town; trees, meadows, corn land, all yielding to the spread of brick and mortar" [1].

This sense of wonderment, even exhilaration, at the rapid development of the town was shared by many, but some observers were shocked by the vulgarity and ignorance which could be found even amongst the merchant class. In 1842 the Rev. William John Conybeare moved to Liverpool from Trinity College, Cambridge, to become the first Principal of the Collegiate

Institution. Later, in his novel *Perversion*, he drew a deliberately crude picture of one merchant family: all its members speak with a "harsh and nasal twang", the women are vulgar snobs who turn "scarlet with indignation" when reminded of their more humble origins, and when the men talk after dinner "the conversation turned principally on trade: the price of cotton, the demand for printed goods, brokerage, freight, interest, discount and investments. The men seemed keen and energetic, thoroughly well-informed on all that concerned their business, but indifferent to more general topics: evidently absorbed heart and soul in the one great object of making money" [2].

This view was shared by Ellen Weeton, a governess who moved to Liverpool from Upholland in 1809; and she too was struck by the distinctive Scouse accent: "When I came to Liverpool I expected to have found it filled with intelligent beings, imagining knowledge to be so generally diffused. I begin to discover that it contains as much proportionate ignorance as any little village in England, where perhaps the curate is the only intelligent man in it. How astonished I am daily to find so many more ignorant than myself, so few more knowing... Here, not one in ten can speak their native language tolerably; not more than one in twenty correctly; and of these last, scarce one-tenth can boast any greater literary acquirement than that of their grammar. I thought myself very ignorant when I came here, expecting to find so many wise, so many learned – I find them not... The people here do not seize the opportunities of improvement that so frequently occur – which they must almost willfully reject – Their ignorance is astonishing! It would almost appear as if ignorance must be taught, as if it were something to boast of. Many intelligent tradesmen may be met with in Liverpool, but generally speaking, those of a similar rank in a little village are equally well informed" [3].

Foreign visitors too reacted to Liverpool with a mixture of emotions. In July 1835 the distinguished French historian Alexis de Tocqueville passed through the town on his way to Ireland. His notes show that, whilst impressed by its rapid development and commercial enterprise, he was also aware of the dark side of this sudden growth and of the effect the influx of vast numbers of rural poor from both England and Ireland was having on it:

"Liverpool. Town destined to become the centre of English trade. A fisherman's harbour three centuries ago. A small town sixty years ago. The slave trade the basis of its commercial greatness. It carried slaves to the Spanish colonies at better prices than all the others. The foundation of the United States, the manufacturing development of Manchester and Birmingham, and the spread of English trade over the whole world, have done the rest. Liverpool is a beautiful town. Poverty is almost as great as at Manchester, but it is hidden. Fifty thousand poor people live in cellars. Sixty thousand Irish Catholics" [4].

A graphic picture of what conditions were like for the thousands of poor who flooded into the town during this period was provided seven years later by a detailed survey of Vauxhall ward, which was carried out by John Finch. This ward consisted of 58 streets and 309 courts in the area lying between Scotland Road and the river, and within it could be found iron foundries, soap, alkali and chemical works, 140 inns and beer houses, and a total population of 23,892 people (about one-twelth of the population of Liverpool at that time). In his survey Finch found that 982 families, or one-fifth of the population were living in cellars. Moreover, out of 4814 families surveyed, 1737 were totally without employment and a further 1587 were only partially employed on a few days a week; 1052 families were supported by pawning, charity or prostitution. [5].

In Liverpool, men such as Conybeare were well aware of the appalling social conditions in the poorer quarters of the town, caused, in his view, by a combination of drink, a "want of proper dwelling houses", and a "want of kindliness between rich and poor... leading the rich to ignore their responsibility". He added that "a great deal of the mischief [is due] to the want of innocent popular amusements, and due space for their enjoyment" [6].

Healthy sports, such as Conybeare had in mind, were hard to come by in Liverpool in the early 19th century. A cricket club had been founded in 1807, which by 1848 had a ground near Edge Hill station and played on 51 occasions during the season, but it does not seem as though the game had become a major spectator sport in the area [7]; and association football did not develop into the pre-eminent working class sport on Merseyside until much later in the century.

More popular in the early years of the century were the traditional rough sports, usually associated with pubs, such as pugilism, ratting, dog racing, badger baiting and dog fighting, all of which were common pastimes in Liverpool. They all also acted as a medium for betting. Descriptions of these "sports" are rare, because they were outside the law and were largely working class recreations. However, the Liverpool journalist Hugh Shimmin, himself of working class origins, attended a number of these events, and has left us with a vivid description of what they were like.

According to Shimmin, "not a week elapses in Liverpool in which several dog-fights do not take place, some more or less openly, many, particularly those involving large sums of money, strictly private". These fights invariably took place at pubs, usually at an early hour in the morning, when the police were going off duty, in order to minimise the risk of being caught. There was also an admission charge (usually of sixpence, but sometimes of a shilling); this was done to "help the poor cove to pay a fine if he should be nailed". Fights could last as long as three quarters of an hour, and often ended in one of the dogs being killed. Shimmin described the scene as "simply loathsome": "The growling of the brutes at each other – the cursing of the men at each other and the dogs – the shouts of delight when the dog which an enthusiastic looker-on is backing obtains an advantage – the crushing to the edge of the pit – the heat of the close room – the sound of money changing hands – the demoniacal expression of the men in the pit, and the terrible excitement of all around, carry the mind far away from happy England in the nineteenth century" [8].

It was also possible to see dogs "killing a few dozen rats in so many seconds", or badger baiting in which dogs dragged the badger "through a sort of tube, amid the yells of the dogs and the shouts of the fancy". Rats were sold at 3d or 4d each, according to size, and, if a young puppy was to be tried against them, they had their teeth torn out or broken off with a pair of pincers. This was called "taking out the stingers", and "to hear the creature squeal, and then hear its teeth fall on the flags of the floor" amidst the "cold-blooded indifference" of the spectators was, to Shimmin, "a revolting spectacle" [9].

Dog racing took place regularly outside the town at Old Swan [10], which was also a noted venue for cock fighting [11].

Liverpool was also a town "where honest stand-up fighting is encouraged". However, this was regarded as more humane than fighting "Lancashire fashion", "whereby some have lost their lives and others only their noses". After one "kick buttock and bite" contest at Bolton when spectators sympathised with a fighter who had lost his nose, he replied "Never moind; I boitend off a pieze of his ———", after which "he spat the amputated portion out of his mouth" [12].

Horse racing was not a rough sport such as these, but it was not an innocent popular amusement either. It was, however, the largest spectator sport at the beginning of the 19th century. For Liverpudlians, the nearest meetings (following the demise of Ormskirk in 1815) were those held at Chester, Newton, Manchester and Preston. Despite racing having taken place at Crosby for more than two centuries, the Liverpool meeting had never been one of the first rank, and the area had never become a centre for the sport. It is, therefore, all the more remarkable that by the middle of the century Liverpool had seen the establishment of two new courses, first at Maghull and then at Aintree, the second of which rapidly developed into a major centre for both traditional flat racing and the new sport of steeplechasing. That this happened was largely due to two men, John Formby, who established the course at Maghull in 1827, and William Lynn, who copied his idea a few miles to the south at Aintree two years later.

The Formby family was long established in west Lancashire, having held at least part of the manor of Formby since the 14th century. John Formby's father, Richard, was a graduate of Brasenose College, Oxford, and held the living of Formby as well as being the local Justice of the Peace. John Formby was born in 1785, and also served as the local J.P. As well as owning land in Formby itself, he had property in Kirkdale [13], thus bringing him more in touch with Liverpool society. His Maghull property, however, came to him through his wife [14].

The land on which Maghull Race Course was to be established formed part of the manor of Maghull, which was owned by the Earls of Sefton until the end of the 18th century when it was sold to William Harper, a wealthy Liverpool merchant who lived in Everton and also owned Davenham Hall in Cheshire. His daughter and heiress, Helen, married Formby in 1811 and in due course the land passed to them; they were certainly in possession of it by 1816, and Formby continued to live at Maghull Hall until his death in 1857 [15]. In the summer of 1826 he received a proposal to form a race course on part of the land, and the following February he agreed to lease twenty-five acres for this purpose to Thomas Jackson of Melow House, near Maryport, Cumberland, and Peter Bretherton, a coach proprietor from Aughton, for eleven years at a rent of £250 per year. He himself calculated that this was £50 a year more than he would receive if he let this area as farmland [16].

Events then moved fairly swiftly. Formby himself spent £500 preparing the ground to make a suitable surface for racing. Amongst other things, this involved filling up a very large pit, levelling a wide and deep ditch, and laying a drainage trench "large enough to admit the body of a man" 500 yards long [17]. These activities suggest the land was quite marshy, as later events were to confirm, and this was to cause many of Formby's subsequent difficulties after the race course had been established. The truth was the ground was probably much less suitable for horse racing than the enthusiastic promoters (who also wanted to make a good deal of money out of the enterprise) realised.

Nevertheless, Formby was keen to incorporate the best practices from elsewhere. At a time when many race courses were unfenced, he ensured that the course at Maghull was railed, and that there were "posts to the same extent as at Chester" [18]. By the time of the inaugural meeting in July a grand stand had been erected. This cost £550 [19] and was described as being a plain stone building, with a verandah or gallery on the second story. There was also standing space on the roof for spectators [20]. Although no picture of this building appears to exist, it was little different to the stand which was to be erected at Aintree a couple of years later and which appears in several contemporary illustrations. The old stand still in use at Ludlow probably also gives a good idea of how it would have looked. Two other smaller stands, built of brick, were placed to the side of the main stand; these seem to have been primarily intended as refreshment rooms [21].

The course itself was laid out in the form of an oval and was rather more than a mile round. The ground was dead level, as one would expect in this part of Lancashire [22].

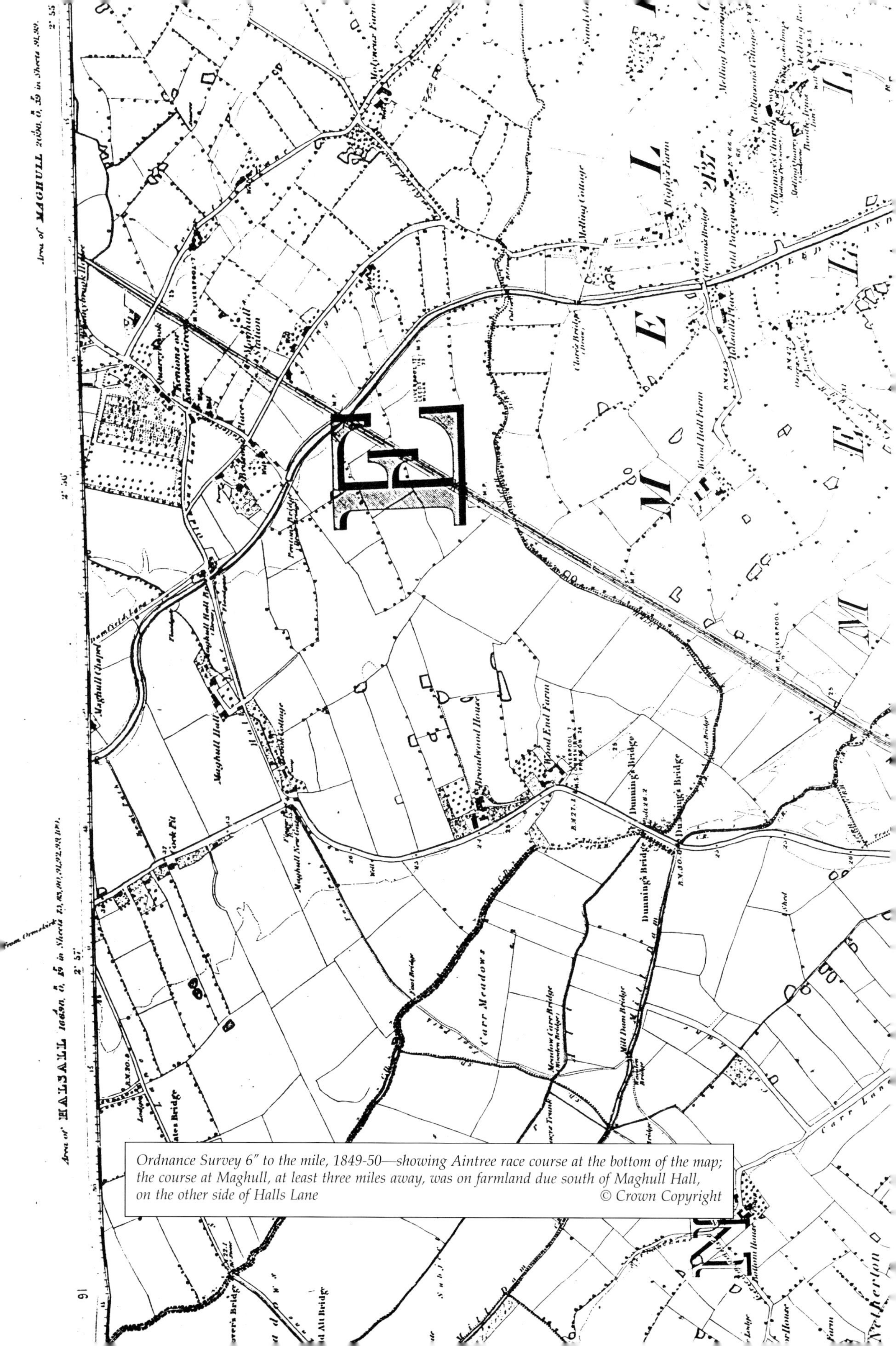

Ordnance Survey 6" to the mile, 1849-50—showing Aintree race course at the bottom of the map; the course at Maghull, at least three miles away, was on farmland due south of Maghull Hall, on the other side of Halls Lane

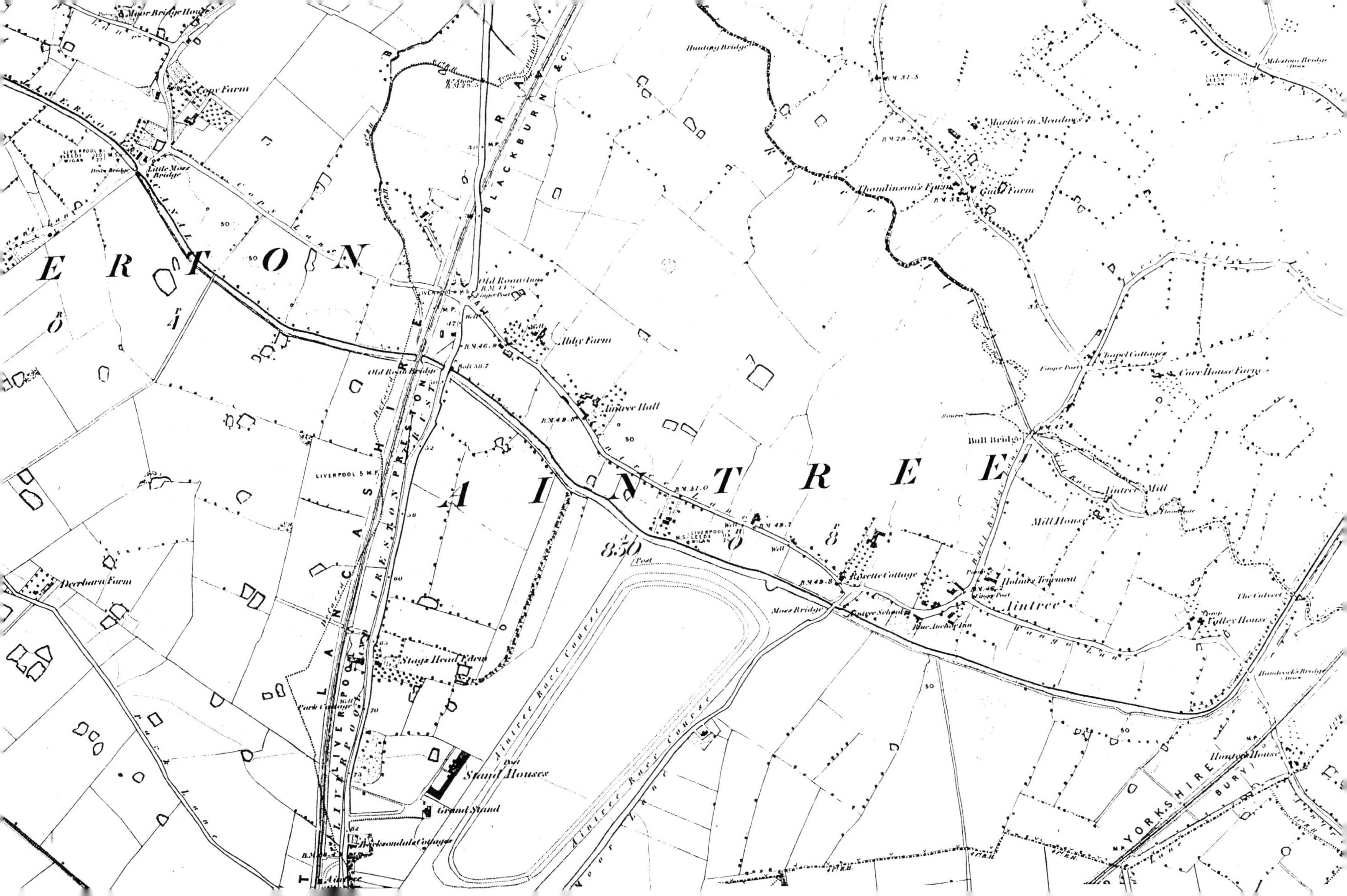

AINTREE
ERTON
Moor Bridge House
Copy Farm
Little Moss Bridge
Hunting Bridge
Milestone Bridge
Martin's in Meadows
Thomlinson's Farm
Gull Farm
Old Roan Inn
Finger Post
Abby Farm
Old Roan Bridge
Aintree Hall
Chapel Cottages
Carr House Farm
Bull Bridge
Aintree Mill
Mill House
Rosette Cottage
Holmes Tenement
Aintree
Moss Bridge
Aintree School
Blue Anchor Inn
The Culvert
Valley House
Hunter's House
Deerbarn Farm
Stags Head Farm
Park Cottage
Stand Houses
Grand Stand
Brooksdale Cottage
Aintree Race Course
BLACKBURN & C.
LIVERPOOL 5 M.P.
850

Teesdale's 1830 map of Lancashire showing the relative position of the race courses at Maghull and Aintree

In view of the confusion which later was to arise over the location of Maghull race course and its relationship to Aintree, with at least one writer implying that the two courses were contiguous, and that some of the early Grand Nationals were run over land belonging to both courses [23], it is important to establish the exact location of Formby's course. Fortunately, contemporary sources make this very clear. The *Liverpool Commercial Chronicle* described it as being "in the meadows opposite the old hall at Maghull... about half a mile from the Red Lion" [24]. It is also clearly marked on Teesdale's 1830 map of Lancashire, which proves conclusively that there was no connection between the two courses; apart from anything else, the line of the canal made this impossible. Teesdale's map [25] also enables us to determine exactly where the course was situated. It shows that the top end of the course was where Hall Lane now meets Liverpool Road South, whence it ran away southwards until it met the River Alt where the bottom turn was situated. It was in this lower part of the course near the river that the drainage problem was most acute. As the River Alt was well-known for its tendency to flood since medieval times [26], this should have been predictable.

'The Meadows' pub, Maghull
Site of the Maghull race course

There is nothing in the area today to show that there was once a race course here. For many years after the end of racing at Maghull the land reverted to farmland, under the appropriate name of Old Racecourse Farm, but the playing fields and buildings of Maghull High School and Woodend County Primary School, together with some modern housing development, now occupy most of the site, and The Meadows Hotel has replaced the farmhouse as the main point of reference. When the last of the old stables and buildings of Old Racecourse Farm were demolished in 1937 to make way for housing on Gainsborough Road the only relic left of the original race course remaining was a low buttressed brick wall, which formed part of the grand stand [27]. The Red Lion was demolished some thirty years ago [28], although the name still survives in the "Red Lion Business Centre", as does the old bridge over the canal where thousands were to alight from barges on their way to the races during the 1820s and '30s. Interestingly, part of the "Red Lion" site now houses the "Chasers" restaurant, but this has no connection with the racing at Maghull, which, as we shall see, was entirely confined to flat racing.

The first notice of the newly planned races appears to have been an announcement in the *Liverpool Courier* on 7 March 1827 that "The Liverpool races will take place on Wednesday, Thursday and Friday following the Preston races. [i.e in the last week of July.] The stakes close on the 1st of May next. Earl Wilton and Sir John Gerard, Bart. are appointed stewards. Mr. T.B. Johnson, clerk of the course. A great number of horses are already entered for the several contests" [29].

The re-establishment of Liverpool races gave much satisfaction to those in the sporting world [30], but as the time of the inaugural race meeting drew nearer it became clear that not everyone in the neighbourhood was equally happy at the prospect. No doubt fearing the threat to law and order a large crowd was likely to pose, especially if alcohol was available, a number of the Ormskirk magistrates threatened with legal proceedings any publican who attended the races [31]. Attempts were also made to get the Liverpool Town Council to prevent the meeting taking place. A letter from a Mr. Bootle Wilbraham was read at the Council meeting on 2 May in which he asked them to "discourage so great a nuisance". The Council's attitude to the races on this, as on a number of subsequent occasions, was ambivalent. They got themselves off the hook by pointing out, correctly, that Maghull lay outside their jurisdiction, but agreed that if any Liverpool publicans attended the races they would be proceeded against for selling alcohol without a licence [32]. In the event this threat seems not to have been carried out, but in the meantime the Council's attitude earned a swift rebuke from the *Liverpool Commercial Chronicle* which, in an editorial stated: "We are sorry the Common Council has joined in the attempt to put down the only project which has ever been started of late years for the amusement and recreation of the Liverpool people... We hope the Common Council will reconsider their determination on this subject and refuse to join in an attempt to suppress these races, whilst those of Manchester, Preston and Newton are allowed to continue" [33].

The *Chronicle*, in common with most of the Liverpool press was a Tory paper, and therefore more likely to support traditional country sports. The *Liverpool Mercury*, which was the voice of the respectable urban middle classes, and which was consistently opposed to blood-sports and cruelty to animals, was more cautious in its views: "Many persons who object to horse racing as a pastime do not wish for its abolition, because it is a source of deep gratification to the people, whose amusements are already too few to admit of abridgement. For our own part, however, we are of the opinion that the people might be amused rationally and usefully without deriving their gratification from seeing a noble animal goaded on by sharp spurs dug into his flanks, from which the blood flows copiously. Horse races, besides, are generally accompanied by the most disgraceful and diabolical of *sports* – cock fighting – to say nothing of the contaminating association of prize fighters, black legs, pick pockets, swindlers and vagabonds, who never fail to frequent the race course and cock pit" [34]. The *Mercury* went on to suggest that the Council would do better to set aside land for foot races, football, cricket and "other healthy and cheering pastimes".

Nonconformists were particularly strongly opposed to racing: "The morals of this town are surely low enough already without being sunk still lower by the introduction of the races" wrote one correspondent, described as a "sectarian Methodist", to the local press [35].

Interestingly, the corruption and chicanery with which racing was associated at this time meant that this was a view which was shared by many sportsmen at the opposite end of the political spectrum. The novelist R.S. Surtees, for example, thought that racing was "an idle lounging pursuit, producing none of the healthful invigorating enjoyment attendant upon sports in which all can take a part". It was, moreover, a sport that "only put money into the pockets of those for whom the public generally have little taste, feeling, or community of interest" [36].

Formby did make some attempts to allay the fears of respectable society by forbidding the setting up of gaming tables on the course [37]; whether or not this particular prohibition was intended to be taken seriously, it was totally ignored on the day. It was also announced that "All dogs found on the course will be destroyed" [38]. This may have been merely a sensible precaution to prevent loose dogs running across the course and interfering with the racing, but it may also represent an attempt to prevent such coarse and offensive "sports" as dog fighting or ratting from taking place at any of the sideshows.

How much effect any of these moves had on public opinion cannot now be ascertained. The apprehension felt by the opponents of the races cannot have been allayed by the events on the Sunday before the races when around 20,000 people took the opportunity of walking the course and the day ended in some disorder with a number of fights breaking out [39]. However, none of the attempts to suppress the races succeeded, and the first meeting on the new course took place as planned from the 25th to the 27th July.

It must have been an extraordinary occasion as many thousands of people, attracted partly by the novelty of the event, made their way out of Liverpool to the course. Perhaps the best way of recapturing the atmosphere is to read the report of the *Liverpool Albion*'s correspondent, which is worth reproducing almost in its entirety (and retaining its original spelling):

"Wednesday was ushered in, in Liverpool, by the early din of preparation for attendance at the races; the yoking of horses and the wheeling out of carriages of high and low degree. Every species of vehicle was put in requisition..., from donkey carts to splendid barouches; coaches, carts, caravans, and wagons were severally announced, at fares suitable to the purses of the several grades of society; and numbers of boats, in addition to the regular canal packets, were fitted up with awnings and stored with eatables and drinkables, for the entertainment of passengers. By far the greater number, however, found their way on foot, a distance of about eight miles. The fineness of the day, after the morning's rain, attracted a dense concourse of individuals, and the whole road was crowded on each side by pedestrians, and in the middle by vehicles, particularly large carts, filled with smiling groups in their holyday dresses. The canal boats, including covered coal barges, were loaded to their gunwales; and the banks of the canal as well as the footpaths through the fields, in every direction, were marked out to the distant observer by strings of passengers. Bands of music were stationed in some of the boats. Fiddlers and pipers plied their weaker instruments in the carts.... Many were the ludicrous scenes which marked the progress of the motley procession, not a few of whom gave early symptoms of their pugnacious disposition, and rolled each other in the dust, with plentiful effusion of loud talk. Several who had begun their potations betimes fell into the canal, to the meriment of the beholders; and no little fun was created by eccentrics, aquatic and terrestrial, amongst the throng who moved to one destination by "flood and field"..." [40].

Those who went by canal could either alight at the Old Roan and walk from there or be carried on a further three or four miles to the Red Lion in Maghull and walk back about half a mile to the grandstand. The canal carriers ran special services on the three race days to cater for the crowds, using their fastest fly boats; these were usually hauled by one horse, but on this occasion, "to make the journey less tedious", additional horses were used. Refreshments and music were available on the boats, and the fares were 1/- to the race ground and a further 1/- back again [41]. Those who went by road had access to the course from the main Ormskirk road. Pedestrians appear to have had free entry to the course, as was common then, but coaches were charged 2s 6d each, and the smaller carts or gigs 1s [42].

On entering the course a no less animated scene met the eye, for the main grand stand was surrounded by an extensive tented village and by all kinds of sideshows, offering a variety of entertainments, many of which would undoubtedly have confirmed those who had opposed the races in their view that they were merely a smokescreen for all kinds of wickedness and ungodliness. Despite the attempts to frighten them off, the local publicans were there in force, and they were accompanied by a motley crowd of gingerbread sellers, jugglers, thimble-riggers and practitioners of other gambling games of chance, pugilists and prostitutes, all there with the object of relieving the crowd of their money. The *Albion* reporter described it thus:

"The whole had the appearance of an encampment, almost every tent being overhung by a flag on a pole, waving in the wind... Besides the tents, perhaps a hundred in number, close to the course, a number of others were erected in the background; as well as theatres of art, dancing exhibitions, and tents fitted up for the convenient rifling of the pockets of those who were hardy enough to adventure their cash at hap-hazard and other games imported from France. For the entertainment of the fancy, caravans were also opened, in which the art pugilistic was exhibited by the milling gentry. The quantity of ale and spirits sent to the ground was, we are told, very great...

"The ground at first sight did not appear to be very densely peopled; but a nearer acquaintance confirmed the conjecture that at least twenty to thirty thousand occupied the booths and surrounding land. Inumerable were the vehicles stationed, with spectators, at the ropes on both sides near the push; but there were only a comparatively small sprinkling of handsome equipages – an indication of the indecision of the gentry as to the respectability of these races. By far the greater number of carriages were carts, chiefly waterside conveniences from Liverpool, with a number of country vehicles. These were occupied partly by the passengers who came by them, and partly by spectators, admitted for pence, to obtain a sight of the race from an altitude of three feet; and we observed bevies of country lassies whose rosy cheeks and smiling looks betokened the hilarity that was going on in their little hearts. There were only one or two carriages and four; but the interior of the course exhibited many fair specimens of hackney-coaches, gigs, curricles, phaetons, cars, buggies, tandems, barouches, wagons, butchers' carts, milk carts and donkey chaises. The bucks of Liverpool and the neighbourhood also looked very large in their boots and spurs, and galloped and trotted and cantered their tits in every direction during the day, to the no small endangerment of the precious bodies of poor pedestrians... In addition to the publicans' tents, there were numerous stands, covered with blankets, for the sale of "best Ormskirk gingerbread", and in every corner the attention of the passenger was arrested by bands of music, soloes on the bagpipe and hurdy gurdy, dancing children, and Chinese jugglers, tossing brass balls and carving knives, to the wonderment of the staring multitude, and ever and anon soliciting donations from those who have derived a certain distinction from the ease with which they part with their money. A deeper game was, however, playing in the tents at the back ground, fitted up with handsome tables, decorated with gilded hazard-boards and finely painted covers, for the amusement of gamblers. At one of these individuals risked their ten shillings and pounds upon the cast of a die; and the banker exhibited a perfect heap of sovereigns enclosed by two hills of silver, and was extremely dexterous in sweeping the board of the superfluous cash of the adventurers. Among the humbler administrators to the speculative taste of John Bull... were providers of rings, nine pins, whirligigs, thimbles, and similar nondescript ingenious contrivances... Swinging-boats, round-abouts, and cars whirling like buckets on a water-wheel were in great repute amongst the youngsters and country lasses...

"To diversify the scene, pugilistic contests between twain votaries of Bacchus drew the vacant spectators here and there into knots; and this truly English amusement, with its usual accompaniments of bloody noses, black eyes, and vociferous talk, thickened towards the approach of night. Amidst all this mass of uproar and confusion, there, however, observed numerous groups of respectable individuals who kept aloof from the scenes of hilarity, and enjoyed the prospect and the race; some in vehicles, others on foot. Amongst these were numbers of genteel females, and whole families, young and old. Many of them obtained comfortable seats in the carts ranged along the line of the course. The frail sisterhood, distinguished by their gaudy dresses and their rouge and feathers, were also seen in handsome hackney barouches, with postillions in flashy jackets" [43]. This is a clear reference to something that was to be a feature of race meetings at both Maghull and Aintree for many years to come, namely the attendance of large numbers of Liverpool's prostitutes, and it seems highly likely that some of the tents on the course formed temporary brothels for the duration of the meeting.

Amongst all the activities going on, one in particular deserves rescuing from obscurity. Perhaps bored with waiting for the racing to begin, one man was observed walking round the course backwards. He had apparently undertaken for a bet to go round the course six times in an hour, three times walking backwards and three times walking "in the usual mode". Sadly, it is not known whether he won his bet or not [44].

After this build up, the racing itself seems to have been something of an anti-climax. Three races took place, a 2 mile sweepstakes for non-thoroughbred horses, a 2 mile handicap for three and four year olds, and a maiden plate of 2 miles, run as two heats on the traditional pattern. The fields were small and the *Albion* correspondent dismissed the racing as "of little interest, nothing like a notable contest having taken place" [45]. Another observer, however, was more charitable, commenting that "All the races were well contested... The day passed off with the best possible effect; every one with whom we have conversed on the subject being charmed with the universal good-humour which prevailed throughout the assembled multitudes" [46]. The first race took place a little after 3pm and was won by Mr. Hudson's four year old filly, Miracle. The other two winners on this first day's racing at Maghull were Predictor, owned by Mr. Thompson, and Sir Thomas Stanley's Grand Duke Nicholas.

At the end of the first day Formby and Bretherton could feel well satisfied with the way things had gone, and the second day of the meeting, at which the principal races were to be run, was eagerly anticipated. In the event, however, the second day turned out to be an almost total disaster, being attended by circumstances which nearly killed off the races at birth and which would colour people's perceptions of them for years to come. The agent of this disaster, as in 1733 and 1781, was the weather. From early in the morning to late at night the course was drenched in heavy rain, and the lack of adequate drainage soon turned the ground into a quagmire, in which spectators were seen standing knee-deep in mud. Conditions deteriorated rapidly, producing scenes which must have far exceeded the worst fears of those who had opposed the races from the beginning. The resulting chaos must have seemed a heaven-sent opportunity to the local reporters, and the *Albion*'s man rose to the occasion magnificently:

"The rain... did not deter thousands of Liverpool folk from going by machines, in boats, and on foot, to the ground. Some, indeed, fortunately returned in despair before they reached the spot; but the greater number were obstinate in pursuit of the gratification of their curiosity, and reached the ground drenched with the rain, against which covered carts and umbrellas offered but a feeble shield. The tents, of course, became densely crowded, and wet without demanded wet within. The ale taps and spirit bottles were plied with unusual activity, and probably double the quantity of the preceding day was served to noisy and disappointed customers. The tents, poorly contrived, became loaded with water in the bagging of the roof, and streams rushed down upon the heads of the distressed guests, from which few could escape. The ground forming the floors was in some places ankle deep. The dresses of the females, particularly those in white, soon became soiled by the penetrating element; and those of the men, who at first deemed themselves invulnerable, soon exhibited similar symptoms of spoliation. The torrent never ceased; and the whole ground, particularly the grand stand, being of a clayey nature and flat, was under water, and became a complete puddle. Numbers of persons were running helter skelter from tent to tent in search of shelter; and many were the falls in the mud, the footing becoming extremely slippery. During the whole day, the most ludicrous scenes continued to present themselves on every side. Thousands were drenched to the skin; and thousands, some sober, and some "o'er all the ills of life victorious", fell and rolled promiscuously in the mire. The races, notwithstanding, were run with spirit, and were witnessed chiefly from the tents, a few persons only who were before drenched venturing to the ropes. Some offered up copious libations to the god of noise and mirth, as if in revenge for the unrelenting state of the weather; and many, jaded out and wet through, lay down on the wet floors of the tents, and under the still wetter hedges and walls. It is impossible to convey an adequate idea of the miserable plight of the thousands who strove against wind and mud and rain to regain their domiciles in Liverpool. Some lay on the road side, in exhaustion and despair, and others, well primed, sang and laughed aloud as they traversed along, each enjoying the cooling benefits of the shower bath. The plight of the females was truly pitiable. The uplifted outside petticoat was of no avail to avert the calamities of the storm; and bedaubed and bedrizzled dresses, that were erst so gay and gaudy, were coated with a layer of mud to the shoulders. Never before was there a scene so remarkable as that which presented itself on the Kirkdale road, by which the draggle-tailed thousands poured into the town; and the astonished cats could scarcely recognise their friends and relatives in their mire-covered habiliments.

"Amongst the thousands of females who were caught in the deluge, without a means of bettering their situation, many were splendidly and fashionably dressed; and all, even the country lasses, displayed their several wardrobes of finery, in blond and Urling's lace, silks of various make, and ribbons from the embossed, or beautifully woven French, to the plain "love". Lamentable was the destruction caused by the watery element to every description of holyday apparel. The broad-cloth of the males appeared, indeed, where thoroughly drenched by upright exposure, to less disadvantage than the habiliments of those gentlemen who had lost their footing in the slippery and puddled fields, and had embraced mother earth. But the slender garments of the ladies gave more distinctive declaration of the unrelenting havoc of the storm; and starch and gum giving way, obedient to the softening influence of the rain, their dresses collapsed, and, in a short time, exhibited the form divine in almost unconcealed charms. We have heard several estimates made of the spoliation to clothes, female robes, bonnets, and caps; and are inclined to believe that the damage would (including the injury to broad-cloth, hats, &c.) amount to several thousand pounds.

"Many of the females, with the precaution of good housewives, kilted their petticoats up to their knees and toddled along with cautious steps; and the "young chevaliers" had an opportunity of obtaining a modest glimpse at legs feminine of the most elegant and delicate taper... Some, by repeated fall, were bedaubed from crown to toe; many lost their shoes; and many were the slender Sunday shoes and boots which, becoming like tripe with the wet, took leave of the feet of the wearers. In some parts the mud was knee deep, and many females, by unavoidable falls, had all their outward apparel drawn or torn off and appeared in their stays; so that the spectators might behold the other half of the charms their downcast modesty concealed" [47].

In view of the appalling conditions, it is remarkable that any racing took place at all, and it seems unlikely that many in the crowd took much notice of the results: Sir Thomas Stanley's Catton won the Great Lancashire Stakes, run over a mile and a half; and Sir William Wynne's Signora took the principal race of the meeting, the Gold Cup, run over three miles and a distance. One not unsympathetic observer noted that the heavy state of the ground and the pace at which they went caused the horses much distress, and added that "if the horses presented a pitiful appearance, the jockeys were not in much better plight: they were literally covered with dirt and drenched with wet – they were really objects for compassion" [48].

On the third day conditions were calmer, and, seemingly undeterred by the debacle of the previous day, large crowds again flocked to the course to see a programme of three races, including one confined to hunters, in which Formby himself had a runner (it came third).

Thus ended what Formby grandly (and inaccurately) called "The First Liverpool Races" [49]. If the races constituted less of a general threat to law and order than had been feared, it nevertheless remained true that they attracted many members of the criminal fraternity. Despite the presence of a large number of constables on the course, pickpockets were active throughout the meeting (as indeed they still are at major meetings today), and there were many instances of robberies in the tents. It also proved impossible to prevent the attendance of thimble-riggers and other tricksters, and even those otherwise favourable to the races thought that greater efforts should have been made to keep them off the course [50].

Especially after the events of the second day, Formby received a good deal of criticism for his conduct of the meeting and the facilities, or lack of them, which he had provided. Whilst admitting that "the Course, and its requisite accommodations, were by no means perfect", he himself felt that the meeting "went off remarkably well, gave general satisfaction, and finished without the least accident" [51]. In fact, there had been one fatality, that of a stone mason who fell in the canal and drowned on his way home during the storm [52], but Formby was probably right not to take any responsibility for an accident that took place away from the course itself and was almost certainly attributable to drunkenness.

The reaction of the crowd to the racing itself is harder to judge. The *Albion*'s correspondent noted a certain lack of enthusiasm, which he attributed partly to the smallness of the fields, and partly to "the novelty of the scene to a Liverpool assemblage" [53].

Despite all the problems he had encountered, Formby does not appear to have lost any money through his venture [54], and he immediately set about planning for the renewal of the meeting the following year. However, "owing to several unforeseen incidents", the planned improvements were "scarcely complete" by the time the 1828 meeting was due to take place [55]. With the events of the preceding year still fresh in people's minds, this meeting was looked forward to "with a degree of anxiety not usually felt respecting similar events" [56], and Formby's inability to complete the improvements to the grand stand in particular can have done nothing to allay the general sense of unease which increasingly began to manifest itself as the time of the races approached.

Fear of another disaster on the scale of the one the year before finally forced some of the leading supporters of the races to act. Just a few weeks before the meeting was due to take place one of the stewards, Richard Willis, called a meeting of interested parties to establish a committee which would take over the management of the races from Formby and his associates (although Formby of course would have retained ownership of the course and continued to receive rent for it). They then sent off the following letter to Formby:

"Rotunda Committee Room,
19th July, 1828.

Sir,

At a Committee of Gentlemen for conducting the approaching Races, it was considered desirable to impress upon you, as joint proprietor of the Grand Stand, the necessity of turning your attention to its fitness for the reception of company, in case the weather should prove wet and unfavorable. At the last meeting, considerable inconvenience was sustained, and it is thought that your own interest, as well as the prosperity of the Races, are so intimately connected with the fitness of the stand, that we trust you will immediately endeavour to improve it.

Sir, your obedient Servant,

WILLIAM FLETCHER, Pres." [57]

Already rumours were beginning to circulate to the effect that the Committee were proposing to move the races elsewhere, and in his reply Formby sought to persuade them not to do so. His main argument was that he would lose a great deal of money – he quoted a figure of £1000 – if this were to happen. To this the Committee somewhat loftily replied that their only concern was "to secure the success and respectability of the ensuing Races, by arrangements for ensuring the safety and increasing the accommodation of the public" [58].

It was in this atmosphere of unease and uncertainty that the July 1828 meeting took place. The weather was once again all-important. During the week beforehand it rained heavily and almost continuously, giving rise to fears that the ground would be "so swampy as to make it almost inaccessible, and certainly to take away every feature of enjoyment from the sports" [59]. However, a break in the weather immediately before the races enabled the ground to dry out to a certain extent, and it was thought that "with the exception of the lower parts, near Netherton" [60] it was in tolerably good condition by the start of the meeting on Wednesday, 23 July.

To begin with, Formby's luck seems to have held. On the first day the rain held off until the end of the afternoon, and a five race card was successfully completed. Disappointingly, however, the principal race of the day, the Waterloo Gold Cup, run over 2 miles and a distance, and with 100 sovereigns added prize money, attracted only two runners and cannot have been much of a spectacle as it was won "off hand" by Corsair who had led throughout.

By means of a petition signed by over 300 people, Formby had persuaded the Liverpool Town Council to overcome their qualms the previous year and sponsor the main race of the second day, the Town Plate, which was worth 120 guineas to the winner and 30 guineas to the runner-up [61]; this was won by Sir Thomas Stanley's Grenadier. Once again, the rain held off, and the day passed off uneventfully.

On the third and last day, however, the rains returned and with them the same chaotic scenes of the previous year. Despite the fact that part of the course was "more than fetlock deep in mud" [62], the programme was again completed, the principal race being the Tradesmen's Gold Cup, worth 100 guineas, plus a further 30 guineas from the Corporation.

There seems to have been general disappointment in the sporting world that the Maghull meeting had once again fallen short of expectation, and local pride was hurt that the "Liverpool Races" did not have the same status as those held at Manchester or Newton. Even Formby admitted that "things were not exactly as might have been wished at the Races" [63], and this view was echoed by more impartial observers. The *Liverpool Chronicle*, for example, said in an editorial that "We wish it were in our power to speak in terms of commendation of every thing connected with the establishment of these races; but our attention has been called by several correspondents to certain practices, which also fell under our own observation, which it is the duty of those who undertake the affairs of such meetings to use their utmost exertions to suppress". The *Chronicle* promised to raise these matters with the managers of the races "whether on the present course at Maghull or elsewhere" [64].

The Racing Committee, chaired by William Fletcher, took a much less charitable view. They seem to have had enough of Formby and his associates, and once the meeting was over they began to take active steps

Lynn's Waterloo Hotel in Ranelagh Street, Liverpool

to move the races to a new venue. Unfortunately for Formby, they did not have very far to look, for it was precisely at this juncture that William Lynn, the landlord of the Waterloo Hotel in Liverpool, brought forward plans to establish a rival course a few miles to the south of Maghull, at Aintree.

There is a suspicion – although it can be no more than that - that some of the more disaffected members of the Committee may have secretly encouraged Lynn to put forward his plans for Aintree in the first place, for it can be shown that he was better known to them than was at first apparent, through a shared interest in another sport for which south west Lancashire was to become famous, that of hare coursing.

Despite a recent revival, coursing, although still legal, is now regarded by many people as barely respectable; its meetings go largely unreported in the national press, and many of them are held clandestinely to avoid attracting attention. In the early 19th century, however, it was quite different. Then it was a sport that was both popular and respectable, supported by many of the aristocracy and gentry. Indeed, even Queen Victoria asked for the famous triple winner of the Waterloo Cup, Master McGrath, to be presented to her at Windsor, long after she had ceased taking any interest in horse racing, even at Royal Ascot.

Locally the principal supporters of hare coursing were the Earls of Sefton, and in 1825 Lord Molyneux, later the 3rd Earl of Sefton, founded the Altcar Coursing Club which rapidly became one of the most important promoters of the sport in the country. Amongst its members were Richard Willis of Halsnead (between Whiston and Cronton), the steward of the Maghull races who had called the meeting which established the Racing Committee, Sir Thomas Massey Stanley of Hooton, who was the leading owner at Maghull, E.G. Hornby, who was later to serve on the Aintree Racing Committee, and of course Lord Molyneux himself, who, for financial reasons, would have been glad to see the race course transferred from Formby's land to his own. One of the rules of the Altcar Club was that "The members of the Club are to dine together, in Liverpool, at six o'clock on the day preceding each meeting" [65], and these dinners were held at Lynn's Waterloo Hotel [66]. A keen supporter of coursing himself, Lynn was surely welcome to join his guests, and it is not impossible to imagine the talk turning to the Liverpool races, and how Lynn might be able to wrest control of them from Formby and then move them from Maghull to Aintree. Formby himself seems to have suspected something of the sort, for he wrote afterwards that "some suspicious movements" on the part of some of the Racing Committee members had led him to believe that they were primarily interested in the "promotion of their own private views or interest" through the establishment of another race course; with hindsight, he believed that they had acted "in a secret, and... not very honourable way" [67].

Whatever the truth of the matter, and whoever first suggested Aintree as an alternative venue, William Lynn was swiftly to make the project very much his own, and it is entirely appropriate that he should be regarded today as its true founder.

Notes and references

1. Aspinall. Liverpool a few years since, pp.186-187.
2. Conybeare. Perversion, ch.14.
3. Weeton. Journal of a governess, pp.169-170.
4. Tocqueville. Journeys to England and Ireland, p.110.
5. Finch. Statistics of Vauxhall ward, pp.9-13.
6. Conybeare. Perversion, ch.14.
7. Walker. The Liverpool Competition, pp.7-13.
8. Shimmin. Liverpool life, pp.77-82.
9. Shimmin. Liverpool life, p.71-77.
10. Shimmin. Liverpool life, p.79.
11. Hoult. West Derby and Old Swan, p.8.
12. *Annals of Sporting and Fancy Gazette*, Vol. 12, 1827, p.27 and Vol. 13, 1828, p.40.
13. *Gore's Directory*, 1827.
14. Foster. Pedigrees of the county families of England. Vol. 1. Lancashire.
15. Victoria History of the County of Lancaster. Vol. 3, p.219; Foster. Pedigrees of the county families of England. Vol. 1. Lancashire.
16. Formby. An account of the Liverpool races, pp.3,8.
17. Formby, pp.8-9.
18. Formby, p.9.
19. Formby, p.9.
20. *Liverpool Courier*, 1 August 1827.
21. *Liverpool Courier*, 1 August 1827.
22. *Liverpool Courier*, 1 August 1827.
23. Bird. A hundred Grand Nationals, p.10.
24. *Liverpool Commercial Chronicle*, 28 July 1827.
25. A map of the county palatine divided into hundreds and parishes, from an actual survey made in the years 1828 and 1829. (Copy in Bodleian Library: (E) C17: 37 (51))
26. Lofthouse. Lancashire villages, p.59.

27. *Liverpool Echo*, 18 February 1937; Rowlands. Lydiate and Maghull in times past, p.29.
28. Rowlands. Lydiate and Maghull in times past, p.18.
29. *Liverpool Courier*, 7 March 1827.
30. *Liverpool Mercury*, 2 March 1827.
31. *Liverpool Commercial Chronicle*, 5 May 1827.
32. *Liverpool Courier*, 8 May 1827.
33. *Liverpool Commercial Chronicle*, 5 May 1827.
34. *Liverpool Mercury*, 27 July 1827.
35. Quoted in *Annals of Sporting and Fancy Gazette*, Vol. 13, 1828, p.124.
36. Surtees. Plain or ringlets?, ch.19.
37. *Liverpool Commercial Chronicle*, 28 July 1827.
38. *Liverpool Commercial Chronicle*, 28 July 1827.
39. *Liverpool Mercury*, 27 July 1827.
40. Reprinted in the *Liverpool Courier*, 1 August 1827.
41. Advertisements by John Kenworthy & Sons, *Liverpool Commercial Chronicle*, 14 July 1827 and Petty & Cooper, *Liverpool Mercury*, 20 July 1827.
42. *Liverpool Courier*, 1 August 1827.
43. Reprinted in the *Liverpool Courier*, 1 August 1827.
44. *Liverpool Mercury*, 27 July 1827.
45. *Liverpool Courier*, 1 August 1827.
46. *Liverpool Commercial Chronicle*, 28 July 1827.
47. *Liverpool Courier*, 1 August 1827.
48. *Annals of Sporting and Fancy Gazette*, Vol. 12, 1827, p.136.
49. Formby, p.4.
50. *Liverpool Courier*, 1 August 1827.
51. Formby, p.4
52. *Liverpool Courier*, 1 August 1827.
53. *Liverpool Courier*, 1 August 1827.
54. *Liverpool Courier*, 1 August 1827.
55. Formby, p.5.
56. *Liverpool Chronicle*, 26 July 1828.
57. Formby, p.8.
58. Formby, p.9.
59. *Liverpool Chronicle*, 26 July 1828.
60. *Liverpool Chronicle*, 26 July 1828.
61. *Annals of Sporting and Fancy Gazette*, Vol. 13, 1828, p.164.
62. *Liverpool Chronicle*, 26 July 1828.
63. Formby, p.21.
64. *Liverpool Chronicle*, 26 July 1828.
65. Altcar Coursing Club. The coursing calendar, p.4. The list of the Club's members is on p.7.
66. Goodlake. The courser's manual, p.lxvi.
67. Formby, pp.6-7.

3.

William Lynn and Aintree

William Lynn is remembered today as the originator of both the Grand National at Aintree and the Waterloo Cup for hare coursing at Altcar, a notable sporting double, but, apart from these two bare facts, historians have tended to pass over the rest of his life in silence, or to make misleading assertions which have served to belittle his achievements; in fact, his involvement in Aintree and the Grand National was both longer and more substantial than is generally thought. There has even been confusion over the location of the Waterloo Hotel, of which he was landlord for half a century. This was not at Waterloo or near to the course at Aintree, as is sometimes asserted, but in Ranelagh Street in the centre of Liverpool, on the site adjacent to the Lyceum which is now occupied by Central station.

Lynn was born in 1792 at East Grinstead in Sussex [1]. He received his early training as a hotelier and caterer in London and came to Liverpool in the 1820s to take charge at the Waterloo Hotel. The Waterloo was at that time Liverpool's second hotel, after the Adelphi, and was one of the leading places of entertainment in the town. Despite this status it was a not a very attractive place. One regular visitor reported that "the whole place had a dingy appearance; from basement to attic it was smoke-begrimed and dirty, few and far between appeared to be the visitors of the painter, and the only redeeming feature about it was the fine old fashioned furniture, which, to the credit of the housemaids, was kept well polished" [2].

It was more as a public caterer than as a hotel keeper that Lynn made his name in Liverpool. In particular, for over forty years he was responsible for all the municipal banquets held at the Town Hall [3]. These were magnificent affairs, combining "all the comforts of a well-appointed private dinner party" with an appropriate display of civic grandeur, and were said to be the equal of those given by the Governor General of India [4]. Lynn showed as much flair and innovation in the ordering of these banquets as he was later to do in promoting horse racing at Aintree and hare coursing at Altcar. He personally superintended the distribution of the soup and the fish and the carving of the joints, and one of his innovations was the printed menu or "Carte du diner", which not only allowed guests to select the dishes and wines they wanted with ease, but also enabled them to spot "any inadvertent omission on the part of the servants". Fortunately, some of Lynn's menus have survived, and we can thus see what kind of meal he served up to his guests; for example, this is what diners at the Town Hall were offered on 3 May, 1853:

	"PREMIER SERVICE
Iced Madeira	*Potages*
	Tortue Claire – à la Reine
Moselle Cup	*Poissons*
	Saumon – Turbot
	Filets de Soles à la Venetienne
	Eperlans
Champagne	*Entrées*
	Côtelettes d'Agneau à la Provençale
	Ris de Veau, Sauce Perigeux
	Timballes de Nouilles à la Sefton
	Boudins à la Richelieu
Champagne	*Table de Côté*
	Piéces de Resistance
	Haunch of Venison. Quarter of Lamb
	Spring Chickens. Round of Beef.
	Spanish Ham
	SECOND SERVICE
Claret Cup	*Rôts*
	Leverets, Green Goose, Ducklings,
	Rice and Curry

Eau de Vie de Cerise ou Curacoa	*Entremets* Gelée de Danzic Abricots à la Regence Charlotte à la Bohemienne Crème du Marasquin Poudins à la Nesselrode* Compôte de Pêches Ecrevisses, Oeufs de Pluviers Le Pâté de Foies-gras de Strasbourg
DESSERT Chateau Lafitte Port, Madeira, Sherry	*Dessert* Ices, &c., &c., &c., &c.

* A small glass of Cherry Brandy poured over a slice of Nesselrode pudding is indispensable at all tables." [5]

After reading a menu such as this it is easy to see why Lord Sefton thought that Lynn was "as great a man in his line as the great Duke of Wellington was in his" [6].

Lynn's meals at his own hotel were served with the same degree of style and dignity. In 1853 the author Nathaniel Hawthorne arrived in Liverpool as the new United States Consul and he spent his first few days in the town at the Waterloo Hotel. This is how his wife, in a letter to her father, described Lynn and his establishment: "The head of the Waterloo House, Mr. Lynn, is a very venerable-looking person, resembling one's idea of an ancient duke – dressing with elaborate elegance, and with the finest ruffled bosoms. Out of peculiar respect for the Consul of the United States, he comes in at the serving of the soup, and holds each plate while I pour the soup, and then, with great state, presents it to the waiter to place before each person. After this ceremony he retires with graceful obeisance" [7].

This description of Lynn is borne out by the only known photograph of him, which came to light during the course of research for this book. Undiscovered by previous historians of Aintree and the Grand National, it is reproduced here for the first time [8]. He also appears on horseback in the centre of Richard Ansdell's painting of 'The Waterloo Coursing Meeting of 1840'.

William Lynn

Like many other publicans, Lynn saw the Maghull Races as an easy way of making money, and in 1827, the first year of the meeting, he rented the grand stand for £40 [9]. With the appalling weather forcing the crowds into the bars and refreshment rooms, he must have recouped this sum many times over during the three days of the meeting, and in 1828 he went one better, not just renting the grand stand again, but also sponsoring one of the main races of the meeting, the Waterloo Gold Cup, to the tune of 100 guineas. Formby was later to complain that this latter gesture was "a sort of desperate effort to obtain a species of imposing popularity" [10], and it may well be that Lynn did use the opportunity to try and win support from amongst the sporting community for his plans to establish a new and better course at Aintree. If so, he succeeded, because immediately after the races the Racing Committee began to put pressure on Formby to improve the course at Maghull with the implicit threat that they would take their support elsewhere if he refused to comply with their demands. These they set out in a letter to Formby on 9 August 1828:

"1st, In consequence of the wet and bad state of the ground, the lessees are forthwith to make such improvements and alterations in it as may appear necessary to the Committee.

"2ndly, The course is to be pastured and not mowed.

"3rdly, The Grand Stand is to be enlarged, and another communication to the roof added. The plan of such alterations to be laid before the Committee for approval, on or before the 1st of February, 1829, and the work to be commenced on or before the 1st of May.

"4thly, The lessees are to place the sum of two hundred pounds in the hands of the President of the Committee, on or before the 20th December, 1828, for the purpose of making, or adding to, the stakes.

"5thly, The Committee are to fix the number of men they may think requisite to keep the course; the expense of which is to be defrayed by the lessees.

"6thly, Everything connected with the Sweepstakes, Handicaps, Plates, Weights, or time of running, is to be fixed by the Committee or the Stewards; and all monies received, either as subscriptions or stakes, are to be paid to the Committee or their Treasurer.

"7thly, The prices of admission to the Stands and the Course are to be the same as last races, and carriages with company going to the Stands are to be exempt." [11]

Formby castigated this ultimatum as "arrogant and imperious in the superlative degree" [12], but he nevertheless instructed Bretherton to agree to all the Committee's proposals. In the meantime, Lynn put forward his own plans for a new course on land owned by Lord Sefton at Aintree, and the Committee agreed to meet to discuss these towards the end of August. Having done so, they replied to Bretherton as follows:

"The Committee for conducting the management of the Liverpool Races, beg to state to the Lessees and others interested in the Race Ground [at Maghull], that they cannot consent to extend their pledge to support the Races on the present Course beyond the ensuing year.

"In making this communication the Committee think it due to the Lessees to release them from the engagement they had entered into for the building of a Grand Stand, the erection of which would be unnnecessary, should the plan which is in contemplation of changing the site of the Race Course altogether be carried into effect.

"The Committee, however, being of the opinion that the Course in its present state is absolutely dangerous in particular places, require, as the condition of their support even for the ensuing year, that such improvements should be made forthwith as were formerly stipulated for by the Committee, and agreed to be the Lessees." [13]

In other words, Formby and his associates had to carry out an expensive series of alterations to the course in the fairly sure knowledge that the races would be transferred to Aintree the following year in any case. Faced with this unpalatable prospect, Formby appealed to Lord Sefton to prevent the development of the new course on his land, no doubt hoping that, as a member of the gentry, his views would carry more weight than those of Lynn, a mere publican. If so, Lord Sefton's disdainful reply must have come as a great shock to him. Somewhat disingenuously, he began by saying that the removal of the Liverpool Races from Maghull to Aintree was "a matter of indifference" to him (thus conveniently ignoring the fact that he could expect a vastly increased rent for his land at Aintree should the course move there), and then went on to declare that in agreeing to a new course being established there he was merely following the advice of "disinterested persons" who had told him that "the present concern cannot go on", the reasons being "the great distance from Liverpool, the nature of the ground, and the system upon which the races have been conducted" [14]. Foolishly, Formby had told Lord Sefton that he estimated the value of his own land to have increased by £10,000 through the establishment of the race course on it. At a time of agricultural depression no landowner was going to turn down a proposal which would increase the value of his land by such a vast amount, and there can be little doubt that Sefton was as interested in making money from the new venture as Lynn was; indeed Formby claimed that Lord Sefton's Steward and Book-keeper had admitted as much [15].

That Formby was right in his assessment of Lord Sefton's motives is confirmed by the evidence of the Molyneux estate rent books. These show that in 1829 Lynn and his associates paid an annual rental of £572 for the land on which the new course was laid out [16]. This was considerably more than Lord Sefton was receiving from any other tenant in the immediate vicinity, but at £10 per acre it was the same as Formby had been charging for his land at Maghull. However, once the success of the new venture was assured, Lord Sefton swiftly raised the annual rental for Aintree to £620 in 1830 and then £645 in 1832 [17], and further increases were to follow.

Having lost his battle with the Racing Committee and Lord Sefton, Formby decided to appeal to the racegoing public, and specifically to the tradesmen of Liverpool, who had sponsored the races at Maghull, and who he now feared might shift their support to Lynn's new course. On 27 September, 1828, he placed the following notice in the Liverpool press:

"To the Tradesmen of Liverpool and the Public

"I beg respectfully to caution you against subscribing to the cups for the proposed new race course at Aintree, and I do so, not only because I have a considerable interest in the present course, but because I feel an attempt has been made, by unfair means, to injure the present establishment." [18]

Specifically, Formby claimed that Lynn's object was not so much to establish a new course with improved facilities as to gain control of the Liverpool races by whatever means was most expedient. He then quoted a letter from Peter Bretherton, dated 10 September, 1828, which reveals that Lynn had made an attempt to buy a controlling interest in the Maghull course [19]. What gives particular credence to Formby's view that he was the victim of a conspiracy aimed at depriving the original proprietors of their just and well-merited reward for establishing the races [20] is the fact that the attempt to buy out the lessees of the Maghull course took place *before* the Racing Committee began threatening to move the course elsewhere if their demands were not met. On 6 August 1828 George Lawrence wrote to Bretherton and Jackson, on behalf of the Committee, asking them "whether you, in conjunction with Mr. Formby, are willing to transfer your interest in it [i.e. the Maghull course] and on what terms" [21]. Formby does not record what his reply to this approach was, but he must have given the Committee a very dusty answer. It was only then that the Committee began to give Lynn's plans for Aintree their full backing, and, odd as it may seem now, it is highly likely that if Formby had agreed to sell, there would have been no race course at Aintree and no Grand National as we know it!

Formby's outrage at the way he had been treated knew no bounds, and he took his revenge by publishing a pamphlet with the title *An account of the Liverpool Races established in the year 1827, with observations on the conduct of the Committee*, in which he gave his version of what had happened. This is liberally peppered with sarcastic comments about Lynn's "munificent and liberal spirit" and Lord Sefton's "disinterestedness and liberality", and with attacks on the Racing Committee for their "assumption of illegitimate authority", "gross dereliction of duty" and "sinister motives" in seeking to move the races from Maghull to Aintree. "Not one of the Committee", he claimed, "ever entered a horse – not one subscribed (I believe) a single farthing towards supporting the Liverpool Races"; not one of them "would... have been sufficiently enterprising and public spirited to have undertaken the formation of a Race Course two years ago", but now they had adopted "a system of the most intolerant and vexatious oppression", for the purpose of promoting their own pecuniary interests. Formby concluded by repeating his claim that his course at Maghull was "as far superior to any land in Aintree for Racing purposes as the light of the meridian sun is superior to that of a farthing rushlight", and by announcing his intention of continuing racing at Maghull, whatever the Committee might decide: "I am fully determined that nothing shall put a stop to the Liverpool Races at Maghull", he declared [22].

The fine quality of the turf at Aintree is now so well known that few have taken seriously Formby's claim that the ground at Maghull was better, especially in view of the muddy conditions that prevailed at the meetings in both 1827 and 1828; yet it is worth noting that one impartial observer thought the course at Maghull consisted of "very fine turf", whilst being less than complimentary about the course at Aintree [23]. The truth is, of course, that the relative merits of the terrain of the two courses did not matter all that much; what did matter was that the Racing Committee, for whatever reason, was not able to work with Formby and was only too glad to seize the opportunity offered by Lynn's alternative plans. Money, and the prospect of financial gain, undoubtedly played a part in their decision, but they may also have preferred Lynn's geniality to Formby's demonstrable irascibility (which shows through so clearly in his pamphlet), whilst Lynn's powers of organization and showmanship at Aintree were soon to prove far superior to anything Formby had shown at Maghull. In the long run their decision was to prove far more significant than any of them can have realised, but at the time it was a close run thing, and no-one then can have foreseen the international fame which Aintree was later to acquire, not through flat racing but through the then illegitimate and upstart sport of steeplechasing.

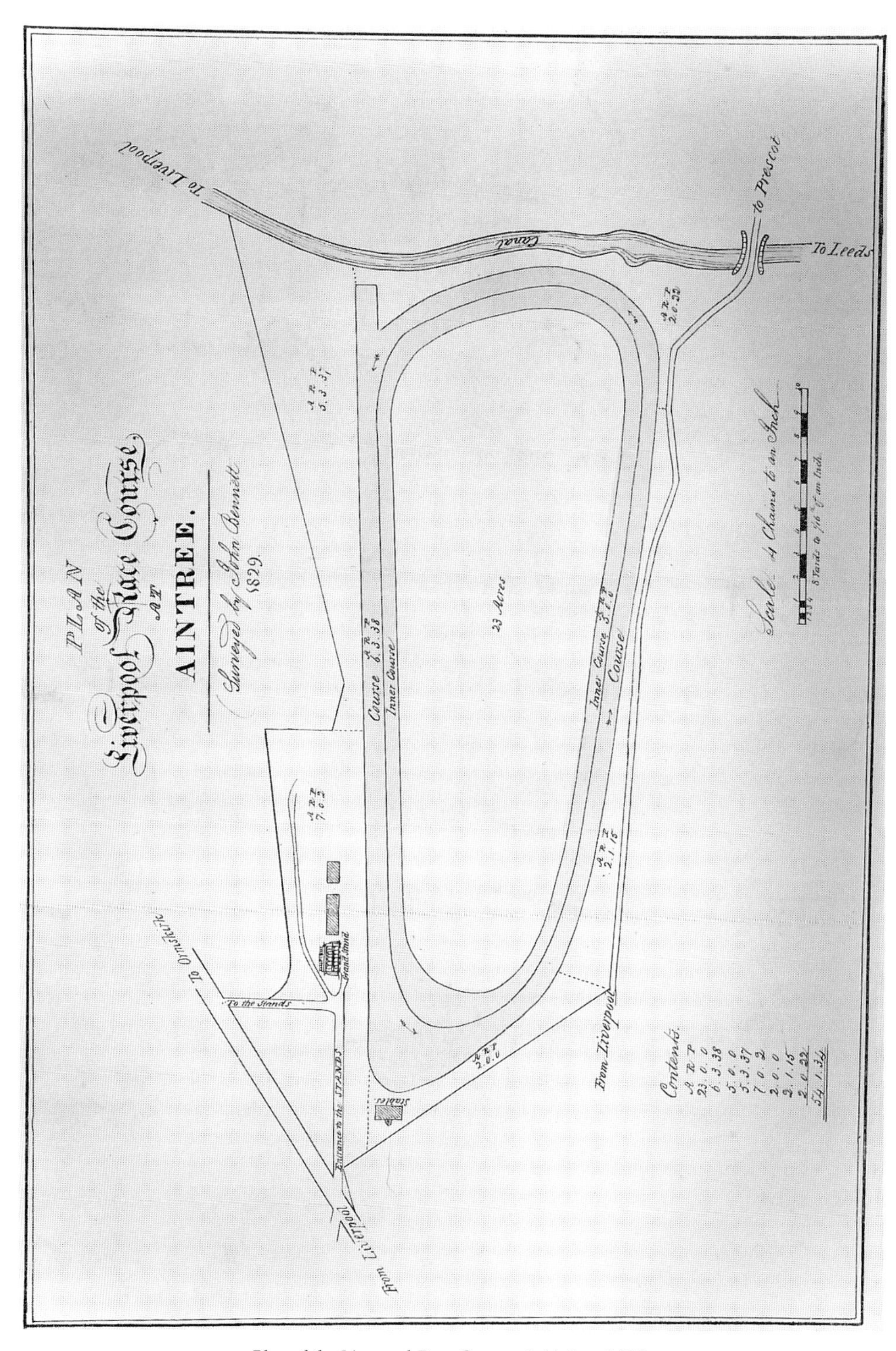

Plan of the Liverpool Race Course at Aintree, 1829

The immediate task was to establish the new course on a firm footing, and win over as much support as possible from those who had previously supported the races at Maghull. As we have already seen, in 1828 Formby had persuaded the Town Council to sponsor the races at Maghull, although this had not been without opposition [24]. Now both rival camps attempted to win the Council over to their side. First off the mark were the Racing Committee, who on 7 January 1829 applied to the Council for a grant of 150 guineas to support the races at Aintree. This led to an interesting debate at the Council meeting at which some members favoured continuing the grant to the existing meeting at Maghull, some were opposed to giving any money to the races because of the shameful scenes of riot, drunkenness and confusion which had taken place there the previous year, or because of the "improper ballads" which had been sung there and "thrust into everybody's face", and others felt that granting money for this kind of purpose was an improper use of Council funds. On the other hand, some members, led naturally enough by Mr. Earle who was also a member of the Racing Committee, were in favour of the grant to the new course. Faced with such a variety of opinion, the Council voted to postpone taking any decision [25].

The following month it was Formby's turn. On 4 February, 1829, he presented a memorial, praying that the Council should either make the same grant as the previous year to Maghull race course or make no grant at all to either course. Mr. Earle then moved an amendment that 150 guineas should be granted to the Aintree course. The Council again found themselves perplexed, and Mr. Drinkwater spoke for the majority when he said that as the opposing parties could not agree the Council should not interfere. Accordingly, it was decided to make no grant to either race course. Formby tried one more time in August 1829, but the Council again declined to pass any resolution on the subject [26].

The Council's decision must have been disappointing to both parties, but it did not deter Lynn from pushing ahead with his plans for the new course at Aintree. On 7 February 1829, a small crowd of about forty gentlemen, some "respectable pedestrians" and "not a few country bumpkins" watched Lord Molyneux lay the foundation stone of the new grand stand. Beneath it he deposited some coins of the realm, and then spread the mortar over it using a silver trowel. Afterwards the gentlemen partook of a cold collation prepared for the occasion by Lynn, and "Success to the Liverpool Races" was toasted in bumpers of sparkling champagne, whilst the workmen were treated to an "ample allowance" of beer and spirits [27]. By this time work on preparing the course was proceeding very rapidly, "the part on which the horses will run being almost finished" [28]. On 27 May the foundation stone of a second, smaller stand, to be known as the Throstle Nest Stand, was laid by George Drinkwater, one of the Racing Committee [29], and this was reported complete by the beginning of July, just in time for the opening of the course [30]. The main stand, however, although usable, was not quite complete by the time of the races, some of the interior decoration still remaining to be done. Quite rightly, it was deemed more important to have the course itself ready on time.

The new course was laid out on a site of rather more than fifty four acres [31]. The circuit took the same irregular oval form which is familiar to racegoers today and was one and a half miles round, with a straight run-in of nearly 1100 yards. Unusually for the time, the entire course was railed, and there was also an inner course for use as a training ground. The turf was described as being "of a light springy nature, which will not easily be put out of order, by either wet or dry weather", qualities which it has continued to hold to this day. At the time of its opening, the course was described as being "as smooth as a bowling green", and there was general agreement that it was a fair course, which gave little opportunity for "the sinister practices of jockeyship" [32]. Interestingly, however, one contemporary source suggests that it was regarded in at least some quarters as "a very distressing course for horses" [33], a comment which has been echoed to a certain extent by some twentieth century flat jockeys who rode the course before flat racing was abandoned in 1976. Champion jockey Doug Smith, for example, said that "The six furlong course was diabolical because the first bend came too soon. The same applied to the Cup course" [34].

Undoubtedly, the most striking sight on the course as far as the spectators were concerned was the grand stand, designed by the distinguished Liverpool architect John Foster. Its general appearance is familiar from old prints of the period, but a more detailed description of it on its opening, which shows how Foster managed to combine elegance with practicality, can be found in the pages of the *Liverpool Chronicle*:

"The building is four stories in height from the ground, with cellars beneath. There are two entrances, from the back and front, to a spacious hall or lobby in the centre of the ground floor, from which two spacious staircases lead to the upper part of the building. On the ground floor are the rooms appropriated for refreshments, consisting of two airy drinking rooms, 27′6″ by 16′9″ each in the rear, and two well-proportioned dining rooms, 29′ by 22′ in front, the windows of which overlook the course; to each of these appartments is attached a bar for the supply of wines, &c. Here tables were laid for 208 persons, and were loaded with every variety of the best quality of the viands, usually constituting a cold collation. Many times were the tables occupied by different visitors, and many a good dinner was there enjoyed. The company was well waited upon, and all the arrangements, as well as the scale of charges, were such as to reflect the highest credit upon the judgement, care and assiduity of Mr. Lynn, the proprietor. Beneath are spacious cellars and kitchens, with every convenience for culinary purposes upon an extensive scale. The principal story contains, to the front (and overlooking the course) an extensive room 91 feet long, 22 feet wide, and 17 feet high, with circular bows at each end, lighted by fifteen arched windows. This room, which was tastefully hung with red and white drapery for the occasion, (neither the plastering of the interior, nor the stuccoing of the exterior being yet begun), presented a very elegant and imposing appearance, and served as a promenade for the ladies during the intervals between the races. The windows of this room open upon a gallery, extending the whole length of the front and round the ends of the building, capable of containing several hundred persons, and affording an ample view of the course. This gallery is supported upon stone piers and iron columns, copied from the columns at the entrance of the Tower of the Winds at Athens, and the whole gallery is covered with an ornamental verandah of novel design and construction. At the back of the large room are two withdrawing rooms, each 28 feet by 17 feet, one for the accommodation of ladies, and the other for gentlemen. Above this story, ascending by a continuation of the same staircases, are two other appartments similar to those last described, and spacious lobbies, which lead to the leads over the large room; and ascending by a commodious staircase, at the back of the upper story, to the upper leads. These leads, which are capable of containing, together, upwards of 2000 persons, command a complete view of the course, and a panorama of the surrounding country, a prospect of much greater extent than can be obtained from any other station with which we are acquainted in the neighbourhood of the town" [35]. Thus right from the start roof viewing was established as a feature of the Aintree stands, a facility which was to become even more attractive when steeplechasing was introduced and the course was extended into the fields on the far side of the Melling Road.

A stable block was constructed to the south of the main grand stand (where Paddock Yard is today), whilst to the north were six smaller stands built of brick and containing more dining rooms and bars, and beyond them were a host of temporary stands and booths, the forerunner of today's tented village. These were gaily decorated, and "in many the sprightly jig, reel or strathspey were footed to the exhilarating sound of every species of music" [36]. Perhaps the most unusual of these temporary stands was a large hay stack at the top of the course, which was used by a crowd of spectators every day of the races.

The first day's racing on the new course took place on Tuesday, 7 July 1829, and was attended by around 40,000 people. It was noted that "the company present comprised a far greater proportion of fashionables than had attended any of the meetings at Maghull. The appearance of the Grand Stand was truly imposing, the roof being literally crowded with gentlemen, and the balcony with ladies, attired in all the dazzling variety of the present fashions" [37]. The weather was unsettled, and there was a heavy shower during the running of the first race, but after that it cleared up and remained fine and dry for the first three days of the meeting; only on the fourth and last day did the rain return, and on that day the crowd was neither so numerous nor so brilliant as on the other days.

The first race, the Croxteth Stakes over a mile and a quarter, was won by Mr. Francis's Mufti. It was reported to be a "very indifferent race" [38], but other races during the four day inaugural meeting were more exciting. On the first day the principal race was the Tradesmen's Cup, which saw Mr. Armitage's Velocipede beat Sir Thomas Stanley's Doctor Faustus by just a head. These two horses were due to meet again the following day in the Stand Cup, but in the event Velocipede had to withdraw because of lameness, and Doctor Faustus was also withdrawn because his stable was "too distant to allow of his arriving in time for the weighing of his rider"; this reduced the field to two, and the race was won by Laurel in a canter. Most commentators were agreed that the best race of the meeting was the Cup given by the Mayor, Bailiffs and Corporation of Sefton for Hunters which, after a "severe race" [39], was won by a horse called Wellington by half a length.

This first meeting at Aintree was generally agreed to have given "universal satisfaction" [40]. Even the *Liverpool Mercury*, normally no friend to horse racing, commented that "the first sporting meeting at Aintree is not likely to be the last. We are not quite sure that this is a circumstance favourable to the course of order and morality in the neighbourhood of so large and populous a town; but as the public voice has declared that the thing shall be, we hope that the national amusement in this neighbourhood will be rendered as free from objection as possible, by every practical endeavour to check the incitements to profligacy, extravagance and demoralization too often to be met with at the race ground" [41]. Lynn, with his aim of making Aintree a place respectable people could go to, would not have objected too much to these words, and he did make an effort to please the crowds with more wholesome entertainment than the gambling games such as thimble-rigging or "prick the garter", which were customarily to be found on the fringes of race meetings at the time. The band of the 67th regiment of foot was on hand to provide musical entertainment between races, and on the third day of the meeting the modern day flypasts by Concorde were anticipated by an ascent of a hot air balloon "of ingenious construction", owned and flown by James Sidney Wood, a publican of Atherton Street, Liverpool [42].

During the meeting, the tradition of "ordinaries", or public dinners, was revived. The first of these was a sumptuous affair at the Adelphi, at which Lord Molyneux made a speech extolling Aintree's merits as one of the finest places for sport in the kingdom, and praising Lynn as the architect of its success. Lynn's health was drunk by the assembled company "with the most flattering testimonials of satisfaction", after which the rest of the evening was spent with "a degree of cordial conviviality not often witnessed" [43].

On the other hand, those who feared that the races would act as a catalyst for lawlessness and disorder had cause for worry by what happened after the last race of the meeting, when it was reported that "a riot of formidable appearance occurred, which originated in an attempt to serve a warrant for bastardy on a plasterer who was a waiter at one of the booths. The fellow resisted the constables, and was supported by a numerous party of his companions, who gathered round them, and being for the most part armed with sticks and bludgeons, proceeded to beat the constables, who were severely mauled by them. One of them, a special constable from Ormskirk, was so dreadfully beaten that he was taken to the Grand Stand in a state of insensibility... The constables, being reinforced by several resolute young men, the rioters were dispersed and pursued in all directions and thirteen of them [were] taken into custody" [44].

Apart from this incident no disturbance took place during the meeting, other than the occasional drunken brawl, which, late at night after the police had disappeared, deteriorated into "that species of *pele-mele* fight which is common in these parts" [45].

Despite losing the battle to prevent Lynn establishing Aintree, Formby carried out his threat to continue racing at Maghull, and for a few years there was an uneasy co-existence between the two courses, with a spring meeting being held in May at Maghull, and the traditional summer meeting taking place in July at Aintree. This was a contest that Formby was always going to lose. As we have seen, the course at Maghull was laid out on swampy and unsuitable ground, whereas the turf at Aintree has always been known for its springiness and fine racing surface. Partly for this reason, and partly because of the bigger prize money he offered, Lynn was able to attract a higher class of entries and provide the better sport. The Maghull meeting, having been moved to May, also suffered through often clashing with the long-established and prestigious Chester May meeting, whereas the summer meeting at Aintree had no immediate rivals, and indeed rapidly became one of the foremost meetings of the season itself.

Most of the horses that ran at Aintree during those early years are now no more than names in the record books, but it is worth noting that within three years Lynn had attracted a Classic winner to the course, the 1830 St. Leger winner, Birmingham, being entered for the Summer Cup in 1832. In 1835 the Knowsley Dinner Stakes, over a mile and a half, was won by the outstanding mare Queen of Trumps, who had already won the Oaks and was to go on to win the St. Leger the same year. At the same meeting the Stand Cup was won by General Chasse, who returned in 1836 to win the race for a second time, despite giving nearly a stone in weight to the Derby winner, Mündig. General Chasse, in fact, was a great favourite in the north west, and in May 1837 he achieved a notable treble in winning the Chester Cup, the Cheshire Stakes and the Liverpool Spring Gold Cup within a period of twelve days.

Mündig, the first Derby winner to run at Aintree, was also the first northern horse to win the Derby. He was both owned and bred by John Bowes, the natural son of the 10th Earl of Strathmore, who was later to found the Bowes Museum at Barnard Castle. Mündig was the first of Bowes's four Derby winners, all of whom were trained by the great John Scott at Malton. From the mid-1830s onwards Bowes regularly entered his horses at Aintree, winning the Liverpool St. Leger with Hetman Platoff in 1839 [46].

Bowes's involvement indicates that Lynn was also successful in attracting the leading owners of the day to enter their horses Aintree. Accounts of the early meetings there invariably stress the numbers of noblemen and gentry present, with names such as Lord Molyneux, Lord Derby, Sir Thomas Stanley, Lord Wilton and Lord Chesterfield regularly appearing.

Lynn's most important supporters were undoubtedly the 2nd Earl of Sefton (1772-1838) and his son Lord Molyneux, later 3rd Earl of Sefton (1796-1855). Nicknamed "Lord Dashalong", the 2nd Earl, who owned the land on which the race course was situated and who had granted the lease to Lynn, was a keen follower of the turf and a noted gambler. Indeed, it is said that on one occasion he lost so heavily at cards that all work on repainting Croxteth Hall had suddenly to be halted, and there was another time when a cheque for £60,000 (approximately £2½ million today) was observed being handed over at Crockford's to pay his gambling debts [47].

The 2nd Earl of Sefton ('Lord Dashalong') by Dighton

Charles Greville, who knew him well, thought that "the one thing needful to him was excitement" and that "he cared for money only as a means of enjoyment". Consequently, although he was an active politician who knew many of the Whig leaders well, he never allowed his parliamentary career to prevent him mixing with "the idle, gay and dissolute frequenters of clubs and race courses". Greville concluded that "he was governed by an intense selfishness, but of that liberal and enlightened character which throws a partial veil over the vice itself, and leaves the superficial observer unconscious of its existence" [48]. The well-known caricature of him by Dighton, which until recently could also be seen on the inn sign of the Sefton Arms at Aintree, indicates his character.

Lord Molyneux, who became the 3rd Earl of Sefton in 1838, was less interested in horse racing than in driving and hare coursing. The last interest, of course, he shared with Lynn; indeed it is said that the very first winner of the Waterloo Cup in 1836, a greyhound called Melanie, was really owned by Molyneux although entered in Lynn's name. As to his driving skills, he once gave curious Liverpudlians a demonstration of his handling powers by driving his team of dark chestnuts up and down the floating landing stage, a feat of no mean skill [49]. He also followed the traditional country sports of hunting, shooting and fishing (he was said to be "a first rate horseman and fine rider to hounds", and "a very good hand at tickling trout"); and despite his relative lack of interest in racing he officiated as a Steward at Aintree from the very first meeting, and later acted as umpire for the inaugural runnings of the Grand National. In character he was "of a quick temper, but very kind to those about him" [50].

Edward, 12th Earl of Derby (1752-1834), is best remembered as the founder of the Oaks and the Derby. By the time Aintree was established he was in his seventies, but was still an active follower of both horse racing and cock fighting. Indeed, he provided a living link with the old Liverpool race course at Crosby, for having run his horses there as a young man, he now entered three horses in races at the inaugural meeting on the new course, one of whom won in a walkover. His first big win at Aintree came the following year when Felt won the Tradesmen's Cup for him. This was the first of a long list of Cup wins for successive Earls of Derby at Aintree, many of which are recorded on the old honours boards recently re-erected in the County Stand. Aged 82, Lord Derby last went to Aintree for the summer meeting in 1834, when he was observed "seated in the round edifice opposite the ending-post enjoying the animated scene" [51]. Before cock fighting was made illegal in 1849, there was a cockpit on the course at Aintree and this was one of the attractions which drew the Earl there; in 1833, for example, a main, or match, of cocks was fought during the race

Portrait of the 3rd Earl of Sefton by Westcott & Ansdell at Croxteth Hall

meeting between Lord Derby and General Yates for 10 guineas a battle and 500 guineas the main. But Derby was also a keen supporter of horse racing at Aintree, and just a few months before he died in 1834 he offered a £70 Plate as an annual gift to the meeting [52].

The Earl of Wilton (1799-1882) was a man of many parts. He was an enthusiastic and accomplished sailor, an anatomist and amateur surgeon (who attended to William Huskisson after he was knocked over by the *Rocket* at the opening of the Liverpool and Manchester Railway), an organist of some note and a composer of music, some of which was "not destitute of merit" [53]. He also wrote a book *On the Sports and Pursuits of the English*. A keen supporter of the turf, who had acted as Steward at the first Maghull meeting, he was also a natural horseman and rode many of his own horses to victory himself. In 1827 he established a race course on his own land at Heaton Park, near Manchester, which quickly established a reputation for corruption and malpractice, exceptional even by the standards of the time. Each year Lord Wilton invited the official handicapper to join his house party for the duration of the meeting; and in return the handicapper was expected to weight his host's runners rather more leniently than they might otherwise have been. It is, therefore, no surprise that Lord Wilton won so many of the races at his home course. Despite this, however, he seems to have been a popular figure on the turf, not least because of his lavish hospitality [54].

Lord Wilton

Sir Thomas Massey Stanley (1782-1841) was head of the Cheshire branch of the Stanley family and had his seat at Hooton Hall on the Wirral. A thoroughgoing sportsman he hunted twice a week with his own pack of hounds from Hooton, held shooting parties there and at Puddington, and owned many successful racehorses who were trained at Hooton itself. In 1824 he won the inaugural running of the Chester Tradesmen's Cup with his six year old Doge of Venice, but his greatest success at Chester came in 1827 when he won all the principal races of the May meeting, including the Tradesmen's Cup again with Grenadier, the Grosvenor Stakes and the Stand Cup with Doctor Faustus, and the Dee Stakes and the St. Leger Stakes with Jocelyn. He had also supported the races at Maghull and won several of the principal races there, so his support for the new venture at Aintree must have seemed especially important to Lynn. Later, when steeplechasing came to Aintree Sir Thomas was one of its keenest supporters, and, as we shall see, he was unlucky not to win the inaugural running of the race that was to become the Grand National with his horse Laurie Todd.

But of all the sporting noblemen who gave their support to Lynn, probably the most remarkable was the Earl of Eglinton (1812-1861). Young, rich and spoilt, he was in 1839 to achieve fame, or notoriety, through his staging of the Eglinton Tournament. This extraordinary attempt to recreate a medieval tournament was said to have cost Lord Eglinton around £40,000 to stage, and in the event it was ruined by the weather in much the same way as Formby's inaugural race meeting at Maghull had been. Around 100,000 people were estimated to have gone to view the Tournament and found themselves struggling home in torrential rain and a sea of mud. The combination of medieval knights in armour and umbrellas proved irresistible to the cartoonists of the day, and Lord Eglinton never quite lived down the ridicule this fiasco engendered.

As a racehorse owner, he was much more successful. Starting in a small way with three horses in 1831, by 1838 he had built up a stable of eighteen. In that year his horse The Potentate won at the Liverpool Craven Meeting, but he was to gain an even bigger victory at the Summer Meeting the same year when St Bennett won the Tradesmen's Cup; this was part of a winning sequence of four races in succession which included the Northumberland Plate. Later Lord Eglinton achieved even greater successes with horses such as The Flying Dutchman; this particular horse won both the Derby and the St. Leger and then took part in the epic match against Voltigeur at York which has gone down as one of the greatest races in British turf history. Eglinton's average winnings have been estimated at £4000 a year, and he was also lucky in his betting; in 1842 he was said to have won £30,000 for an outlay of £650 in one afternoon when Blue Bonnet won the St. Leger. Unusually among the sporting aristocracy, he was also, like Lord Waterford (another of the knights at the Eglinton Tournament), an early follower of steeplechasing. In 1831 he rode to victory in three steeplechases in an afternoon, and when steeplechasing came to Aintree he was a regular supporter. Perhaps even more important than these triumphs was the fact that, at a time when racing attracted more than its fair share of crooks, Lord Eglinton was known as a shining example of the "model sportsman and chivalrous, knightly gentleman". Support of men such as he was vital to Lynn in his campaign to make Aintree a place where the respectable middle classes would be happy to go [55].

In contrast, the races at Maghull declined into low class, bucolic affairs which no respectable person would contemplate attending. This decline set in even before the first meeting at Aintree had taken place, for at the spring meeting in 1829 it was noted that the attendance was "most discouraging in numbers...and in point of character of a vastly inferior description" [56]. Formby fought back. He improved the condition of the course, planned improvements to the stands to make them more commodious, "especially for ladies", and tried to introduce a greater degree of law and order to the proceedings [57]; but none of these measures was sufficient to win back the initiative from Lynn. Liverpool could not sustain two first-class courses in such proximity, and it was Aintree which was the fashionable place to go to and be seen at. One visitor who was present at the very last, seemingly unofficial, meeting at Maghull in 1835 noted the numbers of "tents or low receptacles of drunkenness" and commented that the crowd was "composed of the rougher sort, in and about the great town of Liverpool, being, I sincerely hope, the outpourings of the worst class of inhabitants" [58].

In October 1834, rumours began to circulate within the sporting world that "the Liverpool Maghull races are likely to be discontinued and a Spring Meeting on the Aintree Course substituted for them" [59]. In the event what seems to have happened is that Lynn bought Formby out and gained the right to transfer the meeting to Aintree in return for a quite substantial payment to the Maghull race committee. Thus, in May 1835, the three-day

Liverpool Craven Meeting, as it was now called, took place for the first time at Aintree. The weather was inauspicious, consisting of "heavy rain, accompanied by a chilling blast", but the attendance was greater than had been customary at Maghull, and the sport was generally agreed to have been good. No doubt the inclement weather led to an even greater appreciation of the "abundance of good things" which Lynn provided in the refreshment rooms. As a sop to Formby, the opening event on the first day of the new meeting was named the Formby Stakes, a race on the second day was named the Maghull Stakes, and on the third day the prize money of 100 sovereigns for the Stand Cup was given by "the late Committee of the Maghull Races" [60]. Most of these gestures were not to be repeated in future years, the Formby Stakes being pointedly renamed the Aintree Stakes in 1836 [61]. For their part, the members of the Maghull Race Committee ceased to sponsor the Stand Cup after 1836, when it was replaced by a Gold Cup given by the brewers of Liverpool [62]. As if to add insult to injury, this race was later named the Waterloo Cup after Lynn's own hotel.

Without any serious local opposition, Lynn could now seek to increase the range of attractions on offer at Aintree and, equally important from his point of view, enjoy the greater profits now that Formby's rival course was out of the way. He had no intention of sharing these with his erstwhile rival, and Formby ceased to be involved in horse racing from then on. He continued to live at Maghull Hall, married for a second time, and died aged 72 on 11 February 1857 in St. Helier, Jersey [63]. From what we know of his character, he probably took a malicious pleasure in seeing Lynn forced to surrender control of Aintree only a few short years after he himself had been forced to give up racing at Maghull.

Compared to some of his associates, Formby got off lightly. Peter Bretherton, the stage coach proprietor to whom he had leased the racecourse, lost much more heavily and was forced into bankruptcy [64]. He was the first promoter of racing at Liverpool to suffer this fate, but, as we shall see, he was to be by no means the last.

Notes and references

1. Lynn was baptised at East Grinstead on 12 August 1792, the son of John and Mary Lynn (East Sussex baptism index, 1790-1812). This is in agreement with Lynn's death certificate which gives his age in 1870 as 78. The 1841 census gives Lynn's age then as

45, but this is clearly incorrect. The 1851 census gives his age as 58, and also suggests that Lynn married twice. His wife, Mary Anne, was 35 then, whilst the 1841 census reveals that Lynn's son, another William, was then aged 20. The non-appearance of his first wife in the 1841 census suggests that she may already have been dead.
2. David Brown, writing in the *Greyhound Stud Book*, Vol. 1, 1882, p.35.
3. *Liverpool Mercury*, 12 October 1870.
4. Chapman. The American stranger's guide to London and Liverpool at table, p.32.
5. Chapman. The American stranger's guide to London and Liverpool at table, p.34.
6. *Liverpool Mercury*, 12 October 1870.
7. Quoted in Whale. Lost villages of Liverpool. Pt. 1, p.38.
8. I first became aware of the existence of this photograph through chancing on a photocopy of it in the Molyneux Muniments at Croxteth Hall, where it lay in a file on hare coursing. The original appears in the *Greyhound Stud Book*, Vol. 14, 1895, p.45. I am grateful to Sir Mark Prescott, Bt., a member of the present-day organising committee of the Waterloo Cup, for giving me this information. It is an interesting comment on the lack of contact between the two sports that the portrait appears in Sir Mark's history of the Waterloo Cup, but has remained unknown to writers on the history of steeplechasing, despite a search having been made at the time of the exhibition marking the 150th anniversary of the Grand National at Liverpool Museum.
9. *Liverpool Courier*, 1 August 1827.
10. Formby. An account of the Liverpool races, p.20.
11. Formby, p.12.
12. Formby, p.13.
13. Formby, p.16.
14. Formby, pp.17-18.
15. Formby, p.19.
16. Molyneux estate rent books, 1827-29, Molyneux Muniments DDM 12/117.
17. Molyneux estate rent books, 1830-32, Molyneux Muniments DDM 12/118.
18. *Liverpool Chronicle*, 27 October 1828.
19. *Liverpool Chronicle*, 27 October 1828.
20. Formby, p.21.
21. Formby, p.28.
22. Formby, pp.27-28.
23. Blaine. An encyclopaedia of rural sports, p.375.
24. Touzeau. The rise and progress of Liverpool from 1551 to 1835. Vol. 2, p.836.
25. Touzeau. Vol. 2, p.837; *Liverpool Mercury*, 9 January 1829.
26. Touzeau. Vol. 2, p.837; *Liverpool Mercury*, 6 February 1829.
27. *Liverpool Chronicle*, 14 February 1829.
28. *Liverpool Mercury*, 13 February 1829.
29. *Liverpool Mercury*, 29 May 1829.
30. *Liverpool Mercury*, 3 July 1829.
31. Plan of the Liverpool Race Course at Aintree, surveyed by John Bennett, 1829. Molyneux Muniments DDM 14/18.
32. *Liverpool Chronicle*, 11 July 1829.
33. Blaine. An encyclopaedia of rural sports, p.375.

34. 150 years of the Aintree legend, p.61.
35. *Liverpool Chronicle*, 11 July 1829.
36. *Liverpool Chronicle*, 11 July 1829.
37. *Liverpool Chronicle*, 11 July 1829.
38. *Liverpool Chronicle*, 11 July 1829.
39. *The Times*, 10 July 1829.
40. *Liverpool Chronicle*, 11 July 1829.
41. *Liverpool Mercury*, 10 July 1829.
42. *Liverpool Chronicle*, 11 July 1829.
43. *Liverpool Chronicle*, 11 July 1829.
44. *Liverpool Mercury*, 17 July 1829.
45. *Liverpool Chronicle*, 11 July 1829.
46. Conran. John Bowes, pp. 6-7.
47. 'Recollections of what I heard – the second Earl of Sefton', anonymous memoir in the Molyneux Muniments at Croxteth Hall.
48. Greville. Memoirs. Pt. 2. Vol. 1, pp.138-141.
49. *Sporting Review*, Vol. 34 (1855), p.369.
50. 'Recollections of what I heard – the 3rd Earl of Sefton', anonymous memoir in the Molyneux Muniments at Croxteth Hall.
51. *Sporting Magazine*, December 1834.
52. Cox. Derby, pp.126, 133-34.
53. 'Thormanby'. Famous racing men, p.127.
54. *Baily's Magazine*, November 1863, pp.109-112.
55. Anstruther. The knight and the umbrella, pp.60-63; 'Thormanby'. Kings of the turf, pp.145-163.
56. *Liverpool Chronicle*, 23 May 1829.
57. *Liverpool Chronicle*, 15 May 1830.
58. Head. A home tour through the manufacturing districts of England in the summer of 1835, p.57.
59. *Bell's Life*, 12 October 1834.
60. *Liverpool Chronicle*, 16 May 1835.
61. *Racing Calendar*, 1836, p.43. It is, however, pleasing to note that the Maghull Novices Chase is one of the principal races at the present day Grand National meeting.
62. *Racing Calendar*, 1837, p.45.
63. *Liverpool Mercury*, 18 February 1857.
64. *The Times*, 16 April 1834. However, Bretherton was able to continue running his stage coach business for many years afterwards; in *Gore's Directory* for 1847 he is listed as having his office at Saracen's Head yard, Dale Street.

4.

Steeplechasing comes to Aintree: the first Grand National

Having bought out the opposition and gained a monopoly on the flat racing in the area, although at a cost which was later to contribute substantially to both his own and the Aintree executive's financial problems, Lynn turned his attention to hurdling, and the first two hurdle races at Aintree took place on 24 October 1834.

These were the first hurdle races to be held anywhere in Lancashire, and they attracted great interest on account of their novelty. In the event, the meeting seems to have been a great success; it was reported that the races "were beautifully contested and afforded much amusement". The day was also notable for the first appearance at Aintree of Captain Becher. Riding Milliner in the first race he was twenty lengths behind the leaders at the first hurdle, but nevertheless came through to win the race by almost the same distance, a feat of riding that "excited universal admiration". In the second race no fewer than three out of the seven runners fell at the third hurdle, but fortunately none of them was hurt, and this did not impair the enjoyment of the afternoon [1].

Encouraged by the success of this meeting, Lynn expanded the programme the following year. On this occasion there were four hurdle races, and it was reported that "the sport was excellent and far superior to that of the preceding year". Captain Becher was again present, "so confident of his own superior powers" that he took 40-1 to win every race, but in the event, having won the first three, he could manage only third place in the fourth. Perhaps even more remarkably, and unthinkable in today's conditions, he won two of the races on the same horse, the famous Vivian [2].

At that time Vivian was probably the best steeplechaser in the country; he was certainly the best known. Ridden by Becher, he had already won both the Northampton and the Vale of Aylesbury Steeplechases before coming to Liverpool; the partnership was later to win the Worcester, Dunchurch and Cheltenham Steeplechases and to come second at Leamington. At the time, these were the most important steeplechases of the season, and that a horse of this class should be entered at Liverpool is a clear indication of the rising importance of the meeting.

That Becher and other leading steeplechase jockeys should have thought it worth their while to travel a long way north of their usual haunts to ride at Aintree is also significant. Becher was then at the height of his fame. Born in Norfolk in 1797, he had his first pony at the age of four, and it is recorded that as a schoolboy he often rode the fifteen miles to King's Lynn and back to bring the money from the bank to pay his father's farmhands. On leaving school he obtained an appointment in the Store-keeper General's Department, and in this capacity he was ordered to Brussels, where he was stationed during the battle of Waterloo. He does not seem to have seen any of the actual fighting, but his time in the Low Countries was not without incident. Once at Ostend he quarreled with one of his companions and challenged him to swim to a buoy moored nearly a mile out to sea and back again. The day was cold and miserable with a heavy swell on the sea, but Becher managed the feat, whereas his opponent had to be taken out of the water on reaching the turning point nearly dead from exhaustion.

When peace was declared in 1815, Becher returned to England and was stationed for a time at Ramsgate, where he was in charge of landing the mules and horses as they returned from the continent. He seems to have enjoyed this work well enough, but when his department was transferred to London, he began to get bored, and it was perhaps fortunate for him that as the army was reduced in strength he should find himself made redundant. He moved to the country and indulged himself with hunting, breaking in horses and then entering them for small stakes at county meetings, and in riding in hurdle races.

It was at this time that Becher received his title of Captain, as he was commissioned into the Buckinghamshire Yeomanry. With this corps, he was on duty near Westminster Abbey for the coronation of George IV, and he later also took part in a grand review which was held for the Duke of Wellington at Stowe, the seat of the Duke of Buckingham.

Becher first seems to have ridden in a steeplechase in 1829, when he rode Bantam in the Grand Leicestershire Chase at Melton. Showing the coolness, pluck and perseverance which were to be the hallmarks of his career, he remounted after falling, but finished fourth, a long way behind the leaders. For the next ten years he may almost be said to have lived in the saddle as he travelled the length and breadth of the country in search of rides. During one particular fortnight he was known to have travelled over seven hundred miles, most of it on horseback, to attend the different meetings at which he was engaged to ride, no mean feat in the pre-railway age. Personal comfort did not concern him unduly, and it is recorded that on at least one occasion when he arrived at a country house unexpectedly he was happy to bed down for the night in the stables, saying afterwards that he had had a bed fit for a king. His victories were many, and included the St. Albans Steeplechase in 1835 and 1836, the Northampton in 1834, 1836 and 1838, the Worcester in 1836, and the Dunchurch and Cheltenham in 1837. In 1834 he won 48 races out of 58 starts, and around this time it was said that "Whatever Captain Becher rides, place him on what horse you will, he is

CAPTAIN BEECHER.

pretty sure to win!" There were also plenty of seconds and, of course, not a few falls as well.

In 1834, the year he first came to Liverpool, Becher established the highly successful partnership with Vivian referred to above. A month after their victory in the Vale of Aylesbury Chase, there took place the celebrated match for 1000 guineas a side between Vivian, ridden by Becher, and Cock Robin, ridden by his owner, the "reckless and rollicking" Lord Waterford [3]. So mortified was the latter at his defeat that, unusually for him, he blamed it on his horse. "Well, my Lord", was Becher's characteristic reply, "I am a poor man, but your Lordship shall change horses, and I'll have you back again to where we started for the same money." Lord Waterford did not take him up on the offer.

As a judge of pace Becher was rarely surpassed, and his determination once he had selected his line was proverbial; he also had the reputation of being very clever at spotting the weak parts of the line of country. Perhaps even more important, at a time when horse racing was a far from clean sport, Becher's integrity was never once called into question during his long career in the saddle. He was noted for his cheery spirits and conviviality, often staying on long after racing to regale friends with a host of humorous stories; and he also had an astonishing range of party tricks which included running round the room on the wainscot edge, or up high walls and kicking the ceiling, and giving highly realistic animal impersonations. No better ambassador for the sport he did so much to popularise can be imagined. As one contemporary put it, he was "a thorough sportsman, keenly fond of horses, not so much as a means of making money, but for their good qualities as the partners of his pleasures". His appearance at Liverpool guaranteed the large crowd Lynn was anxious to attract to the course [4].

It seems highly likely that in October 1835 Lynn discussed with Becher and some of the other jockeys the possibility of staging a steeplechase at Aintree. He must also have known of the activities of his fellow publican Thomas Coleman, who had established the St. Albans Chase as the most important race of its kind in the calendar.

Steeplechasing was not unknown in the area, but races tended to be small-scale amateur events which often descended into farce. Typical was a race which took place in January 1836 when two Liverpool gentlemen, Mr. Blake and Mr. Neilson, challenged each other to race from Aintree to Crosby over a distance estimated at three and a half miles. "Unluckily, however, by the time they had reached the Old Roan, about a mile and a half from the starting post, Mr. Neilson's horse stumbled in crossing a low fence, and broke his hind leg. This, of course, terminated the contest, and Mr. Blake was allowed to go to the end of his journey at leisure" [5]. Neilson's horse had to be destroyed, and the whole affair can hardly have provided much of a spectacle for the spectators.

This kind of event was not what Lynn had in mind; he wanted to establish a prestigious new steeplechase which would attract the best horses and the best jockeys, and which would raise the status of Aintree still higher in the sporting world. He must also have hoped that the new venture would make him a great deal of money. The rapid growth of Aintree into a major flat race course had been an extraordinary success story, but the levels of prize money needed to achieve that success meant that it had also been an expensive affair for Lynn. In addition he had had to pay heavily to have the Maghull meeting transferred to Aintree, and there was the annual rent to Lord Sefton to find. The introduction of a major steeplechase, which would attract large crowds, might well ease the financial difficulties which Aintree, and Lynn himself, were beginning to face.

The first intimation of Lynn's plans appeared in one of the local newspapers on 9 January 1836, when it was reported that "the getting up of a grand steeple chase is.... decided upon by a number of our influential sportsmen, on a scale equal in magnitude to those which take place in the neighbourhood of Northampton and St Albans" [6]. It is this race, run as the "Liverpool Grand Steeple-Chase" on 29 February 1836 which should properly be accorded the honour of being the first Grand National.

It is not just the name of the race, nor that most of the top riders of the day were engaged to ride in it, nor that it attracted enormous public interest and a huge crowd on the day, that leads to this conclusion. It is pre-eminently because, as all the contemporary accounts make clear, this race was run over what to all intents and purposes was the same course as that used today. The start was at the top of the race course, near the grand stand, and the line of country then led past Seed's Farm (whose existence is still recalled by Seed's Cottages today) to the turnpike (Melling) road, after which there was a line of fences to be jumped before the course turned and followed the banks of the canal, before coming back on to the race course and finishing opposite the grand stand. As today, the race consisted of two circuits of the course, and, because it was a fine day, the whole race was clearly visible to the crowd on the roof of the stand, especially to those who had furnished themselves with telescopes.

Here lay two examples of Lynn's marketing skills. He followed Coleman's example at St. Albans of making the race start and finish at the same point. Up to this time almost all steeplechases, being run over open country, had started and finished many miles apart, making it impossible for most of the spectators to follow the race in any detail. Perhaps even more significantly, although much of the race took place in the fields beyond the Melling Road (still referred to by race commentators today as "out in the country" even though all semblances of real countryside in the area have long since disappeared), the start and the finish were on an established flat race course; and the crowd were thus able to use the grand stands to get a better view of the race. Given the hostilty of the flat racing establishment to steeplechasing at the time, this was a highly innovative step, and one that was to be triumphantly vindicated. *Bell's Life in London and Sporting Chronicle*, the leading sporting journal of the day, commented that this "admirable arrangement" enabled the spectators "to congregate in one spot instead of being dispersed in all parts to the injury of the farmers as is the case at most other established meetings" [7].

Lynn's other innovation was the appointment of an umpire (Lord Molyneux). At a time when most steeplechase meetings were fairly chaotic affairs, he wanted to introduce a degree of orderliness and punctuality to the proceedings. Race meetings traditionally had been organised to suit the owners; Lynn was one of the first to recognise that the public had certain expectations which needed to be met as well, and this was perhaps the secret of his success. In subsequent years he was to introduce quite a number of further innovations, all with aim of pleasing the racegoers and giving them better information than they had had in the past. Many of these have now become standard practice at race courses, but Lynn's part in their introduction has been forgotten. At the summer meeting in 1840, for example, the runners were numbered in the race card and the results were announced by number for the first time [8]; at the same meeting the betting ring was established on the ground in front of the stands, which, amongst other things, "enabled the ladies above [in the stand] to enjoy the view of the amusements without those encroachments on their comfort which [were] the subject of such general complaint" [9]; and two years later a numbers board giving the names of the riders was introduced [10].

The prospect of the inaugural "Liverpool Grand Steeple Chase" attracted "extraordinary interest, not only in the sporting circles, but with the public generally" [11]; and on the day itself large crowds made their way out to Aintree to witness this historic occasion. Sadly, for reasons which will become apparent later, historians of the Grand National have tended to ignore this first running of the race, so, to redress the balance, this contemporary account must be given:

"On Monday last the first steeplechase ever run in the neighbourhood of Liverpool came off in the enclosed grounds near the Aintree race-course. As it was anticipated, the novelty of the exhilarating scene drew together an immense concourse of spectators, and, singular as it may appear to those who have witnessed the motley groups assembled on the course at the [flat] races, the assemblage was composed principally of the middle classes. There was, however, no want of the mobility experienced, as there was ample supply for any good purpose. The innkeepers who usually attend the races had their booths fitted up for the convenience of sportsmen and the public, and the good cheer provided was highly satisfactory. The country chosen for the race, which was not to exceed five miles in distance, was so appropriately chosen by the noble umpire (Lord Molyneux) to enhance the pleasure of the visitors, that it formed a complete amphitheatre in front of the grand stand, every spectator having the advantage of viewing the whole with the *naked* eye. Those (and there were many) who furnished themselves with telescopes, saw every portion of the race, even to the most minute leap at the most remote distance. The excitement that prevailed touching the contest for "the first Liverpool steeple chase" both *before* and *on* the day of running can only be conceived by the supporters of, and those particularly interested in, field sports. For a considerable time prior to the day, it was the universal theme of conversation and speculation in the sporting circles, with the exception of the Chester Cup, on which latter almost as much money has been ventured as on any great St. Leger. Sportsmen, amateurs, ladies and gentlemen, appeared in great numbers from various parts of the country, and long before the time of starting the main road, lanes and avenues leading to Aintree were thronged with pedestrians, equestrians, and equipages of all sorts. Independent of the superior character of the treat provided, the auspicious appearance of the weather was sufficient to chase away sorrow from the most miserable hypochondriac, and to the beauty of the day, coupled to the fact that the most renowned and daring riders were to compete, is to be attributed the large attendance. The line of road selected for the chase was excellently adapted for the display of the activity of the horses, and the ingenuity and intrepidity of the riders, being intersected with ditches, dangerous fences and ploughed fields. About one o'clock the whole of the company had arrived on the course. The grand stand was filled in every story, as was also several others. The lower part of the former had for its occupants chiefly elegantly dressed females.

"The betting on the first race rather fluctuated from Saturday to Monday. In the first instance the odds were 5 to 2 against Laurie Todd, 4 to 1 against The Duke, 5 to 1 against Percy, 6 to 1 against The Baronet, 8 to 1 against Gulliver, 8 to 1 against Derry, 9 to 1 against Cockahoop, 10 to 1 against [Mr.] Ward's Sweep, and 12 to 1 against Cowslip or any other. On Saturday night and up to Monday morning the odds were 3 to 1 against Laurie Todd, and 3 to 1 against The Duke, and £500 were laid at evens. Polyanthus and Percy were at about 8 to 1, and 100 to 5 was laid against the Sweep. As the first race drew nigh the odds continued to change, but in a trifling degree, as will be seen by the statement at the start. Ten were entered for the great race, and the prize was a sweepstakes of 10 sovs. each with 80 added, for horses of all denominations, carrying 12 stone each; the riders to be gentlemen. The second horse was to receive back his stake, and, as a guarantee that no horse should be entered to carry away the race without a contest, the conditions were that the winner be sold for 200 sovs. if demanded. The horses for the race were:

Sir T. Stanley's b.g. Laurie Todd, aged, purple and crimson (Powell)
Mr. Oswald's b.g. Gulliver, yellow and black sleeves (Denton)
Mr. Kershaw's The Baronet, yellow and black stripe (Kershaw)
Mr. Ward's blk. h. The Sweep, salmon colour (Patrick)
Mr. Aspinall's Polyanthus, yellow (Christian)
Mr. Sirdefield's ch.g. The Duke, lilac and white (Capt. Beecher)
Mr. Thomas's ch.g. Cockahoop, orange (Bretherton)
Mr. Webster's ch.g. Derry, purple crimson (Devine)
Mr. Speed's ch.h. Percy, crimson and white (Tempest)
Mr. Devine's Cowslip, straw colour (Martin)

"Previous to the start the betting was not great, being all in favour of two horses, viz Laurie Todd and The Duke, who were backed safe to win. Most of the animals had been hunted the whole of the season, and the superior qualities of the two, evinced by their exploits 'in flood and field', rendered them the favourites. Laurie Todd had the decided call, and it was supposed nothing would beat him if he could stay on his leap. The odds immediately before the race were 2 to 1 against Laurie Todd, 3 to 1 against The Duke, 5 to 1 against Polyanthus and 6 to 1 against Percy. Nothing else was wasted a thought upon. About two o'clock the horses, mounted by their respective riders, caprisoned in the style mentioned, turned out for a start. The top of the course was the place appointed as the rendezvous to meet and be off, and the line of country was marked by flags, being hoisted at convenient distances from the course down to below Seed's farm. The turnpike road was then crossed, and a turn to the left was then to be taken, where sixteen or eighteen fences had alternately to be leaped. The run was then on the banks of the canal, and from thence to the race-course, coming in opposite the grand stand; this road was to be twice run over. The whole lot came up well for a start immediately at the top of the course, and the word 'Go' being given by the umpire, off went the steeple-chasers. Speed's Percy took the lead, Cockahoop second and The Duke third. Powell on Laurie Todd kept his distance, apparently by design, and was contented with being last but one at the start. The first fence, in front of which was a large ditch, some of the horses shyed at, but eventually all got over, Captain Becher and Percy being the first to cover the ground. By this movement of the horses Polyanthus, Derry and Cowslip lost ground; the former, however, soon took up a more favourable position. Having leaped the sixteen hedges and ditches, on regaining the course the first time round eight only were preceptible. The eight cleared the last two hurdles. Gulliver and Cowslip were distressed. The Duke now took the lead for the second time round, The Baronet second and Cockahoop third, Laurie Todd last but one but still the favourite, two to one being freely offered on him. When at the third fence Laurie came up and challenged The Duke considerable anxiety was now manifested by the spectators, and nothing was heard but the odds on The Duke or Laurie. Previous to arriving at the last fence, Mr. Powell, the rider of the last named horse, was suddenly thrown, in consequence of the impediment of a gate being suddenly and accidentally closed. He was rising on the instant to remount when Cockahoop, ridden by Mr. Bretherton, passed closed by and again threw him. Laurie was consequently distressed and the contest became between Percy, Polyanthus, The Duke and Cockahoop. The Duke and Polyanthus leaped the hurdles at the *finale* almost neck and neck, and in doing so made a complete road through them for the other two. The victory was now evidently either The Duke's or Polyanthus's, and a beautiful race from the hurdles ensued, four to one on The Duke, who succeeded in winning by about a length, his rider coming in with the saddle on his horse's crupper. It was a matter of some surprise and great pleasure to see Polyanthus's performance of such a first-rate character. Few anticipated the result, and it is since the opinion of the sporting circles that he would have won had he not carried four pounds extra weight. Cockahoop came third. The misfortune of Laurie Todd was much felt by those who had speculated their money on him, and it appears they had every reason, as he looked determined to win before the accident befell him. Dr. Grindrod was in immediate attendance on Mr. Powell, and the lovers of the chase and other friends of that gentleman will be happy to hear that he received no serious injuries. The time occupied in the chase was twenty minutes and ten seconds" [12].

Like so many later Grand Nationals, this first race was not free from controversy, for it was far from accidental that the gate at the Melling Road was suddenly closed in front of the favourite, just as he looked a certainty to win. Another spectator gave more detail on this distinctly shady incident:

"Lord Molyneux, the umpire, in his arrangements of the ground had directed a gate in the line to be left open. It was agreeably to his Lordship's directions nailed back to a post; after the horses had gone through this gate the first time round a person who was connected with the owner of one of the horses came up to the gate and, with an oath, declared that they should not go through it again but should leap it, and immediately closed the gate and fastened it with a lock. The consequence was that when the horses came around a second time they found it shut and some of them took the gate while others went over a fence near it into a paved lane. Laurie Todd fell at it and lost the race. Everybody is of the opinion that he would have won in a canter, if this gate had not been shut" [13].

Such was the outcry over this foul play that Lynn offered a reward of £10 for the discovery of who was responsible. It turned out to be the brother of the owner of one of the horses, although which one is not clear. Bretherton's action in riding down Powell as he was attempting to remount suggests that the connections of Cockahoop may have had something to do with it; but this can only be a guess.

Be that as it may, the result was allowed to stand and The Duke and Captain Becher should rightly be accorded the honour of being the first winners of the Grand National. Becher is now remembered only for falling in the brook that bears his name during Lottery's Grand National in 1839, but his contemporaries certainly regarded him as the winner of the first "Liverpool" [14] and it is high time that the record concerning this most generous and sporting of riders is put straight.

The Duke too has received less than his due from turf historians. Described at the time as a hunting sort of cob, his portrait shows him to have been a good looking bright chestnut with one white sock. He was to run again at Aintree on several occasions. Returning first to compete in two hurdle races on the same afternoon in October 1836, he was unplaced in both of them [15]. More notably, he was also a runner in the next two "Grand Liverpools", becoming the first dual winner by his victory in 1837, and coming third in 1838. It is a remarkable fact that in all the years since then only two horses have had a better record over the Aintree fences, Manifesto (two wins, three thirds, one fourth and one eighth), and the incomparable Red Rum (three wins and two seconds). This is the true

The Duke. The first winner of the Grand National

measure of The Duke's achievements, and he deserves to be better remembered.

Both Laurie Todd and Polyanthus also returned to Liverpool to compete in hurdle races at the October meeting, with Polyanthus winning his race (and gaining revenge over The Duke in the process), and Laurie Todd coming second in his [16].

Three final points concerning this first "Liverpool Grand Steeple-Chase" need to be made. First, it sometimes has been objected that this race cannot be regarded as a precursor of the National because of the selling clause in the conditions. Too much should not be made of this. If the conditions as a whole are studied, it is clear that the object of the promoters was to provide a race of the highest quality, and that the selling clause was only there as a device to prevent what was intended as a prestigious event becoming a walkover. In this they were successful, as all the contemporary accounts make clear. In any event, it seems as if the selling clause was not invoked, for when The Duke ran again at Aintree in October he was still registered as owned by Mr. Sirdefield.

Secondly, turf historians have been reluctant to consider this race in 1836 as the first Grand National because it has for so long been believed that the races in 1837 and 1838 took place at Maghull, and that the continuous sequence of races at Aintree started only in 1839. Mrs. Mirabel Topham, who for so long ruled over Aintree, always maintained that any race that took place away from Aintree could not be counted a true Grand National, and in this, of course, she was right; where she was wrong was in believing that these races were held at Maghull, and once it is accepted that they too were held at Aintree, then an entirely different picture of the early history of the race emerges.

Thirdly, it is worth noting that in Liverpool the 1839 race only came to be regarded as the first National many years afterwards; the 1870 Grand National, for example, was referred to in the local press as the 34th [17], and some publications were giving 1836 as the date of the first National as late as the 1890s [18]. It was primarily the national press, based in London, which, for reasons which will appear below, later spread the belief that the race only began three years later.

What is indisputable is that Lynn had a popular success on his hands. "To get up a race of this kind so as to afford satisfaction to all parties is no easy matter with those who have had the benefit of many years' experience; it is no small credit, therefore, to the spirited proprietor of the Waterloo Tavern (Mr. Lynn) and his able coadjutor Mr. Webster [Lynn's Clerk of the Course] that these, their maiden efforts, should have realised such flattering results", commented *Bell's Life* [19]. With words such as these ringing in his ears, Lynn must have thought his fortune made, and he can hardly have needed the suggestion of the sporting press that the event become an annual fixture [20].

Notes and references

1. *Liverpool Chronicle*, 25 October 1834.
2. *Liverpool Chronicle*, 3 October 1835.

3. This description of Lord Waterford is by W.S. Gilbert in *Patience;* as far as I know, Lord Waterford is the only character in these pages to appear, albeit fleetingly, in a Gilbert and Sullivan operetta.
4. *Sportsman's Magazine*, Vol. 1, no. 24, 1 November 1845, p.401; *Sporting Review,* Vol. 52 (1864), pp.400-404; *Bell's Life*, 22 October 1864; *The Times*, 17 October 1864; 'Thormanby'. Sporting stories, pp.105-109.
5. *Liverpool Chronicle*, 9 January 1836.
6. *Liverpool Chronicle*, 9 January 1836.
7. *Bell's Life*, 6 March 1836.
8. *Bell's Life*, 19 July 1840.
9. *Bell's Life*, 19 July 1840.
10. *Bell's Life*, 17 July 1842.
11. *Liverpool Chronicle*, 27 February 1836.
12. *Liverpool Courier,* 2 March 1836.
13. *Bell's Life*, 6 March 1836.
14. *Sporting Review,* Vol. 52 (1864), pp.400-404; *The Times*, 17 October 1864; *Bell's Life*, 22 October 1864.
15. *Racing Calendar,* 1836, p.208.
16. *Racing Calendar*, 1836, p.208.
17. *Liverpool Mercury,* 10 March 1870.
18. *Liverpool Review,* 26 March 1892, p.5. A careful reading of the chapter on Liverpool in John Tyrrel's *Chasing around Britain* suggests that he is the only modern writer on the race to have reached the same conclusion.
19. *Bell's Life*, 6 March 1836.
20. *The Times*, 3 March 1836.

5.

Two Neglected Grand Nationals

In Aintree's County Stand are honours boards which list all the winners of the Grand National from 1837 onwards. However, after the returns for 1837 and 1838 are written the words "The above two races were run over a course at Maghull"; and it is this seemingly straightforward statement which has caused so many writers on the history of the race to conclude that 1839 marks the first true Grand National [1]. The most recent historian of the race, Reg Green, suggests that, as Lynn was still a little cautious about this new form of racing, he "joined forces with Formby for the renewal in 1837 and the race was run at Maghull" [2].

The foundation stone for Aintree's County Stand, dated June 12th, 1886

Examination of the evidence makes it clear that this view is no longer tenable. First, there is the date of the statement itself to consider. The age of the honours boards at Aintree is not known, but the style of the lettering suggests that they date from the late 19th century at the earliest; in any case they cannot predate the building of that part of the County Stand, which is known to have been erected in the late 1880s, and they may even date from after the disastrous fire which destroyed most of the stands in 1892

WINNERS OF THE LIVERPOOL GRAND NATIONAL STEEPLECHASE.

YEAR	OWNER	WINNER	AGES	ST-LB	M-S	RIDER	STRS
1837	Mr SIRDEFIELD	THE DUKE				Mr POTTS	6
1838	Mr THOMPSON	SIR HENRY				OLIVER	10
THE ABOVE 2 RACES WERE RUN OVER A COURSE AT MAGHULL							
1839	Mr ELMORE	LOTTERY		12-0		J. MASON	17
1840	Mr ELMORE	JERRY		12-0		B.BRETHERTON	13
1841	Ld CRAVEN	CHARITY		12-0		POWELL	10
1842	Mr ELMORE	GAYLAD		12-0		T.OLIVER	15
1843	Ld CHESTERFIELD	VANGUARD		11-10		T.OLIVER	16
1844	Mr QUARTERMAINE	DISCOUNT		10-12		CRICKMERE	16
1845	Mr W.S.CRAWFORD	CUREALL	a	11-5		LOFT	15
1846	Mr ADAMS	PIONEER	6	11-12		TAYLOR	22
1847	Mr COURTNEY	MATTHEW	a	10-6	10-39	WYNNE	28
1848	CAPT LITTLE	CHANDLER	a	11-12	11-21	CAPT LITTLE	29
1849	Mr MASON Junr	PETER SIMPLE	a	11-0	10-37	T.CUNNINGHAM	23

YEAR	OWNER	WINNER	AGES	ST-LB	M-S	RIDER	STRS
1880	Mr S.DUCROT	EMPRESS	5	10-7	10-20	Mr T.BEASLEY	14
1881	CAPT KIRKWOOD	WOODBROOK	a	11-3	11-50	Mr T.BEASLEY	13
1882	Ld MANNERS	SEAMAN	6	11-6	10-42⅖	Ld MANNERS	12
1883	Ct C.KINSKY	ZOEDONE	6	11-0	11-39	Ct C.KINSKY	10
1884	Mr H.F. BOYD	VOLUPTUARY	6	10-5	10-5	Mr E.P. WILSON	15
1885	Mr A.COOPER	ROQUEFORT	6	11-0	10-10	Mr E.P. WILSON	19
1886	Mr A.J.DOUGLAS	OLD JOE	a	10-9	10-14⅗	T.SKELTON	23
1887	Mr E.J.THORNEWILL	GAMECOCK	a	11-0	10-10⅕	W. DANIELS	16
1888	Mr E.W.BAIRD	PLAYFAIR	a	10-7	10-12	MAWSON	20
1889	Mr M.A.MAHER	FRIGATE	a	11-4	10-1⅕	Mr T.BEASLEY	20
1890	Mr C.MASTERMANS	ILEX	6	10-5	10-41⅕	A.NIGHTINGALL	16
1891	Mr W.C.JAMESON	COME AWAY	a	11-12	9-58	Mr H.BEASLEY	21
1892	Mr G.C.WILSON	FATHER O'FLYNN	a	10-5	9-48⅘	CAPT E.R.OWEN	25
[illegible]	Mr C.G.DUFF	CLOISTER	a	12-7	9-32⅖	DOLLERY	15

The honours board at Aintree

[3]. It is also clear that the entries themselves are taken from the returns in Weatherbys' *Steeplechases past* which was first produced in 1866/67, thirty years after the events in question and when memories of those early steeplechases were beginning to dim. In contrast, no *contemporary* source mentions Maghull as the location of these races. Nor need this surprise us, for, as we have already seen, racing at Maghull had ceased in 1835. To reinforce the point, not a single source – the *Racing Calendar, Bell's Life*, or any of the Liverpool papers – lists any returns at all from there after that date.

Writing between the wars, T.H. Bird attempted to get round the problem by suggesting that although these races started and finished at Aintree, they may have crossed into the neighbouring area of Maghull [4]. A glance at the map, however, swiftly disposes of this idea, for to reach Maghull from Aintree the horses would have had to cross the Leeds to Liverpool Canal. There were only two ways they could have done this, either by going round the back of the stands and following the main Liverpool to Ormskirk road to the bridge by the Old Roan, or by turning on to the Melling Road and crossing the canal at Anchor Bridge. In either case, they would then have had to race across about a mile of marshy ground and cross the River Alt before reaching Maghull itself. In doing so they would have been out of sight of the crowds in the stands, one of Lynn's main selling points the previous year. This suggestion is, therefore, highly unlikely, to

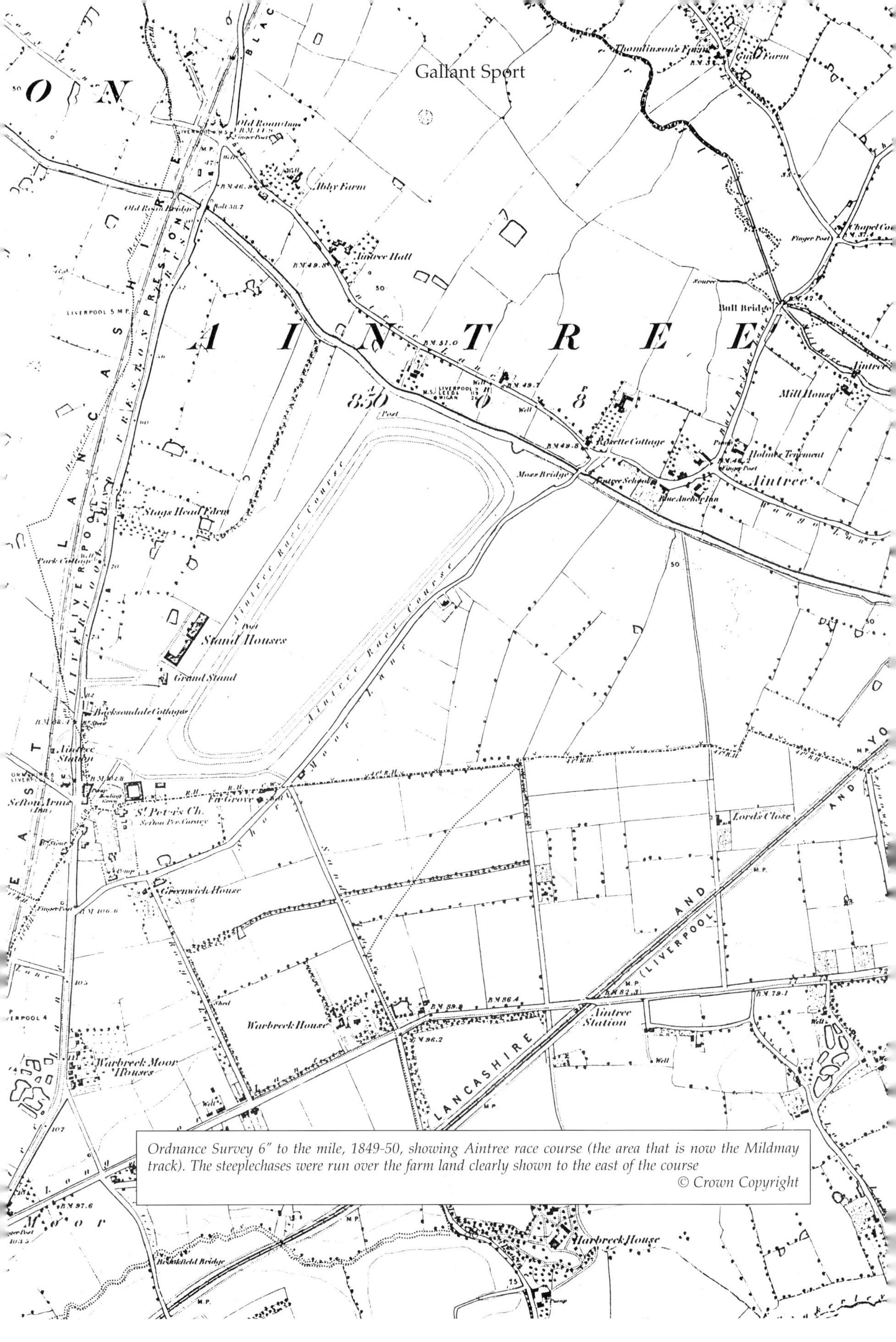

Ordnance Survey 6" to the mile, 1849-50, showing Aintree race course (the area that is now the Mildmay track). The steeplechases were run over the farm land clearly shown to the east of the course say the least, and, in fairness, Bird seems only to have put it forward in a half-hearted way, since most of the evidence he gives supports the view that these early races took place only at Aintree.

Nor was there any reason why in 1837 the race should have been transferred to Maghull. The previous year Lynn had triumphantly staged the first Liverpool Steeplechase at Aintree, and he can have had no possible motive to transfer it elsewhere, least of all into the hands of the man whose deadly rival he had been, and whose course he had forced into closure only a couple of years before. Lynn's view of Formby is not recorded, but the fact that neither Formby nor any of his associates was given a place on the Aintree race committee after the "merger" speaks volumes; whilst, for his part, Formby thought that Lynn was "egregiously ignorant" in all racing matters [5]. The idea of these two men ever being "close associates" [6] goes against everything that we know about them.

Finally and conclusively, there are the contemporary descriptions of the line of country that was raced over in 1837 and 1838. The *Liverpool Standard*'s account of the 1838 "Liverpool Steeplechase" shows beyond all shadow of doubt that all these early races took place over the same course as had been chosen in 1836, and which was also to be used in 1839 and every year since:

"The line of country chosen was the same as that run over on former occasions of a similar nature at Aintree. A part of the line was made up of the race-course, the horses starting from near the stand, breaking off to the right over the country, making a circuit of about two miles and a half, and again joining the course at the opposite end near the bridge over the Leeds and Liverpool Canal, and coming up to the race-course to the left to the winning post." [7]

No-one reading those words can possibly believe that Maghull has any part to play in Grand National history. Nor can it be doubted that the races of 1836-1838 should be restored to their rightful position in the record books.

Following his success in 1836, Lynn became more ambitious in 1837. In particular, he persuaded the Town Council to provide 100 guineas of added prize money; this was a notable achievement given that the Council was then controlled by the Whigs, who were normally no friends to horse racing. In an attempt to attract a greater number of runners, the race was also made a limited handicap, the winner of one steeplechase or hurdle race to carry 5lbs extra, and the winner of two races 7lbs extra.

Lynn did, however, make one mistake. He arranged his race to take place on the day following the big St. Albans Chase, and this explains both the small field and the absence of most of the leading jockeys. Amongst the horses entered at St. Albans that year were Conrad and Lottery, whilst the riders included Jem Mason and Captain Becher. All four were to gain immortality at Aintree two years later in the race which was conclusively to establish the "Liverpool" as the premier steeplechase in the country, but at this time most southern-based owners and jockeys still regarded St. Albans as the more important event. Moreover, until the opening of the railway between Liverpool and the south it was difficult to transport racehorses over such a long distance, especially at short notice. Flat racing faced the same problems, and it is noteworthy that few horses were entered for both the Derby and the St. Leger until after the coming of the railway.

Even without these stars the 1837 race attracted a good deal of attention and promised to be the best of the season [8]. Interest centred on the prospect of a return match between The Duke and Polyanthus, and on the first Irish runner, Dan O'Connell, who came to Aintree a hot favourite. Unfortunately, Polyanthus was a late withdrawal, owing to "peculiar circumstances" which were thought to have to do with a disagreement between his owner and the trainer [9]; and in the event only four horses went to post. In the absence of Captain Becher, The Duke was ridden by Cheshire farmer Henry Potts; Dan O'Connell was ridden by his owner, Mr. Knaresborough; Irish rider Alan McDonogh had his first ride at Aintree on The Disowned; and the field was completed by Zanga, ridden by Mr. Devine. As in the previous year, the race was not without incident, with the favourite coming to grief at the biggest fence on the course, and bringing down two of the other three runners with him. Here is how the correspondent of *Bell's Life* saw it:

"Dan took the lead to the first fence, followed closely by The Duke, The Disowned third, and Zanga fourth. This fence on the opposite side had a wide ditch, over which lead to the main road. He dropped into the road, sprang on to the opposite side in beautiful style, and got well away. The Disowned and Zanga both got cleverly away from the lane and went up to

Dan. Meanwhile The Duke was boggling at the bank in the lane, and lost a whole field's length before he crept out of it. His prospects, however, across the field appeared good, for the great Dan, the violent Zanga and The Disowned were all in a heap, bungling and refusing at a fence (a bank and ditch) in the most ungracious manner. The gallant old Duke spun away at the fence, cleared it in aristocratic style, without in fact noticing the plebeian 'bog-trotters' who were blundering about in the ditch below him; and he went six or seven fields ahead before The Disowned would own the soft insinuation of Mr. McDonogh that his chance was rapidly going to Pott. To gain upon The Duke and get over this difficulty he had to make up half a mile of ground at least while The Duke was sailing away at his own pace over the fallows and taking his fences in a dreadnought style. The Duke was never headed after this, and won by a dozen lengths without distress, to the satisfaction of the friends of his worthy and spirited owner, Mr. Sirdefield; and those who had backed the field against the Irisher came home without the tail, but did not go the second round, The Duke having so much the best of it, that he was nearly round the last time before Dan could gain the second fence on his second essay to go round. Zanga never came round at all, but was just visible to the naked eye in the distant country, dancing in 'Devine' style to the musical voice of his rider" [10].

The race was a great triumph for The Duke, who was now lauded as "as good a heavy-weight steeple chaser as any in the North" [11], whilst "the riding of Mr. Potts was splendid, and the manner of his getting his horse over the bank where Dan failed excited great admiration" [12]. At the time of the race Henry Potts was twenty-seven years old and a bachelor. According to family tradition, he was somewhat ashamed of himself because he rode without his parents' knowledge. He rode at Aintree only once more when in 1838 he finished fifth in a three mile chase, riding his own horse, The Countess. He thus belongs in that select group of jockeys, of whom Dick Saunders is the most recent example, who have ridden in the National only once and won it [13]. After marrying, he retired from race riding, but continued to hunt from his stables at Beeston in Cheshire. He died in 1884.

With a crowd estimated at ten thousand present at Aintree that day [14], Lynn had reason to be pleased with the way the event had turned out.

However, during the next twelve months he suffered a series of setbacks, which contributed to his increasingly pressing financial problems.

The first of these was the relatively lacklustre hurdles meeting in October 1837. Despite the generous prize money on offer, the entries were disappointing, and the withdrawal of Vivian was a particularly severe blow to Lynn's hopes of a large crowd. Moreover, apart from the first race, "nothing occurred worthy of the name of hurdle racing". The day was only partly redeemed by the superior jockeyship of Jem Mason who, on his first appearance at the course, won the principal race on Isaac; his riding attracted "general... admiration, nothing like it having been witnessed in this part of the country" [15].

Secondly, the Town Council, possibly as a result of pressure from animal welfare groups, withdrew their financial support and the added prize money Lynn was able to offer for the 1838 Liverpool Steeplechase was reduced to a relatively meagre 25 sovereigns.

Thirdly, the weather during the spring of 1838 was very bad, and the race had to be postponed from late February to early March [16]. This meant that instead of taking place before the Metropolitan Chase (won by Jem Mason on Lottery), when it might have attracted more interest, the Liverpool Steeplechase now took place a few days after it, with the same adverse effects as in the previous year. On this occasion, however, at least Captain Becher managed to be present, to be reunited with his old partner, The Duke, now attempting his hat-trick. But with the number of runners reduced to three, the race did not excite so great an interest as its two predecessors, and the crowd was well down on that of the year before.

In fact, so quickly was the race forgotten, at least outside the immediate vicinity, that even the name of the winner has become a matter of dispute. The official record, as given in *Steeplechases past*, and repeated on the honours boards at Aintree, is that the winner was a horse called Sir Henry, ridden by Tom Olliver. However, as we have already seen, *Steeplechases past* is not a reliable source for these early races, and all the contemporary sources are agreed that the winner was Sir William, ridden by his owner, Alan McDonogh [17]. Moreover, none of them lists any horse called Sir Henry as having run at the meeting; nor does Tom Olliver appear to have been riding there. The evidence seems conclusive, and it is high time the official record was amended and Sir William and Alan McDonogh given their proper due.

This 1838 race may not have attracted much interest nationally, either at the time or since, but it evidently was the cause of a good deal of excitement locally. It received the following enthusiastic notice in the *Liverpool Standard*, which *inter alia* confirms that although the fences were different the race took place over the same line of country as that in use today:

"The Liverpool Steeplechase

"Yesterday morning this much talked of Steeplechase came off over Aintree Race-course. If it had been possible for the lovers of the sport to choose a day, they could not have fixed upon one more auspicious, or more beautifully fine and vernal. The rain and 'Scotch mist' which ushered in the evening of Sunday had quite disappeared, and on Monday morning it dawned with a clear blue sky, and an atmosphere as mild as that of May. As the day proceeded, the genial rays of the sun, and the wafting of a gentle breeze, made the face of nature delightful and the day most exhilarating. The concourse of spectators drawn to the scene of action was not very great, though speaking comparatively a considerable number were assembled. The ground, notwithstanding the recent downfall of rain, was in excellent condition. During the night it had dried wonderfully; and instead of being heavy and sloppy, the surface was only of an elastic softness and perfectly free from wet; indeed it could hardly be in better condition. The line of country was that run over on former occasions... The principal obstacles were not, however, of so formidable a nature as on previous occasions. The leap which baulked Dan O'Connell... was completely deprived of its former difficulty, and rendered one of very ordinary nature, by the raising of the land on one side and the lowering of the fence, leaving little more than an ordinary gutter, and not a very high bank and fence at the opposite side to get over. The country from the top of the stand presented a beautiful appearance. The atmosphere was so clear that every part of the racing ground could easily be distinguished, and consequently in the chase the riders were never lost sight of. In order to give our readers something like an idea of the country to be ridden over, let them imagine themselves on the stand with the race-course before them, and the starting post immediately in front. After a short gallop to the right, round about four hundred yards of the circle of the course, the steeple chase line branches abruptly off to the right, crossing the road which leads down to the canal. Here the first leap, and one of the worst, presents itself. The road being about two yards below the level of the race-course, the horses had to take a low fence at the top of the bank into the road, which was immediately crossed, and a similar perpendicular bank, with a low stiff fence upon it, was to be got over at the other side of the road, which was evidently the most difficult leap in the line of country. This lead into a fallow field, over which was rather heavy running, but nothing of any great moment, the land being loamy, but not very wet. At the opposite side of the field was the leap of former occasions... which we shall term *Dan O'Connell*'s leap. From this a succession of stubble and grass fields follow in succession down to the side of the canal, the country presenting no particular obstacle, generally low fences with blind gutters. On reaching the side of the canal, the course lay along its right bank, with an occasional low fence, to the bridge over the canal, which is a continuance of the road before crossed. Here the road is again crossed, and the line of the steeplechase comes on to the race-course again; about half a mile of which is in a straight line to the winning post, and in this distance were two hurdles erected. We have now given a pretty good idea of the face of the country.

"The following were the regulations posted up to be observed:

1st – The riders to be shown the ground on the morning of the race.
2nd – To go outside of all the flags.
3rd – A rider going the wrong side of any flag to be considered as distanced.
4th – No person to be allowed to ride on the course without the especial consent of the umpire.
5th – The riders to weigh and be ready to start not later than 1 o'clock.
6th – Stakes to be made good before starting, or not entitled, although the winner.
7th – The money added will not be given if walked over for.

BY ORDER OF THE UMPIRE

"The gambling and thimble-rig gentry were in rather more than the usual force on the course. Upon the grand stand were Lord Mulleneux [sic] (the umpire), and his lady, Lord and Lady Talbot, Lord Stradbroke, &c. There was not much company on the stand until after the first race when the gentlemen mustered there rather strong. Very excellent ordinaries were provided by Mr. Lynn, the active secretary of the course, and by Mr. Towers of the Angel, at his establishment there.

"At two o'clock the bell rang for the first steeplechase: a Sweepstakes of 10 sovereigns, with 25 added, for horses of all denominations. Four year olds 11 st., five 11st. 7lb, six and aged 12 st. Gentlemen riders. Over a line of country not exceeding five miles, to be chosen by the umpire or such person as he may appoint. A winner of one Hurdle race or Steeple-chase before the day of running to carry 5lbs extra; two 7lbs extra. The second horse to receive back his stake. Stakes to be made good before starting, or not entitled, although a winner. Five were down on the list but the following horses only started:-

Mr. McDonogh's ch h Sir William, aged, 12st 7lb. Owner. 1
Mr. O'Moore's b h Scamp, 5yrs, 11st 12lb. Clarendon. 2
Mr. Chawner's ch g The Duke, 12 st 7lb. Capt. Beecher. 3

"The Duke is a strong hunting sort of horse, very steady and rather aged. The well-known abilities, as a steeple-chase rider, of his jockey, Captain Beecher, added much to the favour he was in. Sir William is a very light made chestnut, showing much blood, but apparently of too slight a build for the heavy work of a steeple-chase. Scamp is a very beautifully formed dark brown horse, showing much blood, and apparently better calculated for the work to be performed than Sir William, being a more compact horse and showing better loins. The result, however, proved the reverse.

"At starting, Scamp took the lead at a very easy pace, followed by Sir William at a canter, The Duke bringing up the rear. On getting into the road Scamp bolted at the fence, but at length took it, The Duke being the first over, and taking the lead at a good pace over the fallow field where he cleared in fine style Dan O'Connell's fence, followed by Sir William, Scamp tailing 100 yards behind. The Duke kept improving his advantage at every fence until he was leading his contemporaries by 200 yards; Scamp being about 40 yards behind Sir William. The pace was very slow. This order was preserved till the horses again entered the race-course, the pace continuing very easy. All three horse cleared well the first hurdle. The second hurdle was cleared beautifully by The Duke; he was followed about fifty yards behind by Sir William, and Scamp still further behind. The pace was still easy. The second time round then commenced and the pace began to be more severe. All the horse cleared well the road fences, and also Dan O'Connell's fence, though The Duke, from taking his leaps with more ease and in a more workman-like manner, gained on his competitors at every fence, till he was nearly three hundred yards ahead. On approaching the bridge, where there is a greater distance of free running, Sir William pushed hard to overtake him. This, however, was thought impossible, and the betting was now all on The Duke. Sir William, however, rapidly gained on The Duke, and had decreased the distance between them full one third when they entered the race-course, where it soon became apparent that The Duke had no chance with Sir William as a racer. Scamp also began to catch up and was not far behind Sir William. The scene now was most animating. The Duke was evidently straining every nerve to maintain his advantage, while Sir William and Scamp were absolutely catching him and going twice his pace. It then became apparent that he could win only by very great exertions. On rounding the corner into the last straight half mile, Sir William seemed to be running over him, and when they had arrived at the first hurdle, both went over together and Scamp close behind. The Duke was now evidently breaking down, killed by the pace. He was passed, and the last hurdle cleared first by Sir William, The Duke immediately after him and breaking down the hurdle, with Scamp close at his heels. The Duke was then passed by Scamp and came in last, dead beat, Sir William winning easily by about 40 yards. The race altogether was a very beautiful one. The riding of both Mr. McDonogh and Captain Beecher was very much admired. The betting was 2 to 1 against The Duke; on running 2 to 1 on The Duke, 2 to 1 against Sir William, and 3 to 1 against Scamp" [18]. McDonogh then followed up his triumph in the big chase, by winning both heats of the succeeding hurdle race on The Disowned. He was the first Irish jockey to win over the Liverpool fences.

Alan McDonogh

Alan McDonogh was born in Galway in 1804 and began riding in steeplechases in Ireland around 1830. Sir William was his first good horse, but although he was a fine chaser, he was cursed with a temper. On one occasion in 1837 McDonogh had a bad fall from him in a steeplechase near Chester, and was dragged along the ground for some way, although he then managed to remount, and was still able to win the race. Sometime after their Liverpool triumph, McDonogh was deliberately knocked off Sir William in a race at Dunchurch, breaking his collar bone and two ribs. Whilst recovering from his injuries he sold Sir William to John Elmore, the well-known horse dealer and owner of Lottery, for £350. Elmore promptly resold him to Lord Cranstown for £1000, and Cranstown then proposed a match for £1000 (an enormous sum for a steeplechase in those days) over four miles against Lord Suffield's famous Jerry, who was later to win the Grand National of 1840. This match excited enormous public interest, and as McDonogh was the only man who could ride Sir William, he came over from Ireland especially. It proved a worthwhile journey, for Jerry uncharacteristically refused at the first fence and Sir William won as he liked. McDonogh continued race riding for many years after this, being particularly associated with a mare called Brunette, on whom he won over twenty races and finished sixth in the 1847 National. He never won the race again, but he finished second twice, in 1840 and 1841, and was fifth on The Nun in 1839. In his later years, he liked to recount anecdotes of the old time, told in a rich Galway brogue, and at his death in 1888 he was mourned as one of the most elegant horsemen ever to be seen in the saddle [19].

If the 1838 Liverpool Steeplechase was a success for McDonogh and Sir William, the small field and the relative lack of interest in the race must have been deeply worrying for William Lynn. Nor did the ensuing flat racing season bring about a change to his fortunes. After the Craven meeting in May, the *Liverpool Chronicle* commented that "it is to be hoped for the success of these races, that some measures may be adopted to ensure a better entry of horses" [20], whilst the opening day of the summer meeting in July was ruined by bad weather, with the result that "the number of individuals at the course was not very great; the grand stand was not half full" [21].

Only Lynn and his creditors knew exactly how much Aintree was costing him. It is impossible now to reconstitute Lynn's finances in their entirety, but what is known is that he was beginning to fall behind in his rent to Lord Sefton. By 1837 the annual rental for the race course had risen to £668, and Lynn's arrears of rent stood at £300 [22]. By the following year he had managed to reduce the debt by £200, but he was never able to wipe it out completely. He was perhaps lucky that his consistently late payments were regarded with a certain amount of equanimity by his sporting landlord and the estate officials with whom he had to deal. In May 1839, for example, Lord Sefton's Steward noted that Lynn owed £768, but that "the receipt has always been postponed until after the July races" [23].

These figures would not have been publicly known, but the general picture was clear enough to contemporaries. As early as 1836 it was noted that Lynn had held four race meetings during the year and had provided almost all the prize money, about £1000, himself. He also had "to pay a heavy rent for the ground, to compensate the proprietors of the Maghull course, and to pay for posts, rails, &c., in addition to an immense outlay in the erection of the Stand" [24]. One source estimates the total expenditure on the course at over £20,000 [25]. It may have been true that horse racing had "of late decidedly hit the taste of a vast number of Liverpudlians" [26], but it was also true that few of them wished to pay for their pleasure, and their lack of liberality in contributing to the Racing Fund was noted on more than one occasion [27]. Indeed, the "race fund", with its implication of there being a large number of subscribers, was something of a fiction, for "nearly the whole of the money came from one pocket, and the inhabitants [of Liverpool] were almost innocent in the matter" [28]. By the end of 1838 Lynn's losses were such that he could not carry on for much longer, and it was this financial imperative above all other considerations which led him to stage "the greatest steeple-chase ever known in this or any other country" [29] in 1839. An enormous popular success would restore his fortunes as well as the reputation of Aintree as the venue for the most important steeplechase of the season. Unfortunately for Lynn, his triumphant success in achieving the second of these aims came just too late to save him from his creditors, with consequences which need to be examined in some detail.

Notes and references

1. See for example the books by Munroe, Smyly, King, Holland and Thompson.
2. Green. A race apart, p.10.
3. The foundation stone on the south east corner of the building is dated 12 June 1885. The fire is reported in *The Times*, 30 September 1892.
4. Bird. A hundred Grand Nationals, p.10. But Bird goes on to state (p.11) that Lynn did not run the National "over John Formby's course at Maghull or anywhere but at Aintree", which agrees with my findings.
5. Formby. An account of the Liverpool races, p.24.
6. Green. A race apart, p.9.
7. *Liverpool Standard*, 6 March 1838.
8. *Bell's Life*, 15 January 1837.
9. *Bell's Life*, 5 March 1837.
10. *Bell's Life*, 5 March 1837.
11. *Bell's Life*, 5 March 1837.
12. *Liverpool Times*, 7 March 1837.
13. Bird. A hundred Grand Nationals, pp.19, 22.
14. *Liverpool Times*, 7 March 1837.
15. *Bell's Life*, 15 October 1837.
16. *Liverpool Standard*, 20 February 1838.
17. The *Sporting Magazine*, April 1838, p.468, disagrees to the extent of giving Henry Potts as the jockey, but the rest of the press is unanimous that McDonogh was the rider.
18. *Liverpool Standard*, 6 March 1838.
19. *Baily's Magazine*, June 1888, pp.269-270.
20. *Liverpool Chronicle*, 19 May 1838.
21. *Liverpool Chronicle*, 21 July 1838.
22. Molyneux estate rent books, 1836-40, Molyneux Muniments DDM 12/120.
23. Letter from William Eaton Hall to Lord Sefton, 25 May 1839, Molyneux Muniments DDM 6/14.
24. *Bell's Life*, 16 October 1836.
25. Gore's Directory 1895: annals of Liverpool.

26. *Liverpool Chronicle*, 19 May 1838.
27. *Bell's Life*, 16 October 1836, 3 March 1839.
28. *Bell's Life*, 3 March 1839.
29. *Bell's Life*, 3 March 1839.

6.

Triumphs and troubles: Aintree, 1839-1850

All Lynn's ambitions for Aintree were fulfilled with the 1839 "Liverpool Great Steeple Chase". Although this may not have been the first race in the series it was undoubtedly the one that established the Aintree spectacular as the most prestigious and popular steeplechase of the season, a status it continued to hold for at least the next one hundred years, and to a large extent, the Cheltenham Gold Cup notwithstanding, it still holds today. Famous all over England at the time, it is a race that is still famous today, for, however little else they may know about steeplechasing, many people know that Lottery won the "first" Grand National and that in the same race Captain Becher fell into the brook that still bears his name. It is a story that is so well-known as to need no retelling in conventional prose. What is less recognised is that it is, so far as I am aware, the only National about which a popular song has been written. Sung to the tune of a well-known song of the time, called "Bow wow wow" [1], this told the story of the race as follows, wittily mentioning every runner in the process:

"Ye lads who love a steeple chace, and danger freely court, Sir,
Hark forward all to Liverpool to join the gallant sport, Sir,
The English and the Irish nags are ready for the fray, Sir,
and which may lose, and which may win, 'tis very hard to say, Sir.
Bow wow wow, odds against the favourite,
Bow wow wow.

"More brilliant cattle never ran, in limb as stout as heart, Sir,
In breathless expectation all, and eager for the start, Sir,
The Riders governing the prade with courage and with skill, Sir,
Despising rasper, brook and fence, cold duck and breakneck spill, Sir.
Bow wow wow, neck or nothing are the words,
Bow wow wow.

"The sun in splendour, from on high, smiles sweetly on the chace, Sir,
And warm excitement fills the soul and gladdens every face, Sir,
The young and old and middle aged, in countless myriads pour, Sir,
And such a concourse never met at Liverpool before, Sir.
Bow wow wow, what a chance for prophecy,
Bow wow wow.

"That Lottery don't win the heat, the odds are five to one, Sir,
Twenty to one against True Blue, and six against The Nun, Sir,
While knowing sportsmen make their bets upon the Irish nag, Sir,
And in the chace swore Seventy Four will shortly strike its flag, Sir,
Bow wow wow, Cannon Ball will soon go off,
Bow wow wow.

"That Railroad ought to show good speed, its proud opponents drubbing,
'Gainst Daxon it is 8 to 1, and Rust will soon want scrubbing,
And Pioneer all in the rear, from every hope must roam, Sir,
And long 'twill be ere Charity will find itself at home, Sir,
Bow wow wow, Cramp will soon be doubled up,
Bow wow wow.

"Lord Waldegrave's Mirth will soon look sad, and humble the Dictator,
Fury, 'tis certain, will be spent, Revenge a harmless cratur,
Whalebone will speedily be stiff, Victory no laurels earn, Sir,
And Dan O'Connell with his tail, be very far astern, Sir.
Bow wow wow, sure he didn't want to win,
Bow wow wow.

"Tis nearly three – by Heavens, they're off, do mark each gallant steed, Sir,
And see in what superior style brave Daxon takes the lead, Sir,
His daring rider dashes on despising pale-faced fear, Sir,
Lottery, The Nun and Seventy Four close following in the rear, Sir.
Bow wow wow, splendid creatures every one,
Bow wow wow.

Captain Becher prepares to receive Cavalry
Finch Mason's view of the christening of Becher's Brook in the 1839 Grand National

"See Conrad, frightened by the crowd, refuses the first ditch, Sir,
And Beecher, head over heels, has got a gentle pitch, Sir,
And Cannon Ball is on the turf, and there it may for ever lie,
While Nun, with others that I've named, perform their duty cleverly.
Bow wow wow, darting forward to the goal,
Bow wow wow.

"Barkston is down, and Daxon too, while leading on the fun, Sir,
And in attempting to get up, unkindly floor'd the Nun, Sir,
And Charity now takes the lead, a little in advance, Sir,
A nag which some wiseacres swore would never have a chance, Sir.
Bow wow wow, knowing ones are often wrong,
Bow wow wow.

"But Charity in horse and man too often is asleep, Sir,
And the stone wall it does not like – it will not take the leap, Sir,
Railroad goes over it like a shot, as rapid as the wind, Sir,

True Blue, the Lottery, Nun and Jack, all following close behind, Sir.
Bow wow wow, hard to name the winner now,
Bow wow wow.

"See Lottery is all ahead, o'er rasper, fence and thicket,
Now what a chance for Lottery – Hurrah boys, that's the ticket,
He dashes on at winning pace, all peril he defies, Sir,
And two to one that Lottery is the winner of the prize, Sir.
Bow wow wow, some will look extremely blank,
Bow wow wow.

"The lightning speed of Lottery despises all controul, Sir,
And by two lengths and more, at length he bravely gains the goal, Sir,
Long faces there are quantum suff – some bursts of indignation,
And many a tempting yellow boy chang'd hands on this occasion.
Bow wow wow, money makes the mare to go,
Bow wow wow.

"Then here's success to Lottery, the glory of his race, Sir,
In sporting annals may he shine, a noble steeple-chacer,
And Seventy Four the second horse, for losing is no crime, Sir,
And may he boast of better luck, and win another time, Sir.
Bow wow wow, may his flag in triumph wave,
Bow wow wow.

"And long may sport in Liverpool a station proud maintain, Sir,
And let us drink The Steeple Chace in bumpers of champagne, Sir,
And if Levanters [2] should be found, the more will be the pity, Sir,
So down from Pegasus I drop, and here I close my ditty, Sir.
Bow wow wow, mustn't ride the hack too hard.
Bow wow wow. [3]

That this race generated an enormous amount of excitement and enthusiasm cannot be doubted, but there is still a question that needs to be asked. If, as we have seen, it was not the first Grand National, how did it come to be regarded as such? The answer would seem to lie in a combination of circumstances. First, this was the first year in which Lynn faced no competition from the St. Albans Steeplechase, which had become defunct by then; this meant that a better field, in terms of both numbers and quality, could be expected to contest the Liverpool race. Secondly, this was also the first year in which Liverpool could be reached by train from both London and the steeplechasing counties of the Midlands, the London and Birmingham Railway having been completed in 1838. This made the transport of horses, spectators and journalists alike considerably easier. The result was a larger field, and more publicity nationwide than its predecessors, and this in turn attracted a far larger crowd than had been present in 1838. The sheer scale of the event and the enormous excitement it generated helped to push memories of the earlier races into the background, and it is perhaps not altogether surprising that when the first histories of steeplechasing came to be written a generation later those races should have been entirely forgotten.

Thirdly, the actual words "Grand National" were first applied, albeit unofficially, to this race, the phrase having been coined by a correspondent writing under the name of "Sam Slick" in *Bell's Life* on 30 December 1838. The name reflects the increased status of the race rather than that it was the first in the series, for the course and the conditions were the same in 1839 as they had been in previous years. Lottery's race may have attracted more attention, but this in itself does not invalidate the claim of 1836 to be the first "National".

And finally, of course, there is the fact that the winner of the race, Lottery, was an equine superstar, as famed in his day as Red Rum or Desert Orchid have been in ours. Writing in 1865, "Argus" described him as "the best horse that ever looked through a bridle, combining as he did speed, stoutness, ability to go through the dirt and carry weight, extraordinary power of jumping and quickness over his fences, and in getting off again when over" [4]. His record speaks for itself. During the season 1837-38 he was second in the St. Albans Chase and won both the Metropolitan Gold Cup and the Grand Steeplechase at Daventry. The following year, in addition to his great triumph at Liverpool, he won the major chases at Maidstone, Cheltenham and Stratford, as well as coming third in the Grand Annual at Leamington, and in 1839-40 he won the Metropolitan Grand Steeplechase again, together with the races at Dunchurch, Leamington (the Grand Annual), Northampton, Cheltenham and Stratford. It was after the race at Dunchurch that Alan McDonogh made the immortal comment that "Lottery must be the best horse in the world, for he could trot faster than the rest of us could gallop" [5]. Had he not been burdened with impossible weights after his victory in 1839, there is no doubt that he would have won many more Grand Nationals. As it was, he fell in 1840, was pulled up in 1841 and 1842 and finished seventh in 1843. He won for the last time at Windsor in 1844.

It is a mark of his stature that even today Lottery must be reckoned amongst the very best winners of the Grand National, the others being, in my opinion, Cloister (1893), Manifesto (1897 and 1899), Golden Miller (1934), Red Rum (1973, 1974 and 1977) and L'Escargot (1975). Of these, Golden Miller and L'Escargot are the only horses to have won both the National and the Cheltenham Gold Cup, and Golden Miller is the only horse to have done the double in the same season, although Garrison Savannah came close in 1991 when he won the Gold Cup and came second in the National. More recently still, Rough Quest won the 1996 National after finishing second in the Gold Cup less than three weeks before.

Lottery with Jem Mason up (owner John Elmore, standing)
from a coloured aquatint, published 1839 by J. Moore, London

Sadly, it is said that Lottery ended his days hauling a cart in north London, but the trainer Arthur Yates has a nicer story of the old horse in his retirement. As a very young boy he was taken to lunch at Mr. Elmore's house at Harrow and Lottery was brought out for him to see. "Let the boy see him jump", said Elmore, and the grand old horse, ridden as in all his great races by Jem Mason, came cantering gently up and cleared the luncheon table, soup-tureen and all, with the greatest ease [6].

That the 1839 National was such a brilliant success was almost entirely due to Lynn, but he was not to reap the rewards that were due to him. Shortly before the race the following notice appeared in the press:

"The continued indisposition of Mr. William Lynn, the Proprietor of the Aintree Race-Course, under whose excellent management the Liverpool Races have acquired such a pre-eminence in the sporting world, compels him to retire from the field of active operations, for the purpose of recruiting his health" [7].

The "indisposition" was entirely financial. Lynn's creditors were becoming impatient, and to remain solvent he had to dispose of the whole of the racecourse complex, including the stands, the stables, the Sefton Arms Hotel, the cock pit and the feeding houses. All this was valued at £25,000, and offered for sale in 1000 proprietorships, or shares, at £25 each. The trustees of the new company, for this is in effect what it was, were named as Lord Stanley, Sir Thomas Massey Stanley, William Blundell, James Aspinall and William Earle.

Liverpool Racecourse proprietor's ticket ca. 1840

It is sometimes said that his financial circumstances forced Lynn to withdraw from Aintree's management completely in 1839, but this is not true. He had certainly lost a great deal of money, for in a letter to the artist John Ferneley he wrote that the race course "has been a most unlucky speculation for me. I should have been worth at least £30,000 if I had never had anything to do with it" [8]; but he also declared that it was his intention to retain some shares in the new concern, and to "render his best assistance to the Directors in carrying out the proposed plans of the Noblemen and Gentlemen forming the Racing Committee" [9].

Lynn, in fact, appears to have been Secretary both to the new company and the Racing Committee and to have acted as a general manager of the course. His continued importance in the running of Aintree is shown by the fact that up until 1843 "Lynn & Co." are recorded as the tenants in the Molyneux estate rent books and in the correspondence of William Eaton Hall, Lord Sefton's Steward [10].

The newly formed Racing Committee which took over the management of the races was composed of the Earls of Derby, Sefton, Wilton and Eglinton, Lord George Bentinck, Sir John Gerard, Lord Stanley, Lord Robert Grosvenor, Sir Thomas Massey Stanley, the Hon. E.M. Lloyd Mostyn, Sir R.W. Bulkeley and E.G. Hornby. Most of these had been active supporters of racing at Aintree since the beginning, and it was thought that their "powerful patronage" and "active individual interest and enterprise" would ensure the future success of the course [11].

In some ways the most significant member of the Committee was Lord George Bentinck. Bentinck was not only the creator of 'Glorious' Goodwood and a leading owner and breeder on the flat, he was also the man who more than anyone worked to improve racing's image by rooting out the fraud and corruption which was rife in the sport in the first half of the 19th century. Like Lynn, Bentinck wanted to introduce a greater degree of order and punctuality into the organization of race meetings. Amongst other things, he campaigned for better starts, and he is credited with the introduction of flag starts and the stationing of a recall flag man further down the course directly in view of the jockeys [12]. (Prior to this time races were generally started by the starter shouting 'Go', and there was no means of recalling the runners once they had started.) However, Bentinck was also not averse to bending the rules to his own advantage when it suited him. At the 1841 Liverpool Summer Meeting, for example, when he was both the starter and a Steward of the meeting, he allowed his own horse, Misdeal, to start fifty yards in front of the other runners. When Misdeal won, Bentinck came in for considerable criticism, but the result was allowed to stand. He then answered his critics in a novel way: Misdeal was entered in a second race at the meeting, and this time the jockey was instructed to start two lengths *behind* the other runners – and Misdeal still won easily! [13]

The syndicate soon installed John Etty as the new Clerk of the Course, although Lynn, as Secretary, continued to carry out some of the functions of the Clerk of the Course as well. Very little is known about Etty, although he is an important figure in Aintree's history. He was some six years older than Lynn, and was already Clerk of the Course at Newton and Manchester. He and Lynn may well have known one another already, but in any case they were to form an effective partnership in charge of the day to day running of Aintree for the next few years.

One of Etty's first acts was to negotiate the transfer of the September flat meeting at Heaton Park to Aintree [14], so that there were now three flat meetings at the course each year, together with the steeplechase meeting in the spring and the hurdles meeting in the autumn. Work was also put in hand to improve the grand stand. This was finished in time for the 1840 Summer Meeting, prompting the favourable comment that "Great improvements in this edifice were observable in more ways than one, and it is due to Mr. Lynn to say that in effecting these he has adopted many of the advantages and rejected many of the disadvantages of the other stands throughout the kingdom, with sound judgement and discretion" [15].

However, the most important task facing the new executive was to build on the success of Lottery's Grand National and make the race the undisputed highlight of the whole steeplechasing season. This they were able to do, despite the fact that some of the races in the early 1840s made a far from favourable impression on the public at large.

The 1840 race, for instance, seems to have been a bruising affair. At the sixth fence (Becher's Brook) Weathercock fell, and his jockey, Barker, was so badly injured through falling underneath the hooves of one of the following horses that he "lay in a state of insensibility and every one thought he was dead" [16]. He was carried off to a neighbouring farm house where he lay "stretched on his back, in his gay attire, pale and motionless, with fixed eyeballs"; still more shocking was the fact that "up to a late hour neither the owner of the horse nor those who had charge of him had sent even to enquire whether the rider was dead or alive, nor had anyone who knew him been near him" [17].

Worse was to come at the stone wall opposite the grand stand: "At this juncture Valentine took the lead of Columbine, and first went over. Lottery followed, but in taking his leap, caught it and fell over, carying away a great portion of the wall with him, and Mason lay his full length on the sward, and gave in. The Nun, Columbine and Seventy Four shared the same fate. Olliver, in attempting to rise, was knocked down and kicked on

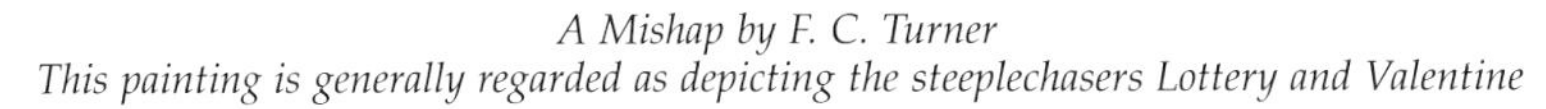

A Mishap by F. C. Turner
This painting is generally regarded as depicting the steeplechasers Lottery and Valentine

the hip by one of the horses, and had his collar bone broken. Powell remounted, but, finding his mare lame, pulled up. The scene at this moment was terrific, four of the five leading horses being down, and the others coming up, but providentially no other accident occurred" [18]. The race was now between Valentine, Arthur and Jerry. Arthur fell at the artificial ditch, and as they came back on to the racecourse proper Jerry took up the running. In the meantime Arthur had been remounted by Alan McDonogh and it was he who took second place behind Jerry, overtaking a very tired Valentine on the run in. Only two other horses finished.

Not surprisingly, this race attracted much adverse comment in the press. Under the sarcastic heading "The beauties of steeple-chasing", the *Liverpool Mercury*'s correspondent wrote of the scene at the wall: "Let [the reader] imagine four or five horses in succession jumping through the gap made in the wall, and, as they passed, swift as lightning, jumping on, trampling and striking the fallen riders and the humane people who were

The Grand National of 1840: the scene at the wall

From a drawing by Henry Alken. THE GRAND NATIONAL OF 1840. THE SCENE AT THE WALL.

endeavouring to drag the wounded somewhat out of danger. Above all, let him imagine one of the prostrate riders, as he lay helplessly on the turf, actually made by the fore feet of a horse in full career striking him, to turn head over heels like a clown at the circus. Let him imagine all this, and think he hears the groans of the wounded and the shouts of the people immediately around the spot, and he may have some faint notion of the scene which we witnessed close to the stone wall on Thursday last, a scene which so shocked our feelings that never again will we place ourselves in a position to witness another so revolting" [19].

1840 was also notable for the first appearance at Aintree of Lord Waterford, who rode his own horse The Sea into a distant last place. Lord Waterford (1811-1859) was a horse mad Irish peer, whose "eccentricities" were legendary. As a young man he once put aniseed on the hoofs of a parson's horse and then hunted the terrified clergyman with bloodhounds. On another occasion he put a donkey into the bed of a stranger at an inn, and he once proposed to a railway company in Ireland that they run two engines in opposite directions on the same line just so that he could see them smash into each other (he offered to pay for this). In the early days of steeplechasing he was a noted amateur rider, who "often used to go out of his way to jump an extra fence". Despite such unorthodox tactics he still won many races, including on one occasion three four mile chases in an afternoon at Eglinton Park. He only rode at Aintree the once, but he continued to enter his horses for the National for several years afterwards, many of them ridden by the McDonogh brothers. It seems entirely

HENRY, THIRD MARQUIS OF WATERFORD.

Lord Waterford

appropriate that he should have died of a broken neck whilst out hunting in Ireland. In his memory a Celtic cross was erected on the spot by members of the Waterford Hunt [20].

The 1841 race was a much more sporting affair than the previous year's succession of damaging falls. Lottery was again burdened with a colossal weight, and Jem Mason sensibly pulled him up. The race was won by the mare Charity who, in a thrilling finish, beat Cigar by just a length, with Peter Simple only half a length further back in third. Charity was ridden by Powell, who thus gained some compensation for having been cheated of victory in the inaugural running of the race in 1836 when he rode Laurie Todd.

In 1842 Tom Olliver recorded the first of his three victories in the race, riding Gaylad. Along with Captain Becher and Jem Mason, Olliver was probably the best of the early steeplechase jockeys, but he was a very

Gaylad, winner of the 1842 Grand National

different character to either of them. Possibly of Gypsy or Spanish descent, Olliver was born at Angmering in Sussex, rode his first pony at the age of six, and then became stable boy to his uncle, a Mr. Page, who was a trainer at Epsom. Later he moved north to Liverpool where he served as foreman to a man called Farrell who was a well-known Irish horse dealer. A "juvenile indiscretion" (the first of many) forced him to move from Liverpool to Southampton, where he assisted with Mr. Hewitt's horses. It was while working for Hewitt that he saw his first steeplechase at Egham. Immediately he decided that he wanted to become a steeplechase jockey, like Becher or Powell.

Olliver had his first ride in a steeplechase at Finchley, where he rode a horse called Columbine. It was an inauspicious start to his new career, for he fell in a ditch the second field from home, and "going home in his wet clothes took a violent cold and lay speechless for six weeks, receiving for his mount the magnificent remuneration of a sovereign". After this, he rapidly established himself as one of the most successful steeplechase jockeys, but he was also something of a rough diamond, always in debt and often in dispute with the law. On one occasion he had to flee into Wales to escape arrest; another time he was arrested as he dismounted after a race and spent a month in Northampton gaol. It was said of him that "in ethics he cannot be said to have taken a high degree. Bred up in a school where the fine distinction between honesty and cunning is not so distinctly laid down... it is not surprising if he adopted the common code of steeple-chasers for his own guidance, or that his elastic temperament should have made him a tool in the hands of others". It was, in fact, his generosity to others that often led him into debt.

Olliver was renowned for his skill at putting his horses at their fences and for his judge of pace, but his own judgement on when he rode best is somehow more endearing: "Squire, when you've got the traps in the house and the bums after you, and you say to yourself, within three fields of home, 'If my nut is screwed on a little better than these other beggars, and I can beat them, how pleased my poor wife and kids will be!', that makes you ride!" [21].

Olliver also won the National on Vanguard in 1843 (the year the race became a handicap) and Peter Simple in 1853. On the latter occasion he is reputed to have said to Lord Sefton at the start, when speaking of his mount, "Sometimes he means it and I don't, sometimes I means it he don't, but today we both mean it" [22]. That day they certainly did mean it, for, on soft ground which suited Peter Simple, they went on to win a fine race, beating the previous year's winner Miss Mowbray by three lengths, with the famous Abd-El-Kader, winner in 1850 and 1851, back in fourth place. Peter Simple had won the race previously in 1849, so this victory made him the third dual winner. It was one of the classiest of the early races and is appropriately commemorated in a fine series of aquatints by R.G. and A.W. Reeve after paintings by G.H. Laporte. Olliver's other National winner, Vanguard was one of his favourite horses, and after his death he used his skin to cover a sofa in his home.

Tom Olliver on Vanguard

THE GRAND NATIONAL STEEPLE-CHASE—CROSSING THE BROOK.

The 1845 Grand National, as depicted in the Sportsman's Magazine

The 1845 National saw one of those fairy tale wins for which the race has become famous. The winner, Cure-All, had been injured jumping some rails, and as a result was sold for just £60 to Walter Loft of Healing in Lincolnshire. Loft's groom, Kitty Crisp, restored the horse to soundness, and Loft thereupon decided to enter Cure-All for the National. Horse and groom then walked the entire way from Healing to Liverpool together. At first it seemed as though their efforts were to be in vain, for on the day of the race there was a sharp frost and it was doubtful whether the National could be run at all. Eventually at 5pm the stewards decided to go ahead, even though many people thought the ground was still unfit for racing. For Cure-All and his jockey, the decision was soon to be vindicated, for, in walking the course, Loft had spotted a tow path running alongside the heavily ploughed stretch of the course which bordered the canal; by making use of this Cure-All was able to conserve his energy and win easily, despite being virtually ignored in the betting. Afterwards Kitty Crisp and Cure-All walked all the way back to Lincolnshire again, to be greeted by the ringing of church bells. This victory inspired one anonymous writer to compose a lengthy poem; a fine example of the sporting verse of the time, the full text of this is reproduced in the appendix on p.282 [23].

The enormous popularity of steeplechasing during this period cannot be doubted – one source lists 92 different courses, ranging from Paisley and Edinburgh in the north to Totnes and Dover in the south, as being in use by 1853-54 [24]- but it was also a very new and raw sport, and one which was capable of arousing considerable opposition from very disparate groups.

Then, as now, much of this opposition came from those who believed it was a cruel sport which inflicted unnecessary suffering on the horses which were forced to take part in it. This early 19th century campaign for improvements in animal welfare formed part of a much wider humanitarian and evangelical movement which also concerned itself with such matters as child labour and temperance reform. In 1823 it achieved its first major success with the passage of the Ill-Treatment of Horses Act, and the following year saw the formation of the Society (from 1840 Royal Society) for the Prevention of Cruelty to Animals.

Many people in Liverpool shared these concerns; indeed the formation of the national R.S.P.C.A. was pre-empted locally by a Liverpool Society for the Prevention of Wanton Cruelty to Brute Animals, which existed as early as 1809, amongst whose aims was the abolition of hunting, shooting and fishing [25]. This society seems to have been in existence for only a short time, but in January 1834 a new society whose aim was "the prevention of cruel practices towards animals" was established in the town [26]. One of the leading members of both societies, and a long-term campaigner for the better treatment of animals, was Egerton Smith. In 1836 he published a book called *The Elysium of Animals: a dream*, in which a representative group of animals describe the terrible cruelties they have suffered at the hands of man. Amongst them is a former racehorse who tells how "in consequence of being urged beyond my natural capacities by a cruel infliction of the whip and spur, I broke down during one severe contest" [27]. Smith's position as owner and publisher of the influential *Liverpool Mercury* enabled him to put the case against cruelty to animals to a much wider audience, and just a few days after Lottery's victory in the 1839 National, in which at least one horse died, an editorial in the *Mercury*, almost certainly written by Smith himself, pulled no punches in its opposition to steeplechasing on precisely these grounds:

"It was, no doubt, a very exciting spectacle, but we can no more be reconciled to it on that account, than we are to cock-fighting, bull-baiting, or any other popular pastime which is attended with the infliction of torture to any living being. That these steeple-chases are of this nature will hardly be denied even by those who are most ardently attached to such sports.

"All the objections which may be urged against hunting the hare or the fox apply with still more force to such scenes as those which were witnessed in our neighbourhood on Tuesday. In ordinary hunting the sportsman can choose his ground, and avoid those perilous leaps which might endanger his own life and that of his horse; but in these steeple-chases, the most formidable obstacles are artificially placed in the course which the horse must necessarily take, and the almost certain result is the death of some of the noble animals thus wantonly urged on to their own destruction" [28].

Somewhat fancifully, the *Mercury* then went on to suggest that those who entered their horses in steeplechases should be punished by being compelled "whether rich or poor, titled or untitled, to go through the purgatory of a steeple chase, with sturdy drivers at their heels to urge them over hedge and ditch, until they reached the goal, and when they had arrived at the end of the steeple chase, they should do penance in white sheets, or horse cloths, in the church, until they confessed their iniquities, and promised for the future to be more merciful to their cattle" [29].

It is interesting to note that many American visitors to England at this time shared these views. Steeplechasing was hardly known in the United States before the Civil War, and some Americans were quick to seize on it as an example of English degeneracy. One such was Warren Isham, who visited England in the early 1850s and then produced a book with the splendid title of *The Mud Cabin, or the character and tendency of British institutions*. In this he castigated steeplechasing as the same kind of amusement as "the gladiatorial and other inhuman shows of heathen Rome at which men and wild beasts were slaughtered for the gratification of excited myriads who feasted their eyes upon the scene", adding the rhetorical question "Can anything be more savage and demoralising? Is not this a refinement of barbarism at which American sensibility would revolt?" [30]

That steeplechasing could (and still can) be a cruel sport cannot be denied. One journalist, walking the course after the 1849 Grand National, found Equinox "lying in a pool of his own blood. At the next fence, scarcely a hundred yards beyond, lay The Curate, in exactly the same situation, and at the next, Kilfane, the knife having put an end to the sufferings of each" [31]. Around this time several other sports, including cock fighting, bull baiting and dog fighting, were outlawed on account of their cruelty, but steeplechasing and hare coursing were left untouched by legislation, probably because they numbered so many influential peers amongst their supporters. This was, however, an issue that refused to go away. In the 1862 Grand National three riders were thrown at the hurdle opposite the stands, one of whom died as a result of the fall, leading one well-known Liverpool writer to comment that "the loud shouts and screams which resounded as a horse or rider slipped or fell could hardly be reconciled with national or innocent sports". And, rather pointedly, he added that "steeple chasing in general and... this race in particular" were events which brought no good at all, other than to create business for professional betting men, "throngs of whom were met at every turn" [32].

Opposition to steeplechasing on grounds of cruelty was predictable. It is rather more surprising to find that there was also considerable hostility to the sport amongst the foxhunting fraternity, a group of people who can hardly be accused of sentimentality towards horses, or indeed anything else. No better portrait of this extremely tough world exists than that given by Surtees in his novels *Mr. Sponge's Sporting Tour* and *Facey Romford's Hounds*, across whose pages march a veritable army of hard-boiled country squires, slovenly servants, cheats, imposters, touts and crooked horse dealers; even the women are menacing, ranging from predatory mothers plotting the most advantageous marriage alliances for their daughters, to the cigar-smoking denizens of the *demi-monde*, such as that accomplished horsewoman, “the beautiful and tolerably virtuous” Lucy Glitters of Astley’s Royal Amphitheatre.

Surtees, a Master of Fox Hounds himself, disliked steeplechasing. His lampoon of the ’Grand Aristocratic’ in *Mr. Sponge’s Sporting Tour* presents a rather sordid picture of what a typical steeplechasing meeting of the 1830s and ’40s could be like. In part Surtees’ opposition to the sport lay in its poor organization: “Steeple-chases”, he wrote, “are generally crude, ill-arranged things... There is always something wanting or forgotten. Either they forget the ropes, or they forget the scales, or they forget the weights, or they forget the bell, or – more commonly still – some of the party forget themselves.” Perhaps more fundamentally, Surtees also found it hard to come to terms with the, as it seemed to him, hybrid nature of steeplechasing. As he said, “it is just the mixture of two sports that spoils both; steeplechasing being neither hunting nor racing. It has not the wild excitement of the one, nor the accurate calculating qualities of the other. The very horses have a peculiar air about them – neither hunters nor hacks, nor yet exactly race-horses” [33]. On another occasion Surtees went even further and called steeplechasing “neither fish, fowl, nor good salt herring”, adding that in his opinion “a bunch of good salt herrings drawn at random over a hunting country, with ten or twelve couple of good hounds to hunt it, would be infinitely superior to any steeplechase that ever was arranged” [34]. Given Surtees’ known opposition to drag hunts this was a damning comment indeed, but it was one with which many traditionally-minded sportsmen of the time concurred.

With his keen eye for the social scene, Surtees was quick to spot the connection between steeplechasing and drink. “Nine tenth’s of the steeple-chases and coursing matches are got up by innkeepers, for the good of their houses”, he wrote [35] in a comment that might well have made William Lynn blush.

There was a certain amount of snobbery involved. Foxhunting was seen by many of its supporters (however incorrectly) as a noble sport for gentlemen in which the thrill of the chase was its own reward. Steeplechasing, on the other hand, was seen as an illegitimate offspring, and one, moreover, in which professional jockeys rode for money. The great sporting journalist, “Nimrod”, expressed this view when he wrote that "unaccompanied by the soul-inspiring music of hounds, which excites both man and horse, a Steeple-chase is run divested of all such stimulus as far as the horse is concerned, whilst the rider is excited only by the anticipated acquirement of so many sovereigns earned with great risk and no inconsiderable exertion" [36]. However, "Nimrod" also opposed the new sport because he believed it exposed horses to unnecessary cruelty, and because he was unconvinced by the arguments, put forward by some of steeplechasing's proponents, that it acted as an inducement to people to breed the kind of good staying horses which were also in demand for foxhunting.

The general atmosphere of sleaze and corruption which surrounded many of the early steeplechasing meetings also aroused opposition from those who might otherwise have been amongst the new sport's fervent supporters. The compiler of a contemporary *Manual of British rural sports*, for example, dismissed the accusations of cruelty against steeplechasing, and described a steeplechase as "a beautiful sight [which] might well challenge the admiration of all those who delight in that wonderfully graceful animal the horse", adding that "to see 20 or 30 of these graceful creatures start across country, taking everything in their stride, and charging a brook or a bullfinch at the rate of 20 miles an hour, is a glorious sight indeed; and I confess it is one which has afforded me much gratification on many occasions". But he also expressed concern at the "numerous evils" to which the sport was exposed, and concluded that because it was "injurious to the people" there could be no question "as to the propriety of its discontinuance, especially if its laws and practices are not remodelled" [37].

This kind of opposition cannot have helped, but perhaps the greatest problem Aintree faced during the early 1840s was the old one of money, for the titled grandees who made up the executive after 1839 proved no more able to make the race course pay than William Lynn had been able to do. As a consequence, they raised the admission price to the grand stand to half a sovereign in 1840 [38], but this measure on its own was not enough to make the course profitable. In his standard history of the Grand National, Reg Green notes that in 1842 the entry fee was raised to 23 sovereigns and that, for the first time, no added money was provided by the executive. He calls this decision "strange" [39], but the explanation is obvious enough –

they were strapped for cash and simply could not afford to put up any added prize money. That this was so is confirmed by the fact that later in the same year the autumn flat meeting was reduced from three days to two, and there was even talk of it being cancelled altogether, on the grounds that it would never make a profit "commensurate with the exertions of the stewards and their officers" [40].

It is against this background that the decision to turn the Grand National into a handicap needs to be seen. A handicap might attract a larger field and more stake money, lessening the need for the executive to provide added prize money; by making the race "a more sporting affair", it would also increase interest amongst the betting public at large and attract a larger crowd on to the course. The race would no longer be the kind of true championship test which only races at level weights could provide, but the Aintree authorities had already moved away from that kind of event when from 1840 onwards they effectively handicapped Lottery out of the race. By 1842 they were desperate to make the race more of a spectacle, thereby to generate more income; and turning it into a handicap was the obvious way to do that. Accordingly, an announcement was made in *Bell's Life* on 18 December 1842 that the 1843 "Liverpool Great National Steeple-Chase" would be a handicap. Entries were to be made to Weatherby's in London, Lynn at the Waterloo Hotel in Liverpool, or Etty in Manchester [41].

The decision did not meet with universal approval, and the speed with which the decision was taken appears to have surprised some of the subscribers. Lord Maidstone wrote to Lynn, as Clerk of the Course, as follows:

"Sir – The race which I subscribed to at the Liverpool Steeple-chase last year was not then a handicap. If the conditions of the race are changed, without any notice being given to the subscribers with a view to ascertain their intentions respecting the new race, it has always been held that the subscription is null and void.

"I therefore give you notice, as clerk of the course, that I do not consider myself a subscriber to the race in its present form. I object most strongly to the system of handicapping steeple-chase horses, and beg that the name of the horse entered in my nomination may be forthwith struck out" [42].

Lynn's reply to this letter has not survived, but others made the case for him. "Grimaldi", for instance, wrote that the change was a good one because "it brings large fields of horses to the post and almost invariably causes a closer contest than would have been the case at even weights", and he added that "I think a good field and a sporting race may be anticipated" [43].

The man Lynn and Etty appointed as official handicapper for the 1843 National was Edward William Topham, known as the "Wizard". A native of Middleham, Yorkshire, Topham moved to Darlands Hall near Rossett, between Chester and Wrexham, in the 1830s, and became Clerk of the Course at Chester in 1842. For over thirty years he was handicapper for the Chester Cup, then one of the biggest betting races in the calendar, and it was in this capacity that he made his name. At his death, it was said that he had "introduced the flattering system by which every animal seemed to have a chance, but which generally proved the most fatal in results to people who meddled with it". The same writer went on to add that year after year the Chester Cup "was a 'gift' to something or another, the result generally being that the gifted one was nowhere" [44].

Topham had a genius for handicapping horses, but, from the outset, it seems that he wanted to play a much greater part in the management of Aintree. He is said to have bought some land adjacent to the course and offered to build stables on it for the race course [45]. He owned a steeplechaser named Cruickshank who won a four mile chase at the Old Roan meeting in February 1848 [46]; and family tradition has him as one of the members of the syndicate which ran Aintree in the mid-1840s [47]. However, his name never appeared in the press as a member of the Racing Committee, and his principal role for the next five years remained that of official handicapper.

Turning the National into a handicap undoubtedly enhanced its appeal both as a spectacle and as a betting medium – it is significant that no-one seems to have suggested reversing the decision during the succeeding years – but it appears to have done little to alleviate the executive's financial problems. The crunch came during the spring of 1843, when "it became advisable... to dispose of the entire property of the Liverpool race course, stands, stables, tavern, &c", the shareholders retaining only their silver tickets of admission. The course thus passed back into the hands of Lord Sefton, who then sought to find a new leaseholder. This was not an easy task for by this time people were beginning to realise that there was less money in running a race course than they had imagined. The correspondent of *Bell's Life* noted that "the rental is large, the taxes, expenses of advertising, printing, servants and etceteras, exceedingly heavy, and the risks great"; and he concluded that "It must be obvious, therefore, that without the most liberal support from the public, the spec must be a losing one, and even at the best, including the Steeplechase, we question if a fortune is to be made" [48].

The details of the negotiations that followed are rather obscure, but what is clear is that from the outset John Etty, the Clerk of the Course, was the only person who showed a serious interest in taking over the course. To begin with he seems to have considered leasing only the course itself and not the stands, for on 20 April 1843 William Eaton Hall wrote to Lord Sefton, "I have not heard anything particularly from Mr. Etty for some time past. I believe he has not let the House [i.e. the stand] but the land"; and he added "It can hardly be expected any tenant would do much on the present uncertain tenure" [49]. In May Etty was due to meet Lord Sefton, presumably to finalise the arrangements, but the meeting had to be postponed because Lord Sefton delayed his visit to Croxteth [50]. In June, the bargaining was still going on, with William Lynn taking a hand in the negotiations, which seem to have been carried out during the Derby meeting at Epsom. Anxious to have the matter settled before the Liverpool Summer Meeting, Hall wrote "I hope Mr. Lynn made good progress with the deed when he was at Epsom last week. He promised he would use every exertion" [51]. This seems to have done the trick, for by the beginning of July it was known that Etty had leased the course, initially for one year only [52]. However, he does not seem to have regretted his decision, and he was happy to renew the lease for the next five years, until his death in 1848.

In the midst of this uncertainty, a certain amount of work was carried out to improve the look of the course, and particularly the stands, which appear to have become somewhat dilapidated. It was arranged for the Grand Stand to be cleaned, whitewashed and painted for £50 [53], and a new iron staircase was installed [54]. There were also plans to erect new iron gates at the entrance to the course, the design of which had to be approved by Lord Sefton personally [55], and for a new small stand, the location of which was chosen by John Etty [56].

During the next couple of years Etty and Lynn (who was still Secretary) continued to work together to improve the facilities at Aintree, and by 1845 they had made the Grand National the centre piece of a whole week's carnival of sport, which included two days' hare coursing at Altcar (including the Waterloo Cup), two days' racing at Aintree and a further steeplechase meeting held at Hooton Park on the Wirral. This last was the

The race card for the 1846 Grand National (on which John Etty is named as Clerk of the Course)

PRINTED BY EVANS AND CHEGWIN.

LIVERPOOL

GREAT NATIONAL STEEPLE-CHASE,

WEDNESDAY, 4th MARCH, 1846.

THE EARL OF SEFTON AND GEORGE PAYNE, ESQ. STEWARDS.

The Cap, is black, unless otherwise expressed.

To start at Two.

50 Sovs. given by the Earl of Sefton, to a Sweepstakes of 10 Sovs. each, five forfeit. For horses that never won more than 200 Sovs. at any one time. Three yrs old, 6st 7lb; four 8st 3lb; five, 8st 10lb; six and aged, 9st. Fillies allowed 3lb. One mile. The second to save his stake.

1—Ld Chesterfield's b h *The Poor Soldier*, 6 yrs..red, blue slvs, red cap
2—Lord Howth's ch h *Switcher*, 5 yrs ....white
3—Mr R Bell's b f *Rosina*, by Romulus, 4 yrs .... green
4—Hon E M Ll Mostyn's b c by *Phœnix*, out of L'Hirondelle, 3 yrs, yellow ....
5—Sir J Gerard's br f *Camelia*, by Voltaire, out of Camelina, 3 yrs, crimson and white stripe, cap same.......................
6—Mr Binnie's b f *Apparition*, by Taurus, out of Young Duchess, by Walton, 3 yrs ....white, red cap
7—Mr R J Mostyn's b c *The Premier*, by Tory Boy, out of King Cole's dam, 3 yrs..............................light blue, white cap

Three o'clock.

A Handicap Sweepstakes of 20 Sovs. each, 10 Forfeit, and 5 only if declared on the 12th February, with 100 Sovs added. The owner of the second horse to have his stake returned, and the winner to pay 10 Sovs. towards the expenses.

1—12 8—Lord Waterford's ch g *Firefly*, aged................ light blue
2—12 4—Mr W G Loft's br h *Cure-all*, aged....................yellow
3—12 4—Lord Howth's *Switcher*, 5 yrs ....white
4—11 12—Mr Adams' b g *Pioneer*, by Advance, 6 yrs ....blue
5—11 12—Lord Waterford's b g *Regalia*, aged.............. light blue
6—11 12—Mr C E Brooke's *Eagle*, aged.................... prim, pur cap
7—11 12—Captain Campbell's b h *Crœsus*, aged....................white
8—11 12—Mr Atkinson's b g *Golden Pippin*, aged ....blue
9—11 12—Sir R Brooke na gr m *Alice Gray*, aged..............crimson
10—11 6—Mr Windham's b h *Major A*, 6 yrs ....
11—11 6—Mr Austin's b g *Troubadour*, aged, (h b) .....blue, white st
12—11 4—Mr Payne na ch g *Culverthorpe*, aged, (h b).. scar, wht cap
13—11 4—Mr G Lambden's b g *Carlow*.............blue, white stripe
14—11 4—Mr Hammond na b m *Brenda*, aged, (h b).............. black
15—11 4—Mr Robertson's gr g *Tinderbox*, aged................. tartan
16—11 2—Mr Ekins' gr h *Peter Simple*, aged ....crimson
17—11 0—Mr H L Carter's b g *Homihiharriho*, aged, (h b)....pale blue
18—11 0—Mr Hey's br g *Lancet*, aged, (h b)...............blue, wht strp
19—10 12—Captain Barnett's *Mameluke*..............blue, white sleeves
20—10 10—Mr G Lambden's *Pickwick*..................blue, white stripe
21—10 8—Lord Sefton na b g *The Artist*, 6 yrs................. scarlet
22—10 8—Hon F Craven na b m *Perambulator*, 6 yrs, (h b) purple, orange cap ....
23—10 6—Mr S Crawfurd's b g *Veluti*, 6 yrs, (h b)......blk, white cap
24—10 2—Mr Pearce's ch h *The Scavenger*, 6 yrs.................black
25—10 0—Sir R Brownrigg na gr m *Lady Gray*.....................pink

Half-past Four.

A Free Handicap Hurdle Race of 10 Sovs. each, 5 Forfeit, with 50 Sovs. added. Over Six Hurdles. Two Miles.

1—12 0—Mr. Clifton's br h *Pedlar*, aged ....scarlet, white stripe
2—11 12—Captain Campbell's b h *Crœsus*, aged .... white
3—11 10—Lord Chesterfield's br g *New Brighton*, 6 yrs, red, blue sleeves, red cap ....
4—11 7—Mr Duckworth's b g *Clear the-Kitchen*, aged .... blue
5—11 4—Mr Ralph na gr h *Everton*, 6 yrs..................... green
6—11 0—Mr Roberts's gr g *Quicksilver*, 6 yrs ......straw, white cap
7—10 10—Mr M Heap's br g *Chints-Print*, 6 yrs ....light blue
8—10 8—Mr Cross na b h *Single Peeper*, aged ....pink
9—10 6—Mr W Turner na ch g *Sands*, 6 yrs ..... blue, crimson cap
10—10 6—Mr Henderson's b g *The Artist*, 6 yrs .... scarlet
11—10 2—Mr E R Clarke's b h *Sir Edward*, agd, light blue, trim crim
12—10 0—Mr Dymock's ch m *GraceDarling*, (h b) agd, purple, crim cp
13—9 13—Mr Sutcliffe's b m *Alice*, (h h) ....
14—9 10—Mr King's br g *Artful Dodger*, aged ......violet, white cap
15—9 9—Mr Quin's b m *Violet*, 5 yrs, (h b) .....orange and purple

Mr. ETTY, Clerk of the Course.

brainchild of Sir William Stanley, who had succeeded his father in 1841. The race was for horses owned and ridden by gentlemen who had hunted with the Hooton Fox Hounds, and it was run over a three mile course from Storeton windmill towards Barnston and back. The fences were all natural (as were the majority of the fences at Aintree at this time) and they were reported to be "rather stiff with big ditches, but all fair hunting jumps" [57]. Sadly, this meeting did not last for long for Sir William, already heavily in debt when he inherited the Hooton estate, was ruined by his extravagance, and in 1848 the whole property, which had been in the Stanley family for five centuries, had to be sold.

Another feature of the week, and one which no doubt gave almost as much pleasure as the racing itself, was "Lynn's sumptuous banquet of turtle and every other delicacy with wines of every country decking the festive board" [58].

A further change took place in 1847 when the race was officially named "The Grand National Handicap Steeplechase" for the first time. It had previously been called "The Liverpool Grand Steeple-Chase" (1836), "The Liverpool Steeple Chase" (1837-38), "The Liverpool Great Steeple Chase" (1839), "The Liverpool Great National Steeplechase", "The Liverpool Grand National Steeplechase" or "Liverpool Grand Steeplechase" (all three used more or less interchangeably, 1840-42), and "The Liverpool and National Steeplechase" (1843-46); but most people seem to have called it the "Grand National" ever since the name was first coined at the end of 1838.

Around this time Lynn seems to have gradually withdrawn from active participation in the running of Aintree. This may well have been a consequence of his continuing financial problems, for his creditors were losing patience with him, and as a result of a petition by one of them, a grocer named John Benyon, he was offically declared bankrupt in June 1844 [59]. By 1848 he had even given up the lease on the refreshment rooms, as in that year it was announced that Mrs. Sillitoe of the Bath Hotel, Waterloo, had undertaken the management of the grand stand and would be providing "the choicest delicacies on the most reasonable terms, together with wines of her own importing" [60]. So far as is known, Lynn never again promoted steeplechasing, although he retained his interest in hare coursing, acting as Secretary (at least in name) to the committee which organized the Waterloo Cup until his death [61]. To put this into perspective, it should be remembered that at that time the Waterloo Cup was one of the biggest events in the sporting calendar, attracting crowds of up to 80,000 people. Betting was enormous – in 1886 two individual dogs were backed to win £200,000 each – and even the Stock Exchange closed down so that its members could learn the result.

Lynn also continued to run the Waterloo Hotel with great aplomb and to superintend the municipal banquets, for which he was justly famous, until only a few months before he died in 1870. Indeed, he only gave up the Waterloo Hotel when it was compulsorily purchased by the Cheshire Lines railway and demolished to make way for the new Central station. It is sometimes said that Lynn died in impoverished obscurity [62], but this is not entirely true, for he remained a well-known figure in Liverpool life, and at his death was given a grand funeral in St. James's Cemetery, then a fashionable burying place. On the other hand, his obituary in the *Liverpool Mercury* noted that he "at one time took a deep interest in sporting matters, and, like many others who have engaged in turf speculation, lost largely thereby" [63]; and when his will was proved it emerged that he was worth less than £1000 [64]. Nevertheless, his place in history, as the man who founded the most famous steeplechase in the world, should be secure.

Lynn's associate and successor as Clerk of the Course at Aintree, John Etty, died at his home in Erskine Street, Liverpool, aged 62, on 18 May 1848. He was mourned as a "worthy man, and [a] respected and upright lessee of the course" [65]. His contribution to the history of Aintree was rather greater than that rather anodyne statement suggests. On the honours board in the County Stand it states that the Grand National was "named and framed" by Edward William Topham; this seems to be a clear case of later generations of Tophams rewriting history, for, as we have seen, it was Etty and Lynn together who turned the race into a handicap in 1843, and probably Etty alone who was responsible for the official change of name to "Grand National" in 1847.

He was initially succeeded as Clerk of the Course by his son, Thomas Etty, who was commended by the sporting press for his efficient organization of the summer meeting [66]. Behind the scenes, however, all was far from well, for on taking over the course Etty discovered that his

Printed by W. Mc. Call, by Order of Mr. ETTY, Clerk of the Races.

LIVERPOOL JULY MEETING,

Thursday, July 15th, 1847.

☞ The Bell for saddling will be rung at a Quarter before Two o'Clock, and Grooms are required to have their horses at the Starting-post at the appointed time.

As soon as each jockey is weighed, his name and number will be exhibited to the public; and the number of the winning horse will be shewn immediately after each race. In case of a dead heat, the numbers of all the horses in the dead heat will be exhibited in an horizontal line, and in ordinary cases the 1st, 2nd and 3rd will be put up in a perpendicular line.

Stewards—The EARLS of MARCH, EGLINTON, and GLASGOW.

The Cap is black, unless otherwise specified.

The FOAL STAKES of 100 sovs. each, h. ft., for foals of 1844. Colts, 8st. 6lb.; fillies, 8st. 3lb. Once round and a distance. (5 subs.)

Two o'Clock.

1—Col. Anson's b c Lazarillo .... white jacket and cap
2—Lord G. Bentinck's br c Sloth .... light blue, white cap
3—Mr Hesseltine's ch f Mary Stuart .... green
4—Lord Stanley's ch c Bowstring (3lb) .... black, white cap

The DERBY HANDICAP of 10 sovs. each, p.p., with 80 Sovs. added by the Right Hon. the Earl of Derby. One mile. (45 Subs.)

Half-past Two.

1..8st.3lb Mr Meiklam's br h Lightning, 6 yrs ....*blae & wht stp, wht cap*
2..7 10 Mr Nunn's bl c The Prior of St Margaret's, 4 yrs ....*black*
3..7 8 Mr J Lillie's br c Spithead, 4 yrs ....*black, crim garter*
4..7 7 Sir W M Stanley's b m Picnic, 5 yrs ....*blue & orange*
5..7 6 Mr Worthington's ch c Sharston, 4 yrs ....*drab, red cap*
6..7 3 Mr B Green's b f Princess Alice, 4 yrs ....*pink, scar slvs & cap*
7..7 3 Mr Merry's bl c Pilgrim, 4 yrs ....*yellow*
8..7 0 Lord Eglinton's br m Plaudit, 5 yrs ....*tartan, yel slvs and cap*
9..6 12 Capt Knight's ch c Jolly Beggar, 6 yrs ....*green white cap*
10..6 7 Mr Mostyn's b f Sagacity, by Theon, 3 yrs ....*yellow*
11..5 7 Mr Mostyn's b f Queen Mary, (late Twyoges,) 3 yrs ......*scarlet, white cap*
12..5 7 Mr Heap's br f Brownfly, 4 yrs ....*blue*
13..5 3 Sir J Gerard's b f Dipthong, 3 yrs ....*pink & wht strp jacket & cap*
14..4 11 Mr Allen's b f by Yaxley, 3 yrs..*wht body & cap tied with yel ribbon, yel sls*

MATCH FOR 100 SOVS., h. ft. T. Y. C.

Three o'Clock.

1—Lord Stanley's ch c Abdiel, 8st. 2lb ....black, white cap
2—Lord Glasgow's Discontent, 7st. 13lb. ....white, red slvs & cap

The LIVERPOOL CUP or Plate value 300 sovs., given from the Racing Fund, added to a Handicap Sweepstakes of 25 sovs. each, 15 ft., and 5 only if declared on or before July 3rd. 2 miles. The winner to pay 30 sovs. to the Judge. 2nd to receive 50 sovs. from the Stakes.—(135 subs.)

A Quarter Before Four.

1—8st 5lb. Mr Meiklam's br h Lightning, 6 yrs......*blue and white stripe, white cap*
2—8 5 Sir J. Gerard's br h Pantasa, 5 yrs....*pink and white stripe jacket and cap*
3—8 4 Mr St. George's gr c Chanticleer, 4 yrs..............*sea-green and white*
4—8 3 Mr Meiklam's br m Inheritress, aged....*blue and white stripe, white cap*
5—7 12 Mr B. Green's b c The Conjuror, 4 yrs........*pink, scarlet sleeves and cap*
6—7 8 Mr Fraser nas ch m Rowena, 6 yrs ....*crimson, green cap*
7—7 5 Mr Cook's b c Inglewood, 4 yrs..............*blue*
8—7 5 Lord Warwick's b h Gwalior, 5 yrs......*brown body, white sleeves and cap*
9—7 4 Sir W. M. Stanley's b m Picnic, 5 yrs....*purple, orange sleeves, quar. cap*
10—7 2 Lord Glasgow's br f Conspiracy, 4 yrs.....*white body, red sleeves and cap*
11—7 1 Mr Merry's bk c Pilgrim, by Don John..............*yellow*
12—7 0 Mr Stephenson's b c Sheraton, 4 yrs..............*scarlet, white cap*
13—7 0 Mr Wormald's ch c Quadruped, 4 yrs..............*geranium red, green cap*
14—7 0 Lord Eglinton's br m Plaudit, 5 yrs..........*tartan, yellow sleeves and cap*
15—6 11 Mr Igoe's ch c Woodpecker, 4 yrs..............*pink, white sleeves*
16—6 6 Sir W. W. Wynn nas br f Romance, 4 yrs..............*blue*
17—5 10 Lord G Bentinck nas ch f Camera Obscura, 4 yrs..........*blue, white cap*
18—5 10 Mr Mostyn's ch c Wiseacre, by Lanercost, 3 yrs ....*yellow*
19—5 8 Mr F Villier nas b f Miss Castling, 4 yrs..............*chocolate*
20—5 5 Mr Mostyn's b f Queen Mary, 3 yrs..............*scarlet, white cap*

The GROSVENOR STAKES of 15 sovs. each, 5 ft., with 30 sovs. added. For three and four years old. Three years, 7st. 4lb; four, 8st. 10lb. Mares and geldings allowed 3lb. Four years old, being maiden at the time of nomination, allowed 3lb. 1 mile & a quarter. (14 subs.)

Half-past Four.

1—Mr T. Dawson ns br c St Leon 3 yrs...pink & wt stp jacket & cap
2—Mr A W. Hill's b f Burlesque, 4 yrs, crim and wh str hoop wht cap
3—Mr Baindridge's b f Mary, by Colwick 3 yrs ......yellow, wht cap
4—Mr B. Green's b c The Conjuror 4 yrs ..pink, scarlet slvs and cap
5—Mr B. Green's b f Princess Alice 4 yrs, pink, scarlet slvs and cap
6—Mr Nunn's bl c The Prior of St. Margaret's 4 yrs ....black

HER MAJESTY'S PLATE of 100 gs.; three years old, 7st. 5lb; four, 9st. 1 lb; five, 9st. 11 lb; six and aged, 10st. 2lb. Heats, two miles.—(13 subs)

Five.

1—Mr W Tempest's b g Deceiver, 6 yrs ....yellow, wht cap
2—Mr Stewart ns br f Comme il-faut, 3 yrs..... drab, crimson sleeves
3—Mr B Green's b c The Conjuror. 4 yrs ..pink body & cap, red slvs
4—Mr B Green's b f Princess Alice, 4 yrs ..pink body & cap, red slvs
5—Mr Shelmerdine's b c Walmgate Bar without, 3 yrs..crim, wht cap
6—Mr Carter's ch m Fair-Rosamond, 6 yrs..............pink
7—Mr Roberts' ch c Lush, Brother to Winesour, 3 yrs..........blue
8—Mr Mostyn's b f Sagacity, 3 yrs ....yellow
9—Mr A Johnstone's ch m Rowena, 6 yrs ....crim, green cap
10—Mr Meiklam's br m Inheritress, aged......blue & wht stp, wht cap
11—Mr Cook's b c Inglewood, 4 yrs ....blue
12—Mr Dawson's bk c M'Gregor, by The Provost, 4 yrs......dark blue
13—Mr Stephenson's b c Sheraton, 4 yrs ....scarlet and white cap

Mr. CLARKE, Judge.—Mr. HIBBURD, Starter.

Race card for the Liverpool July Meeting, 1847

father's financial affairs were not as healthy as had appeared, and he was unable to find the money to pay the rent owing to Lord Sefton [67].

This gave Topham his chance and he proposed taking over the lease on the same terms as Etty. Although Lord Sefton's agent thought that Topham was "a much more suitable tenant than young Etty", he appears to have felt some qualms about dispossessing Etty so peremptorily, and proposed that Topham buy him out with a lump sum. This Topham firmly declined to do, but he did agree to pay Etty £100 per annum for five years by way of compensation. By the end of July 1848, less than two weeks after the summer meeting, the deal had been done and Topham had become sole lessee and Clerk of the Course, initially for a period of seven years [68]. It was a momentous change, for the Topham family were to remain in control of Aintree for the next one hundred and twenty five years, until Mrs. Mirabel Topham sold the course to Bill Davies in 1973.

Notes and references

1. The true title of this song appears to have been 'Sit down neighbours all'; it was originally composed in the 1780s as a satire on William Pitt the Younger and Henry Dundas.
2. Levanter was a slang term for someone who made off without paying their debts.
3. *Bell's Life*, 3 March 1839.
4. Quoted in Bird. A hundred Grand Nationals, p.37.
5. Quoted in Bird. A hundred Grand Nationals, p.36.
6. Yates. Arthur Yates, trainer and gentleman rider, p.38.
7. *Liverpool Mercury*, 1 March 1839.
8. Quoted in Seth-Smith. A history of steeplechasing, p.27; I have been unable to trace the original letter.
9. *Liverpool Mercury*, 1 March 1839.
10. See for example letter from William Eaton Hall to Lord Sefton, 31 May 1842, Molyneux Muniments DDM 6/73.
11. *Liverpool Mercury*, 1 March 1839.
12. 'Thormanby'. Kings of the turf, pp.13-14.
13. Seth-Smith. Lord Paramount of the the turf, pp.55-56.
14. *Liverpool Standard*, 22 February 1839.
15. *Bell's Life*, 19 July 1840.
16. *Sporting Magazine*, April 1840, p.419.
17. *Liverpool Mercury*, 13 March 1840.
18. *Sporting Magazine*, April 1840, pp.419-420.
19. *Liverpool Mercury*, 13 March 1840.
20. Nevill. Sporting days and sporting ways, pp.7-9; *Sporting Review*, Vol. 41 (1859),

pp.239-240.
21. *Sporting Review*, Vol. 41 (1859), pp.249-254.
22. 'Recollections of what I heard – the 3rd Earl of Sefton', anonymous memoir in the Molyneux Muniments at Croxteth Hall.
23. The poem can be found in the *Sportsman's Magazine*, Vol. 1, no. 1, 15 March 1845, p.7.
24. Walsh. Manual of British rural sports, pp.388-389.
25. Smith. The elysium of animals, p.100.
26. *Liverpool Mercury*, 10 January 1834.
27. Smith. The elysium of animals, p.34.
28. *Liverpool Mercury*, 1 March 1839.
29. *Liverpool Mercury*, 1 March 1839.
30. Isham. The mud cabin, pp.211-213.
31. *Illustrated London News*, 10 March 1849.
32. Hugh Shimmin in *Porcupine*, 15 March 1862, p.283.
33. Surtees. Mr. Sponge's sporting tour, ch.68.
34. Quoted in Welcome. The sporting world of R.S. Surtees, p.162.
35. Surtees. Mr. Sponge's sporting tour, ch.67.
36. *Sporting Magazine*, April 1839, p.469.
37. Walsh. Manual of British rural sports, p.389.
38. *Bell's Life*, 8 March 1840.
39. Green. A race apart, p.18.
40. *Bell's Life*, 25 September 1842.
41. *Bell's Life*, 18 December 1842.
42. *Bell's Life*, 22 January 1843.
43. *Bell's Life*, 26 February 1843.
44. *Baily's Magazine*, June 1873, pp.362-363.
45. Barton. Where the dream of 'The Great Chase' was born, pp.1-2.
46. *Steeple Chase Calendar*, 1847-48, p.32.
47. James Bidwell-Topham in conversation with the author, May 1995.
48. *Bell's Life*, 16 July 1843.
49. Letter from William Eaton Hall to Lord Sefton, 20 April 1843, Molyneux Muniments DDM 6/81.
50. Letter from William Eaton Hall to Lord Sefton, 15 May 1843, Molyneux Muniments DDM 6/84.
51. Letter from William Eaton Hall to Lord Sefton, 8 June 1843, Molyneux Muniments DDM 6/91
52. *Bell's Life*, 16 July 1843.
53. Letter from John Lathbury to Lord Sefton, 3 June 1843, Molyneux Muniments DDM 6/87.
54. Letter from John Lathbury to Lord Sefton, 16 June 1843, Molyneux Muniments DDM 6/94.
55. Letter from Wiliam Eaton Hall to Lord Sefton, 18 June 1843, Molyneux Muniments DDM 6/95.
56. Letter from John Lathbury to Lord Sefton, 16 June 1843, Molyneux Muniments DDM 6/94.

57. Aspinall. Birkenhead and its surroundings, p.81.
58. *Bell's Life*, 2 March 1845.
59. *Perry's Bankrupt and Insolvent Gazette*, 1 June 1844.
60. *Bell's Life*, 27 February 1848.
61. *The Field Quarterly Magazine and Review*, Vol. 2, 1871, p.42. A Mr. T.J. Williams is stated to have been "for many years the acting manager for the late Mr. Lynn".
62. Smyly. Encyclopaedia of steeplechasing, p.157.
63. *Liverpool Mercury*, 12 October 1870.
64. Lynn's will can be seen at Somerset House, where it is listed in Vol. 12 of the Index of Wills for 1870. Lynn left his entire estate to his wife during her lifetime; after her death it was to be divided equally between his grandchildren "notwithstanding their father shall be living".
65. *Bell's Life*, 9 July 1848.
66. *Bell's Life*, 16 July 1848.
67. Letter from R. Ledger to Lord Sefton, 29 July 1848, Molyneux Muniments DDM 6/174.
68. Letter from R. Ledger to Lord Sefton, 29 July 1848, Molyneux Muniments DDM 6/174.

7.

A forgotten Liverpool race meeting: the Old Roan steeplechases

By the mid-1840s a number of other sporting events had been established around the Grand National meeting. The Waterloo Cup and the Hooton Park steeplechases have already been mentioned; less well-known than either of these was a further steeplechase meeting which was held in fields near the Old Roan, hardly more than a mile away from Aintree.

The first references to this meeting occur in 1845, when on 27 February, just six days before the Grand National, there were six entries for a steeplechase "for horses regularly hunted with the Earl of Sefton's harriers, or other hounds in the neighbourhood, and *bona fide* property, for two months at least, of gentlemen residing within six miles of Liverpool" [1], to be run "just beyond the Old Roan at Aintree" [2]. The race was promoted by "a few of the influentials of Liverpool", and was "intended to be an annual one, as a precursor to the 'Great National'"; it was run "over fine level country in a ring fence, with upwards of thirty fences" [3]. The *Liverpool Courier* reported it as follows:

"Sankey made the running for near the whole distance, with The Artist nearly abreast, both horses taking their leaps in beautiful style. After getting well over the last fallow-field The Artist shot ahead, and went in, an easy winner by ten lengths. The Artist and Sankey were beautifully ridden by Mr. Henderson and Mr. Thomas. Copeland on Ewbank fell. Louise and

Runaway did not get once round, having refused their leaps at an early period of the race. The gray mare came in a very bad third" [4].

This inaugural meeting attracted "a strong muster of the right sort" and gave "great satisfaction" [5].

None of the accounts of this race give any indication of its distance, but the fact that it was run over thirty fences suggests that it was around four miles. The following year a race with similar conditions was run over this distance. On this occasion it must have been more of a spectacle as Single Peeper beat The Iron Duke by just a head, with the third horse, Lady Grey (the "gray mare" of the previous year), close up third. A second race, over an unspecified distance, was also added to the card [6].

The exact location of this course is now impossible to determine. There is no trace of it on the 1849-50 Ordnance Survey 6" survey, but as the races were clearly held over open country, this is not surprising; even the steeplechase course at Aintree is not marked on the same survey. After examining the map, my feeling is that the fields between Aintree Lane and the River Alt to the east of the main Liverpool to Preston road and, after 1849, the railway line, are the most likely location. It would have been easy to mark out a circuit of around two miles in this area without encountering any natural or man-made impediments, whereas this would have been difficult in the land on the other side of the Ormskirk road.

Hunt steeplechases, of which the Old Roan meeting was clearly one, occupied an intermediate position between point to points and the smaller National Hunt meetings that were common before the Second World War. The courses tended to be less developed, and the majority of the jockeys were amateurs, many of them riding their own horses. One of the better-known riders at Old Roan was Mr. Bretherton, who had ridden Cockahoop in the inaugural Grand National, and who had subsequently won it on Jerry in 1840. In some cases the horses were ridden by their grooms or lads, another indication of the low status of the meeting.

How long these races at Old Roan lasted is unclear. The meeting was still in existence in 1849, as it is listed in the *Steeple Chase Calendar* for that year, but I can find no trace of it after then. It does not appear in the list of steeplechase meetings in the 1856 edition of Walsh's *Manual of British rural sports* [7]; and by 1866 the Croxteth Hunt (presumably the successor to the Earl of Sefton's harriers) was holding its race at Aintree during the Grand Sefton meeting in November [8].

There were also attempts to establish steeplechase meetings at Ormskirk (1849), Croston (1861) and Southport (1853); and the Liverpool Hunt Club held an annual steeplechase on the race course at Hoylake between 1854 and 1876. Apart from Hoylake, these meetings lasted only a few years, and none of them could rival Aintree in prestige [9]. As Will Ogilvie put it:

"There are many famous courses
In the width of English ground
Where the steeplechasing horses
And the racing silks go round:
But it's Aintree, Aintree, Aintree,
Where the champion horses run
Where there's courage to be tested
And there's glory to be won" [10].

Notes and references

1. *Steeple Chase Calendar*, 1845-46, pp.9-10.
2. *Liverpool Courier*, 5 March 1845.
3. *Bell's Life*, 2 March 1845.
4. *Liverpool Courier*, 5 March 1845.
5. *Bell's Life*, 2 March 1845.
6. *Steeple Chase Calendar*, 1845-46, p.67.
7. Walsh. Manual of British rural sports, p.389.
8. *Racing Calendar: steeple chases past*, 1866-67, pp.10, 16.
9. There is an invaluable list of former race meetings in the appendices to Chris Pitt's *A long time gone*. However, his dates need to be treated with caution as those given for Crosby, Maghull, Ormskirk and Old Roan are all wrong. For Hoylake see Thompson. On the turf, pp.24-27.
10. Ayres and Newbon. Over the sticks, p.29. A framed copy of this poem hangs over the entrance to the weighing room at Aintree.

8.

Early Steeplechase Jockeys

Delabere Blaine, who compiled an early 19th century *Encyclopaedia of rural sports*, thought that "the origin of the jockey... is in most cases low, and too many of them are not wanting in low cunning, and too frequently they even exhibit consummate villany", but he added that "nevertheless, many others among them rise on fair fame to high respectability and competence" [1].

When he wrote those words, Blaine probably had flat race jockeys rather than steeplechase riders primarily in mind. Nevertheless there is no reason to suppose that there was much difference in this regard between the two sports, even though many early steeplechases were restricted to "gentlemen riders". This seems to have been a condition that was more honoured in the breach than in the observance, as it is clear that many of the leading early riders, such as Captain Becher, whilst calling themselves "gentlemen", were in practice professional jockeys in all but name. The distinction seems to have been fluid, not least because of the difficulty in defining who was and who was not a "gentleman" satisfactorily. There is a story, perhaps apocryphal, of a "gentleman" rider at a Yorkshire meeting in 1836 defending his status on the grounds that he subscribed to a pack of hounds, hunted three days a week, drank wine with his dinner, and kept a mistress [2]. Perhaps, as Roger Munting has suggested, the restriction was designed less to keep out professionals as such than the "lower orders", such as tenant farmers [3].

From the very beginning steeplechase riders formed a class "quite separate and distinct from the jockeys of the flat race". They rode at heavier weights, from 11 stone down to 8 stone, and by the middle of the 19th century their riding fees were from £5 upwards. [4]. This was a large sum by the standards of the time, and it has been calculated that it would take a rider only seven losing rides to exceed the average annual money wage at the time [5]. There was thus quite a temptation for grooms and other agricultural workers who knew something of horses to try and become professional jockeys. How many of them there were is hard to assess, although it is clear that their number grew as rapidly as the sport itself. In 1846 Henry Corbet published a list of 32 in the *Steeple Chase Calendar*; by 1849 the number had risen to 48; and by 1854 to 110 [6]. However, these lists are not complete, being resticted to those who were more or less openly professional. Riders who rode only their own horses or those belonging to friends, or the lads and grooms who rode many of the entries at the smaller meetings, were not included.

The first man who can fairly be described as a professional steeplechase jockey was probably Dick Christian. Christian was born in 1779 at Cottesmore, and, after spending his early years as a groom and Second Whip to the Cottesmore Hunt, he turned to regular "rough riding" and training in 1817. His first patron was Lord Plymouth, by whom he was retained for £21 and 15/- a horse; later he also trained for Berkeley Craven and Lord Forester, and in 1820 he was working for Matt Milton, a well-known horse dealer, for £5 5s a week, plus his keep and clothes. He is reckoned to have taken part in most of the major steeplechases between 1809 and 1841 (by which time he was over 60). He finished second on Polyanthus in the first "Liverpool Grand Steeple Chase" in 1836, and rode The Augean in 1840 when he failed to finish. At the age of 61 he went as Stud Groom to Lord Scarborough at Rufford and remained there until Scarborough died in 1856. Sadly, he was left in poverty in his old age, until the sporting writer Henry Hall Dixon ("The Druid") started a Fund on his behalf. He suffered a severe stroke on Christmas Day 1860 from which he never recovered; he died on 5 June 1862, aged 84, and was buried in the Dissenters' Burial Ground, Melton Mowbray.

Christian was widely regarded as one of the finest steeplechase riders of his day, and this despite the fact that he was lame, riding two holes shorter on his left stirrup leather than his right, and using only one spur. Despite all his successes, he is said to have been "the perfect servant who knew his own place and respected it as he did that of his superiors", a trait which no doubt endeared him to his aristocratic employers. He was a deeply religious man, but one who was also prey to supersitition, believing that there were witches who could turn themselves into hares or black foxes. Although a grave man, who did not laugh a lot, like Becher he liked a good joke and was something of a prankster. He married three times, on the last occasion to a Belgian tight rope dancer from Sanger's Circus, and had twenty one children [7].

Dick Christian

Also riding in the 1836 "Liverpool Grand Steeple Chase" was Bartholomew Bretherton on Cockahoop. He was a local man, who may have been related to the Peter Bretherton who was John Formby's partner at Maghull. Certainly they shared the same occupation for by 1844 Bartholomew Bretherton had become a coach proprietor based in Worcestershire [8]. But, despite moving away from the area, he still had strong family ties to south Lancashire and continued to be a member of the Liverpool Hunt Club [9].

After the inaugural running in 1836, Bretherton had six more rides in the Grand National. In 1840 he won it on Jerry; in 1841 he rode Goblin, fell at Becher's and then remounted to finish seventh; in 1842 he failed to finish on Satirist; in 1843 he rode Goblin again and finished fifth; and in 1848 and 1849 he rode Wolverhampton, failing to finish on the first occasion and falling at the fence after the Canal Turn on the second.

Despite being remembered as "one of the best of the self-styled gentleman riders in the earliest days of steeplechasing" [10] and having won a Grand National, Bretherton did not receive many rides. In the 1846-47 season, for example, he had just three rides, at Wolverhampton, Leamington and Lincoln, on each occasion riding the same horse, Glaucus. The following year he rode Wolverhampton on four occasions, at Worcester, Wolverhampton (where most appropriately he won), Wakefield and Liverpool, and had only one other ride, in a hunt chase at Ormskirk. Glaucus and Wolverhampton were both owned by a Mr. B.H. Jones, Wolverhampton being a son of Glaucus. After riding Wolverhampton in the 1848 Grand National Bretherton purchased him before riding him again in the race the following year [11].

Bretherton was also represented as an owner in the Grand National on two other occasions: in 1844 by Marengo, who finished seventh, and in 1853 by Chatterbox who was pulled up.

Bretherton's career suggests that not all those who called themselves gentlemen riders were in reality professional jockeys in the way that Captain Becher, Tom Olliver or Jem Mason were. In 1846-47, when Bretherton had three rides on the same horse for the same owner, Tom Olliver had thirty four rides and Jem Mason at least fifteen (including winning the Grand French Chase in Paris). Bretherton and men like him may have been willing to accept payment for riding, but this clearly was not their main source of income in the way it was for Olliver or Mason.

Towards the end of his life Bretherton moved back to Liverpool, and he died aged 67 at his house in Bedford Street South on 29 March, 1874 [12].

Another local rider in the inaugural "Liverpool Grand Steeple Chase" was John Devine who rode Derry. Even less is known about him than about Bretherton. He clearly continued riding for some years, as he appears in Henry Corbet's list of professional steeple chase riders for the 1847-48 season [13], yet he does not seem to have been given a single ride that season. At that time his address was the beer house, 2 Mount Street, Everton [14], and this suggests that his primary occupation was that of a publican; although listed as a professional rider he would today be more likely regarded as an amateur.

The careers of men such as Bretherton or Devine were very different from those of the leading steeplechase jockeys, such as Becher or Jem Mason. Mason, the third son of a breeder of and dealer in hunters, was born at Stilton, near Peterborough, in 1816. He was educated at Huntingdon Grammar School and then became a rough rider for a horse dealer named Tilbury who was based at Pinner in Middlesex. It was there that his steeplechasing capabilities were first discovered by Lord Frederick Beauclerk who declared that "that boy picks his ground out better than any of them" and engaged him to ride The Poet in the St Albans Chase of 1834; despite The Poet refusing at the first fence, the partnership eventually won in a canter. After this victory Mason rapidly became the leading steeplechase rider of his generation, especially after he teamed up with John Elmore who owned many of the best chasers of the time. In 1837 he won the Leamington on Jerry, and the same year he rode Lottery for the first time. The following year he won the Leamington again on The Nun, and in 1839, of course, he gained his memorable victory on Lottery in the Grand National. This partnership was also successful at Cheltenham, Stratford, Leamington and elsewhere, leading one observer to remark that "Those three words 'Mason on Lottery' have long represented the *beau ideal* of the crack cross-country rider on the crack steeplechase horse".

Other notable horses on which Mason was successful included Gaylad, Peter Simple and St. Leger. In riding style, he was said to combine "a firm, elegant seat, with fine hands, good eye to a country, quick decision, and great judgement in picking his ground". But it was at putting his horse at a fence that he excelled, and he was regarded as unrivalled in getting horses over water.

Mason's record at Aintree would surely have been better had Lottery not been burdened with impossible weights after his victory in 1839. His other rides in the Grand National were Veluti who broke down in 1846, Clinker who fell in 1847, and Rat-Trap on whom he finished sixth in 1851.

Mason's career, like that of Dick Christian, shows that it was possible to rise from humble beginnings to national fame through becoming a steeplechase rider, but, also like Christian, he had a "simple knowledge of his own position, which was never spoiled by either public or private flatteries"; in other words he knew his place. It is also worth noting that despite his fame and his success as a rider, he died a far from wealthy man.

Mason was married twice, first to John Elmore's daughter, and then to a Miss Seckham of Oxford. On his second marriage in 1857 he gave up race riding and concentrated on his horse dealing business, which was based at 114, Mount Street, London and at Hendon. He died of cancer of the throat on 23 October, 1866 in London, and is buried in Kensal Green Cemetery [15].

Another leading rider in the early days of Aintree was Mr. Powell, who was based at Cheltenham. As we have seen, he rode Laurie Todd in the inaugural National in 1836 and won it on Charity in 1841. The following year he landed over the last first on Seventy Four, but was then caught on the long run in by Tom Olliver on Gay Lad and had to be content with second place. His other rides included Railroad in 1839, on whom he finished sixth, The Nun in 1840, who fell, Charity again in 1844, when he fell at the water, Peter Swift in 1845, who failed to finish, Brenda in 1846, who fell, Culverthorpe in 1847, on whom he finished fifth, Variety in 1848, who failed to finish, and The Curate in 1849, who fell and broke his back.

Powell had the reputation of being a "bruiser". On one occasion in 1835 he rode at a steeplechase meeting in Norfolk at which the course was exceptionally severe. He was heard to say that he was going to show the natives how to ride in a steeplechase, but, as he lost his first mount and killed his second, a local reporter remarked that they remained satisfied with "admiring his style, without imitating it" [16]. Like many of the other leading steeplechase riders of the time he was prepared to travel large distances; during the 1845-46 season, for example, he rode at places as far apart as Pembrokeshire, Usk and Hereford in the west, Teignbridge in Devon and Harleston in Norfolk [17].

It is worth remembering, however, that the leading riders such as Mason or Powell were exceptional. Many steeplechase winners were ridden by their owners, and although the big races tended in the early years to be the preserve of the professionals or near-professionals, there too it was not uncommon for the genuine amateur to triumph, as the history of the Grand National itself shows, particularly in the last third of the 19th century, when, for example, in the twenty years from 1873 to 1892 there were fourteen winners ridden by amateurs as opposed to only six ridden by professionals.

Amongst the genuine amateurs who won the National in its first two decades were Henry Potts on The Duke in 1837 and Alan McDonogh on Sir William the following year. They were followed by Captain Little on The Chandler in 1848. Little, who had a colourful career, was born at Chipstead in Surrey in 1821, where his family had lived for generations. He was gazetted a cornet in the 1st Dragoon Guards in 1840, later being promoted to captain, and he began his riding career in military steeplechases, winning a 3 mile chase at the 1st Dragoon Guards meeting at Exeter. However, his military career suffered a major setback when the bank in which all his money was deposited failed and he had to resign his commission. The story is that Captain Little was at Worcester races, having his first ride on The Chandler in November 1847, when he heard of the bank's collapse. Davies, the "Leviathan" bookmaker, who was present, shouted out "Twenty 'ponies' against your horse, The Chandler, Captain", to which the Captain immediately responded "Put it down, Davies". A few minutes later, having won his race, he found himself £500 richer and able to start his career once more; however he later transferred to the infantry, becoming a captain in the 81st Foot. He won on The Chandler again at Leamington in December 1847, and the partnership started third favourite at 12-1 for the 1848 Grand National. In an exciting finish, they just beat The Curate, ridden by Tom Olliver by half a length. As Olliver had coached Captain Little in the arts of steeplechase riding, this was very much a case of the pupil turning the tables on his former teacher.

Captain Little's triumph was even more notable because he was also the co-owner of The Chandler, and this is one of only six occasions when an owner has ridden his own horse to victory in the race, the others being in 1838 (Alan McDonogh on Sir William), 1877 (Fred Hobson on Austerlitz), 1879 (Garry Moore on The Liberator), 1882 (Lord Manners on Seaman) and 1883 (Count Kinsky on Zoedone). It was said Little and his partner Captain Peel, also a noted amateur steeplechase rider of the day, won £6-7,000 between them in bets on the race.

Captain Little continued riding for several more years after this, both on the flat and over jumps. He rode The Chandler again in the next two

Captain Little on The Chandler

Grand Nationals finishing fifth in 1849 and falling at the fence before Becher's in 1850. Away from Aintree, in 1850 he won the Hunt Cup at Warwick, and as late as 1860 he won on the flat at Brighton. He was also lucky as an owner, as he won the National again with Peter Simple in 1853, ridden by his old mentor Tom Olliver.

Known as the "captivating captain", Captain Little was renowned for his store of entertaining anecdotes, which no doubt became considerably embroidered over the years. One of his favourite stories told how once, having weighed out for an important steeplechase, he was approached by an impecunious individual who proposed a cunning plan to him. Captain Little was to remove the leads from his saddle cloth and hand them over to his accomplice. He would then win the race (this was unquestioned); then, according to the plan "when you pull up, I will be there, Captain, with ten pounds of shot, which I will pour into your boots. You understand, Captain? Your BOOOTS!"

One of his friends also recalled the Captain warning her against entering a railway carriage with only one other person in it, as a result of an "*awful* experience" he once had on travelling home from York races: "My only fellow-passenger kept his eye on me, and, needless to say, I did the same. At last he made a spring at me. I was ready, however, and managed to push him down and hold him until the train stopped, which it did in the nick of time, for... I couldn't have held him another three minutes". Little had indeed had a narrow escape for his attacker turned out to be an escaped lunatic and a very powerful man. In those days there were no corridor trains and no emergency communication cords, and the train he was on, being an express, stopped only once between York and London. As his friend said "It was indeed an awkward predicament for the Captivating Captain".

Captain Little died on 17 February 1877 at the Hotel Clarendon in Paris. The immediate cause of death was congestion of the liver, caused by a severe cold, but, about eighteen months before, he had contracted gout which had spread to his left eye, resulting in his losing its sight [18].

Little was regarded as a very talented amateur rider, who could hold his own with most of the professionals of the time, but not all amateurs who rode in the Grand National were equally skilled, for then as now it seems to have attracted its fair share of eccentrics. One such, who also rode in the 1848 National, was the pugilist Johnny Broome. Broome was born in Birmingham in 1818 and fought seven prize fights, the most notable of which were in 1841, when he defeated Jack Hannan for £500, in a contest of 47 rounds which lasted an hour and nineteen minutes, and one the following year when he beat the Australian Bungaree in a contest which lasted 42 rounds. By this time he had married and become the landlord of the Rising Sun, in Air Street off Piccadilly [19].

In 1848 Broome was said to have taken a bet of £10,000 to £100 that he rode a horse called Cavendish in the National and won. Cavendish, however, became lame and never started so the bet was lost. There is some mystery over this bet as Cavendish's owner later said he knew nothing of it and had never been approached by Broome to ride the horse. Broome then bet Captain Alleyne £500 that he would be within four fields of the finish when the winner passed the post. He intended to buy a horse called Proceed to ride in the race, but this deal too fell through, and it was only at the eleventh hour that he secured the ride on a horse called Eagle, which was lent to him for the purpose. A further bet of £500 to £5 was struck that another horse called Blue Pill, whose rider was wearing exactly the same colours as Broome, red jacket and black cap, would win the race.

Broome rode Eagle "with great pluck", and kept up with the rest of the field on the first circuit, but he then began to lose ground and was in the last four as the runners approached Becher's Brook second time round. Here Eagle bucked and threw Broome heavily, with the result that he was "so much shaken that he was unable to leave the cottage to which he was assisted by the bystanders for upwards of an hour". Meanwhile, Blue Pill, whose rider was wearing the same colours, continued in the race until he broke down on re-entering the race course. Not surprisingly, many of the spectators in the stands confused Blue Pill with Eagle and assumed that Broome had won his bet of being within four fields of the winner at the finish. However, that evening Broome went to Lynn's Waterloo Hotel and presented Alleyne with his cheque for £500, "to the ineffable surprise and delight of the gallant captain". Impressed by Broome's honesty, Alleyne then offered to return a considerable proportion of the money "as an acknowledgement of the promptitude with which he came to scratch" [20].

Broome's later life was tragic. He was said to have had quite a lot of money at one time, but lost much of it in a court case after he was accused of cheating at cards. "Not a man of sober habits", he turned increasingly to drink, and became further depressed after the government rejected his invention of a gun which he claimed could fire a 50lb weight for two miles. He also suffered from the effects of sunstroke and began to have hallucinations, saying to one of his friends "Did you see those five men following me; they are continually watching me". He quarrelled with his family and moved from Birmingham to London, where, on 31 May 1855, at the Wrekin Tavern in Broad Court, off Bow Street, he cut his throat with a large carving knife; the jury at the inquest returned a verdict of insanity [21].

Notes and references

1. Blaine. Encyclopaedia of rural sports, p.358.
2. Quoted in Vamplew. The turf, p.162.
3. Munting. Hedges and hurdles, p.125.
4. Walsh. Manual of British rural sports, p.388.
5. Munting. Hedges and hurdles, p.132.
6. Walsh. Manual of British rural sports, p.388.
7. Paget and Irvine. The flying parson and Dick Christian, pp.127-153.
8. Information from Bretherton's will, held at Somerset House.
9. *Steeple Chase Calendar*, 1848-49, p.23.
10. Richardson and Mason. Gentlemen riders past and present, p.39.
11. This information has been drawn from the returns in the *Steeple Chase Calendar.*
12. Index of Wills, 1874, Vol. 2; *Liverpool Mercury*, 2 April 1874.
13. *Steeple Chase Calendar*, 1847-48, p.vi.
14. *Gore's Directory*, 1847.
15. *Baily's Magazine*, December 1866, pp.229-236; *Bell's Life*, 27 October 1866; *Gentleman's Magazine*, December 1866, p.840; *The Times*, 6 November 1866.
16. Richardson and Mason. Gentlemen riders past and present, pp.46-49.
17. *Steeple Chase Calendar*, 1845-46.
18. *Bell's Life*, 5 March 1848, 24 February 1877; Blew. A history of steeple-chasing, pp.103-105; Richardson and Mason. Gentlemen riders past and present, pp.93-95.
19. Dowling. Fights for the championship, pp.370-378.
20. *Bell's Life*, 5 March 1848.
21. *Bell's Life*, 3 June 1855.

9.

Dandy rats at play: low life at Aintree

Horse racing in the early 19th century was closely connected with the criminal and semi-criminal underworld, yet it was also a popular and fashionable sport, which was supported by people from virtually every social class. Indeed, there was probably nowhere else in early Victorian England where the nobility and other members of polite society rubbed shoulders quite so closely with the tricksters, beggars, pickpockets and prostitutes who flocked to the races in the search for easy pickings.

This mixing of classes at the races was sufficiently unusual for it to be noticed by foreign visitors to England. The French writer, Hippolyte Taine, for example, tells a nice story of how at Epsom on Derby Day he saw gentlemen amicably lunching with their coachmen, but then he comments that "on the morrow distinctions of rank will be as strong as ever, and the coachman will be respectful, distant, as is his wont". Not all social contacts were quite so innocent, however, for Taine also noted that, under the influence of drink, "these people so proper, so delicate, indulge in strange conduct... the animal nature had full vent" [1].

Writing at around the same time, the American Warren Isham noted that at race meetings the noblility and gentry could be found "perched upon the most prominent look-out", whilst "the acclivities swarm with human beings of the plebeian stamp". During the larger three day meetings, Isham found the neighbouring towns to be often "in a state of perfect uproar; and it is generally a three days' siege, during which people move about warily, with their hands upon their purses. The din is kept up through the live-long night, and it is in vain to think of seeking repose. The gangs of gamblers, jugglers, mountebanks, thimble-riggers, whirligigs, pickpockets and swindlers of every description who follow the races, and grace the grounds during the day, come pouring into town during the night, and together with the accompanying rabble, both noble and ignoble, constitute a medley over which Satan himself might be well pleased" [2].

The lewdness, brutality and disorder that writers such as Taine and Isham were referring to were present at every race meeting and aroused increasing opposition from some sections of society during the first half of the 19th century. Nonconformists, as part of their general concern with reform of popular manners, had a long history of opposition to traditional sports, particularly those associated with gambling and drink; and the Evangelicals within the Church of England also took up the cause with vigour. On Sunday, 17 June, 1827, for example, the Rev. F. Close preached a sermon at Cheltenham, in which he stated that in his view "The Heathen festivals of Venus and the Bacchus are exceeded on a Christian race ground", going on to add that "the roads, and fields, and pathways leading to the emporium of vice and folly are strewed with the victims of riot and vicious excess". Getting into his stride, he listed the vices that during the races "stalk abroad in all the impudence of emboldened profligacy" as "adultery, fornication, uncleanness, lasciviousness – hatred, variance, emulations, wrath, strife – envying, drunkenness, *revellings*, and SUCH LIKE". For the time being, Close's congregation was left to wonder what nameless horror was meant by "SUCH LIKE", delivered with such emphasis, but later in his sermon he returned to this "master sin of the week, the most frightful demon of this moral storm", which turned out to be "the foul spirit of gaming". According to Close, "every vile passion of our corrupt nature is excited and inflamed by it; envy, malice, revenge, the lust of money, pride contention, cruelty, and, as we have on one occasion known, murder" [3]. Close clearly didn't believe in pulling his punches, but the Anglican clergy in Liverpool do not seem to have condemned the races at Aintree in quite such forthright terms, perhaps because the senior Rector of Liverpool, Jonathon Brooks, was an old-fashioned sporting parson of the 18th century school; indeed it was said of him that during the shooting season he kept his carriage, together with his guns and dogs, outside the church door, so that no time would be lost once the service was over [4].

Nevertheless, as we have already seen, there was considerable opposition to the races in the town, which found its most vocal expression in the pages of the *Liverpool Mercury*. Racing's association with the triple evils of drink, gambling and sex made it an easy target for the moralists and reformers, whilst underneath the surface there was also the ever-present fear of riot and disorder by an unruly crowd drawn in large part from amongst the disreputable classes. Not all the Anglican clergy shared Rector Brooks's *laissez-faire* attitude to sporting events. Between 1843 and 1865 the Rev. John Saul Howson was on the staff of Liverpool College, latterly as Principal. Later, as Dean of Chester, he condemned the races there in forthright terms. "Each season", he wrote, seems to indicate an increasing tendency to fraud, obscenity, profanity and debauchery" as some of the "vilest and most degraded" people descended on Chester "like an army of locusts", resulting in "a state of wild and reckless excitement, which, with too many, obliterates the sense of right and wrong" [5]. It seems unlikely that his views had changed much since his time in Liverpool.

Nonconformist ministers in Liverpool, as elsewhere, tended to be strongly opposed to the races. Augustine Birrell, who was the son of the Pembroke Place Baptist minister and who was born in 1850, remembered that in his youth there was a marked distinction between the inhabitants of Liverpool who were not allowed to go to the Grand National and those, "the large majority", who were; he was "as usual", in the minority [6].

From the very beginning the races at Aintree attracted large crowds of people from all over the country. And what a motley crowd it was: "Visitors from all quarters, and by all sorts of conveyances, have poured in upon us – from north and south, from Scotland, Wales and Ireland, by steamers, railways, coaches, chaises, gigs and waggons. Our inns have been crowded with gentle and simple; the taverns and private houses have been everywhere in request for the accommodation of the sporting fraternity of all descriptions. Count Whiskerandos from Germany and France, hard-riding horse dealers from Ireland, knowing ones from Scotland, and sporting manufacturers, tradesmen, butchers, graziers, &c., &c., from Manchester, Bolton, Wigan and the neighbourhood surrounding. Croxteth, Knowsley, and the mansions of our country gentry have been crowded with guests, who exhibited their 'swell turns out' in our streets, jostling the equipages of our merchants, and astonishing not a few of the natives, who have heretofore looked with singular self-complacency on their tiny tilburies [7] and tardily-trotting-tits [8]. In short, our streets have exhibited an accession of bustle, with an assemblage tolerably motley, as is usual in such cases -peers, Corinthians, and peasants, jostling with -

Knowing faded kids [9]
And dandy rats in bloom" [10]

The races were used as an excuse by most of the working population of the town to take a holiday, and the Summer Meeting in July became the nearest equivalent Liverpool had to the Wakes Weeks of the Lancashire mill towns. As well as the races themselves, there was the arrival of a large travelling fair to look forward to. This was situated on the upper part of Scotland Road and contained "travelling menageries, aerial machines, hobby-horses, swinging boats, and booths, accompanied by bands of... strolling players, most of whom [were] wretchedly ragged and miserably foot-sore" [11]. There were also shooting galleries, toffee stalls, fortune tellers and exhibitions of freaks such as five-legged dogs. Hundreds of children roamed around the fairground, "many ragged and shoeless, all dirty and mischevious", whilst "the riotous conduct of the young men and women riveted the gaze of all beholders". Huddled together under coats and shawls, they sang "ribald songs" and indulged in "disgusting conduct and disgraceful language" [12]. It was no doubt a lively and uninhibited scene, shocking to some middle class observers, but, as one proprietor of a merry-go-round philosophically put it, "The races will last only three days [and] the lads in a town like this must have their fun" [13].

In fact, the degree of sexual licence enjoyed by Liverpool's youth at this time was the subject of considerable comment. William Bevan, the minister of Newington Chapel, thought that they were "notorious for their disregard of morality and law" [14]; that this state of affairs was not new is shown by a song written in 1810 called *All alive at Liverpool*, one verse of which ran:

"But what most made me stare
Was to see the Washing Fair

Where the lads are all so witty
And the girls are all so pretty
For in spite of wind and weather
They jumped in Pell Mell together
And said that they had Physic in the Water O
Together yok'd – ladies douk'd
Water dashing – kicking, splashing
Indeed it's true – Buff and Blue
Men and women – all a swimming
Cheek by jowel – upon my soul!
Hey down, oh down derry, derry down
O Liverpool's a wonderful town O!" [15]

On race days, "as early as nine o'clock the road leading to Aintree was crowded with pedestrians of the usual class, including pie-men, chimney sweeps, cigar-sellers, thimble-riggers, and all the small fry of gaming-table keepers. As the day advanced the road swarmed with passengers of all descriptions, 'from noblemen to tailors', from merchants and wealthy manufacturers to butchers and tinkers, all hurrying to the scene of action as fast as their several means of conveyance would permit... It was one dense mass of people, in some of the more *recherche* points wedged together, so as to defy motion in those who had once got enclosed" [16].

Nor was it just the horse racing that drew these people to Aintree. There was cock fighting, there was pugilism, there was archery, and a host of sideshows offering gambling games of all descriptions. Of these, the most common, and the one which seems to have aroused the most opposition from the opponents of horse racing and the race course authorities alike, was thimble-rigging. This was a game usually played with three thimbles and a pea, which was ostensibly placed under one of them; the thimble-rigger then challenged the bystanders to guess under which the pea had been placed and to bet on the result. The whole thing was, of course, a fraud, and how it was done was neatly exposed in a letter to the *Illustrated London News* in 1842:

"First, then, know that the player has the game entirely in his own hands, and you can never win by any chance without his will. The 'pea', as it is called, is a piece of new bread, worked up in the hands till it assumes the blackness of, and is softer than a piece of India rubber, and is, moreover, very adhesive. When the player places it on the board, he takes the thimble between his fore-finger and thumb, and so he pretends and appears to place it over the pea: he then takes the pea adroitly up with the thumb nail. This, by practice, can be done with either hand, and completely deceives the eye. Of course the pea is not under any of the three thimbles, and when you select one, he instantly raises one of the remaining two, and drops the 'pea' at the same moment, to convince you that it really was under one of them" [17].

Thimble-rigging, as illustrated in the ***Illustrated London News****, 1842*

Another game often seen at Aintree and other courses in those days was called Prick the Garter. This was an old swindling game, sometimes also known as Fast and Loose, which seems to have first been introduced to Britain by the gipsies in the 16th century. It was played with a belt or strap and a stick, the belt being doubled and rolled up with the loop at the centre and placed on the edge of a table. The player then had to catch the loop and make the belt fast with the stick as it was unrolled, but this was done in such a way by the trickster as to make the feat virtually impossible.

There were also board games such as roulette or rouge et noir, but the most popular of these was probably E.O., a game which was a kind of cross between roulette and pin-ball, in which the appropriation of the stakes was decided by a ball falling into one of several niches which were marked E or O. This too was a fraudulent game, for underneath the board was a cloth which could be manipulated by a stooge in the crowd to ensure the ball fell into the hole which would best profit the owner of the stall.

It was not just the nature of these activities that caused offence, it was the sheer scale of them. The thimble-riggers tended to congregate in large gangs, and were "as desperate a set of ruffians as could be found" [18]. They were thus easily able to intimidate racegoers, and it was not unknown for them to strip their victims of everything they had and beat them up as well. Nor were the sums of money involved always small ones; at a case which came to court in 1823 plenty of evidence was produced to show that gentlemen would often stop their carriages by a thimble-rigger's table, get out, and lose twenty or thirty pounds in a few minutes.

With so much money at stake, it is hardly surprising that the thimble-riggers and their allies resisted all attempts by the authorities to remove them from the race course. The most famous incident occurred at Doncaster in 1830 when a force of one hundred policemen, aided by mounted volunteers drawn from the gentry and their servants, fought a pitched battle with four or five hundred thimble-riggers in full sight of the crowd in the grand stand [19]. Occasionally, too, the tables could quite literally be turned when racegoers became incensed at the thimble-riggers' trickery and attacked them in their turn. At Lincoln in 1831, a crowd of country people began to break up the thimble-riggers' tables. The disturbance spread until around two thousand people were involved, who, after destroying the gaming tables, attacked the thimble-riggers' tents and carts as well, and "if the owners made any resistance they were beaten untill they became insensible"; two children were so badly injured during the affray that they were thought unlikely to live [20]. Nothing on quite this scale ever appears to have happened at Aintree, but at the steeplechase meeting in 1840 there were 150 Liverpool policemen present, one of whose tasks was to keep the thimble-riggers from getting on to the course [21]. They appear to have been successful, as it was reported that only one thimble-rigger was seen on the course that year, "and he seemed to be in continual terror of the police" [22]; the following year there was "a total absence of all gambling concerns" [23].

Even with the thimble-riggers removed, there were plenty of other temptations on offer at Aintree, not the least of which was sex, for, as William Bevan put it, "The incidents of sin attendant on the race-course would be incomplete without the fascination... of bartered womanhood" [24]. Nor is this surprising when it is remembered that, as a major seaport, Liverpool was notorious for the large numbers of prostitutes who lived within its boundaries. A French writer who toured the town in the company of Michael Whitty, Liverpool's first police chief, thought that it was infected with vice to a much greater degree than any other English city [25]; and even a retired ship's officer, presumably a fairly hardened character, considered it "the most immoral of all immoral places" [26]. In 1836 it was estimated that there were 300 brothels in the town containing 1,200 prostitutes. These figures rose sharply in succeeding years. The police recorded the number of known prostitutes as 1,902 in 1838, 1,695 in 1839, 2,394 in 1840, 2,683 in 1841 and 2,900 in 1842 [27]. By this time the number of brothels and other "houses of bad character" in the town had risen to 770 [28]. It was estimated at the time that each house of resort received 70 visits each week, which, if true, meant that no fewer than 2,802,800 visits were being made annually to Liverpool's prostitutes [29], a figure which, staggering as it may seem, may well have been an underestimate.

We have already seen that large numbers of prostitutes were present at the very first race meeting at Maghull in 1827, and they continued to see the races as an ideal opportunity to ply their trade more or less openly for the whole of the period.

On race days the roads out to Aintree were crowded with "coaches filled with harlots". The drivers in most cases were trimmed out in some sort of lace and the horses' heads were decorated with large pink or blue

'A rather fast steeplechase'. *Sporting ladies depicted as jockeys*

rosettes, and many of the girls were also decked out in their finery, wearing brightly coloured satins and hats decorated with plumes of feathers. The Liverpool journalist Hugh Shimmin described what happened next as follows [30]:

"At every coach you see well dressed men dancing attendance on these women... Cards have been distributed amongst the fashionable and sporting gentlemen during the morning, and in imitation of the cards of the horses these ladies' cards have written on them the colours in which their owners will appear, and are in this style – 'Matilda, primrose and pale blue,' 'Fanny, pink and French white,' 'Sarah, white and green,' 'Jemima, pink and blue,' &c., &c., the colours corresponding with the bonnets and dresses. The great event being over, lazy-looking and fashionably attired men cross the course and enter the ploughed gallop, drawing from their pockets the cards they have received, in order that they may the more easily distinguish their favourites. The girls, flushed with wine, waited on by bullies and pimps, watched keenly by their keepers, who are hovering about, are thus decorated to captivate the turfites."

Out in the centre of the course were a number of tents set apart from the rest which were clearly temporary brothels: "a canvass screen protects the visitors from the gaze of the vulgar crowd... 'Come in, come in', cry half a dozen damsels, 'what are you going to stand?' The waiter is opening a bottle of champagne, and a young man... hands a sovereign in payment. Do the obscene remarks of the women offend the visitors here? Not at all, this is what they seek. The Aintree meeting affords them extensive gratification in this way. Here publicly, in face of day, men can display their utter want of common decency, and by their conduct induce the poor unfortunate outcasts to display their utter want of modesty and shame".

Nearer to the grand stand was another tent with "a very aristocratic title" suspended over the entrance. This was frequented by supposedly respectable merchants who, as members of the Exchange, formed Liverpool's commercial elite, but here, quite openly, they consorted with "young girls and women – their faces daubed with paint, their persons profusely adorned with highly coloured dresses", whilst "persons in the humbler walks of life" gazed on with astonishment. This tent was presided over by a "notorious brothel-keeper and procuress".

An entire new Liſt of the

SPORTING LADIES,

Or PETTICOAT AMBLERS,

With a particular account of their ſeveral Pedigrees, Performances &c.

YE bucks and bloods of ev'ry claſs,
Who range the globe for pleaſure,
From race to race and place to place,
To ſpend your time and treaſure;
Draw near and you ſhall quickly hear,
The names of theſe fine laſſes,
Belonging to the ſporting train,
According to their claſſas.

AMong the foremoſt of all theſe ſweet creatures muſt be ranked Miſs H—, juſt arrived from Cock-Court ſhe is thought to be as fine a filley as ever appeared in the field of pleaſure, beſides a handſome face and fine ſhape ſhe has as genteel a pair of Legs as any Buck would wiſh to have thrown over him.

Miſs E——, and her ſiſter are juſt arrived to teach young Bucks a new mode of amorous enjoyment (in the modern taſte) as taught by Madam Springwell in the Hay-Market.

Miſs J——, a fine tall genteel filley 15 hands high and well made, has lately been afflicted with the dropſy, but is now perfectly recovered, and may be met with moſt evenings at the ragged Tour.

O——B——, is juſt arriv'd and may be met with near petticoat bridge on ſmock alley.

Miſs P——I——, is likewiſe arriv'd and may be met with at the ſame place, has been much us'd of late but is now in good repair.

Miſs B——, and her ſiſter are juſt arrived from New-Bride, where they have been to bring themſelves into good condition, they have fine buſhy muffs are very fond of the ſport and in high ſpirits while running.— They are rather ſtiff at firſt but when they grow warm will afford great diverſion to their jockeys.

Miſs R——, from the ſame place is a fine tall filley 16 hands high, has a remarkable fine fore-hand and has every perfection (only ſhe turns in her toes when ſhe walks.)

Miſs S——H——, is a pretty ſmall filly in good repair and may be met within the Horſe-Fair.

Miſs J——, from the Horſe Fair is but juſt broke up, and as not yet learn'd her paces ſo well as could be wiſhed, however in a little time 'tis thought ſhe'll be as pretty a filley as needs be mounted.

Miſs E——, from Rambleſhame is a fine full cheſted filley goes well on her legs, but if the Jockey does not hold a tight reign he will be very liable to [illegible] rown, as when ſhe's firſt mounted runs ra[illegible]

Miſs B——I——, is a fine genteel filley free from all epidemical diſeaſes except (that of poverty,) ſhe may be met with on Tripe-Hill.

C——B——, is a fine plump aged ginger has no defect but her heels a little greaſy.

N. B. *Any young filley that has not yet learn'd her pace (for a trifling acknowledgement) may be inſtructed in thoſe various Actions and Movements, which ſhe has practiſed ſo many years and with ſuch ſucceſs.*

Ch——r B——, is juſt arrived to exhibit to the Bucks a new mode of amorous enjoyment. She is in excellent condition and able to exerciſe herſelf with great dexterity and eaſe——She will inſtruct young Maſters in the fine arts and ſweet endearments of pleaſure and delight,— She may be met with at Petticoat Booth near the new Windmill on the Courſe.

Miſs J——B——, Miſs D——J——, and Miſs B——E——, takes this method to acquaint thoſe gentlemen who purſue the dictates of Nature, and deteſt that of B——y, that at their Chambers on Tripe Hill they will perform every evening in the neweſt taſte as taught by Madam Rampant at the grand Accademy in Drury-Lane.

Several from C——and other places are expectted to enter at the Poſt.

Amongſt the clan there's ſporting Nan,
With blowſy Beſs and Jenny,
Now Beſs will work for half a crown,
And Jin for half a guinea;
There's ragged Moll and dirty Sal,
Both theſe are fond of billing,
They'll trot the ground for eighteen-pence,
And throw you back a ſhilling.

'Sporting Ladies'. *Prostitutes described as fillies. Sheets like this were sold openly at Aintree in the 19th century*

At Aintree in the 1850s even the race-card sellers formed part of this semi-criminal underworld for, as well as their legitimate stock, they also dealt in pornography. They were all females "with sunburnt faces, gaudily trimmed bonnets, bright coloured plaid shawls, white aprons and shoes with buckles", and in their pockets they had "filthy and obscene prints, which they sell at high prices, and by such means pander to the taste of many to be found at such gatherings – men whose sole aim and object in life appear to be indulgence in gross sensuality and animal pleasure".

By the end of the day drunkennness was rife. "Carts have brought loads of the lowest grade of prostitutes, and females of the humbler classes are very numerous. In the booths dancing is general, and men half and wholly drunk stagger about in all directions." Nor was it just the "humbler classes" who were beginning the feel the effects, for the policemen had "quite enough to do in keeping the respectable people within bounds, for drink is now telling on all".

Drunkenness was endemic in 19th century Liverpool. In 1821 it was noted that "the vast number of public houses in this town has long been a subject of remark with strangers" [31]. One of these was the well-known novelist Mrs. Craik (author of *John Halifax, Gentleman)*, who wrote that "This Liverpool is an awful town for drinking. Other towns may be as bad; statistics prove it; but I know of no place where intoxication is so open and shameless. Not only in bye streets and foul courts, where one expects to see it, but everywhere" [32]; even "gentlemen", she claimed, could be found drunk when travelling home on any of the local trains.

The Beer Act of 1830 exacerbated the situation. This extraordinary measure attempted to reduce the level of alcoholism, caused mainly by spirits, by making it legal for any ratepayer to open his house as a beer shop on payment of two guineas to the local excise office. In fact, it had precisely the opposite effect. It has been claimed that within nineteen days of the Act coming into force no fewer than 800 licences to open beer shops were taken out in Liverpool [33]. Giving evidence to a parliamentary inquiry in 1834, the Liverpool Dock Master Charles Purnell reckoned that there were 1,150 pubs serving beer and spirits and a further 570 serving beer only, most of which opened between 4 or 5 o'clock in the morning and 11 or 12 o'clock at night [34]. By 1855 the police were reporting the number of public houses at 1,452 and the number of beer houses at 937; and that year there were no fewer than 12,819 convictions for drunkenness in the town [35].

Seen against this background the incidence of drunkenness at the races does not seem so out of the ordinary. There is, however, some evidence to show that there was a greater degree of drinking at Aintree than at other race meetings. One journalist who attended the 1870 Grand National, for example, thought that the crowd differed from that at all other sporting gatherings, and that one of its distinguishing characteristics was the openly expressed desire for "a big drink afterwards" [36].

Hugh Shimmin too thought that drinking was one of the main reasons why Liverpudlians went to the races, and he described a typical day out there by "a very Liverpool man" as beginning by stopping at every public house on the road between Liverpool and Aintree and having something to drink there. "By the time he reaches the race-course he is a good deal muddled, and becomes coarser and noisier than before. He wanders over the ground, lounges in a few tents, plays a few games at shying sticks and such like on the course; drinks at every possible opportunity; leers vacuously and coarsely at the fine flashy women in the carriages...; straggles about vociferous and vulgar all the evening; comes roaring home in his spring cart with his roaring companions; and believes he has spent a most delightful day of it, even although he should conclude by getting locked up all night" [37].

A graphic description of the drinking habits of racegoers a hundred and fifty years ago appears in a contemporary poem by John Stanley Gregson. Although written about Manchester races, there is no reason to suppose that the scene was very different at Aintree:

"Next, to the booths descend the men to bet,
And deluge their insides with heavy wet;
Some claim their winnings with a joyful face,
And risk more chances on the coming race;
Others edge off to clear their losing debts,
And curse the luck of all their former bets.
Then, when the porter runs in strong flood-tide,
Such cries as this resound from side to side:-

'Here! waiter, waiter! come, be quick as fire!
Bring us two quarts of Whitbread's stout entire'-
'Three brandy bottoms'; – 'Three of gin too here'
'A squib of rum in half a pint of beer!'
(Cider and brandy then were all the rage,
Unknown the bliss of this improving age;
To thirsty souls the name be ever dear
Of Jewsbury's 'celebrated ginger beer';
And let the meed of cool-tongued praise be paid
To Whitlow's 'effervescing lemonade'!)" [38]

The raffish, pleasure-seeking and potentially disorderly crowds that were to be seen at Aintree in the 19th century seem a world away from the stereotype of mid-Victorian moral earnestness. The race course, in fact, was one of the last places where the more free and easy morals of an earlier age survived – at least in public. It was a place where people went to enjoy themselves in an uninhibited way, and where things that were frowned on elsewhere could be indulged in without fear of censure. This was, no doubt, a large part of its attraction to men, and indeed women, of all classes, living in an increasingly strait-laced society.

The police no doubt had their hands full dealing with the drunkenness and petty crime which inevitably occur, even today, at large scale sporting events, but serious crime appears to have been rare at Aintree. An exception occurred at the summer meeting in 1846, when the body of a woman called Eliza Bateson was found in a pond near the course, and Robert Farmes, a strolling clarinet player was arrested on suspicion of her murder. Bateson, who was described as "middle-aged and extremely well-looking" was a dancer and actress at a booth on the course owned by John Shaw. Late in the evening, after the end of racing, she was observed "very drunk" in conversation with Farmes, apparently imploring him to take her home with him. The next day she had disappeared, and Farmes was heard to give contradictory and somewhat strange accounts of what had happened to her. At first he said that she had been committed to gaol for three months, but then he said he had left her drunk and did not know what had happened to her. As a consequence of this careless talk, Farmes was arrested at Croxteth and examined by one of the county magistrates, after which a surgeon from Knotty Ash called Thomas William Christie was asked to carry out a post-mortem on Eliza Bateson's body.

In order to do this, the body had first to be exhumed from Sefton churchyard, where it had been buried. Christie then found that "the head, face, chest and shoulders were swollen and livid, particularly the head and face. On the side of the neck and left side there were four or five marks, similar to the imprint of a thumb and fingers", and he concluded that "there must have been a struggle before death, and that the marks were produced by pressure before death". It seemed that "the only imaginable reason he [Farmes] could have for committing the deed is that he wanted to accomplish an unlawful purpose and that the woman... resisted him. A fierce struggle took place between them, but eventually she was strangled and thrown into the pit" [39].

Farmes, who was aged about sixty, was committed for trial at the Liverpool Assizes, but when the case came up the grand jury "ignored the bill", a legal phrase which suggests that the case was dropped for lack of sufficient evidence [40], and Farmes, who had been remanded in custody, was presumably released.

No further violent death appears to have occurred at Aintree until 1875, when a pugilist named Looney was killed in a prize fight at the course. This was precisely the kind of event which gave pugilism a bad name, as it does boxing today, and Looney's opponent in the ring, a man named Mahoney, together with five others who were present at the fight, were taken into custody and charged with manslaughter [41].

This incident is interesting in revealing that well after it was declared illegal, and even after the introduction of the Queensberry Rules and the move towards the supposedly more humane sport of glove boxing, bare knuckle prize fighting was still taking place openly at race courses such as Aintree, despite its well-known connections with the criminal underworld.

Old fashioned pugilism, however, was by no means the only illegal sport which continued to take place at Aintree. Cock fighting was outlawed in 1849 and the cock pit by the Sefton Arms was then converted into a church [42]; but despite this remarkable transformation there are reports of cock fighting taking place at Aintree for many years afterwards. In 1875,

THE COCKPIT.

Cock fighting as depicted in Pierce Egan's Book of Sports, 1832

for example, the police raided a building on the course where they suspected that a cock fight was being held. "When the officers succeeded in gaining admission to the room, one or two men got out through the doors, 40 or 50 ran upstairs to another room, some broke down a wooden partition dividing two of the booths, smashed one of the windows and, passing through the aperture thus made, dropped a distance of 14 feet; others broke down a shutter and so escaped". In all about a hundred people were thought to have been present, of whom the police contrived to arrest thirteen, "some of whom gave false names and addresses". They also found "a large number of dead fowls", about thirty live ones, and sets of weights and scales. Although it was suspected that many of the participants occupied "high positions in society", almost all those the police arrested were publicans or artisans. However, it must have been a major event as some cocks had been brought over from Ireland especially for it. Indeed, one farmer from Ireland was so concerned over the loss of his birds that he went to the police station the next day to claim them back, only to find himself under arrest for his part in the affair. Another of those arrested, an iron britler from Rochdale, offered the police a bribe of two guineas "to say nothing about the affair", but this was refused, and all the defendants were brought before the magistrates, who fined them £5 each. Considering that the owners were said to have staked as much as £3000 on the match, a fine of this size can hardly have acted as much of a deterrent [43].

Lynn and later Topham worked hard to make Aintree respectable, but events such as these show that even as late as the 1870s this aim was still far from having been achieved. Much of the corruption associated with horse racing earlier in the century had been eradicated, but links with the underworld were still very much in evidence. Given the close connection between racing and gambling, which, after 1853, was illegal off-course, this was perhaps inevitable. On the other hand it must always be remembered that there was another side of the coin, and that not everyone who went to Aintree was a criminal, a prostitute or a drunkard. Even such a hostile witness as Hugh Shimmin, after describing "all the repulsive and disreputable features of the racing ground", had to admit that one could see "another phase of life" on the course when he wrote: "cross over the ploughed gallop, and notice what a neat style of pic-nic can be done. How speedily bottles can be opened and emptied, and how pleasant and affable even Liverpool merchant princes may become under the influence of good air and healthy appetite" [44]. This is an altogether more pleasant picture of what it was like to go racing at Aintree in Victorian days, and it would be nice to think that this was the experience of many, perhaps even the majority, of the people who made up the crowds that flocked to the course.

Notes and references

1. Taine. Notes on England, pp.42-43.
2. Isham. The mud cabin, pp.209, 213.
3. Close. The evil consequences of attending the race course exposed, pp.7-9.
4. Hiley. Memories of half a century, p.172.
5. Quoted in Bevan. The Roodee, p.30.
6. Birrell. Some early recollections of Liverpool, p.10.
7. A tilbury was a light open two-wheeled carriage.
8. A tit was a small horse, or one not fully grown; the word was generally used as a term of deprecation.
9. In sporting circles a kid was a term of admiration for an expert young thief or a pugilist.
10. *Liverpool Standard*, 1 February 1839.
11. Shimmin. Liverpool life, 2nd series, p.13.
12. Shimmin. Liverpool life, 2nd series, p.19.
13. Shimmin. Liverpool life, 2nd series, p.18.
14. Bevan. Prostitution in the borough of Liverpool, p.8.
15. Broadbent. Annals of the Liverpool stage, p.125.
16. *Liverpool Standard*, 1 February 1839.
17. *Illustrated London News*, 11 June 1848, p.78.
18. 'Thormanby'. Tales of the turf and the chase, p.30.
19. 'Thormanby'. Tales of the turf and the chase, pp.30-33.
20. A correct account of the dreadful riot which took place at Lincoln Race Course in the afternoon and evening of Friday Sept. 30th, 1831, with other matters connected therewith. Broadsheet printed by R.E. Leary, Lincoln; Copy in John Johnson Collection, Bodleian Library.
21. *Liverpool Mercury*, 6 March 1840.
22. *Liverpool Standard*, 6 March 1840.
23. *Liverpool Standard*, 5 March 1841.
24. Bevan. Prostitution in the borough of Liverpool, p.9.
25. Faucher. Etudes sur l'Angleterre, p.175.
26. Our mercantile marine, p.38.
27. Faucher. Etudes sur l'Angleterre, pp.160-161.
28. Bevan. Prostitution in the borough of Liverpool, p.10.
29. Bevan. Prostitution in the borough of Liverpool, pp.11-12.
30. This and subsequent references from Shimmin. Liverpool life, 2nd series, pp.20-36.
31. *Liverpool Mercury*, 7 December 1821.
32. Craik. A life for a life. Vol. 2, pp.147-148.
33. Winskill. The temperance movement and its workers. Vol. 1, p.18.
34. Report from the Select Committee on Inquiry into Drunkenness, p.369.

35. Quoted in Winskill. The temperance movement and its workers. Vol. 3, p.136.
36. *The Field Quarterly Magazine and Review,* Vol. 1, 1870, p.138.
37. *Porcupine*, 27 July 1861, p.193.
38. Gregson. Gimcrackiana, pp.44-45.
39. *Liverpool Mercury,* 31 July 1846; *The Times*, 5 August 1846.
40. *Liverpool Mercury,* 21 August 1846.
41. *The Times*, 5 August 1875.
42. Harkins. Aintree past and present, p.58
43. *The Times*, 17 April, 19 April and 5 May 1875.
44. *Porcupine,* 15 March, 1862, p.283.

10.

Betting in Nineteenth Century Liverpool

Although betting on horses has existed as long as horse racing itself, the development of off-course betting and the establishment of betting houses only really began in the 1840s. Improved communications through such means as the railway and the telegraph were partly responsible, as was the development of the sporting press from the 1820s onwards, but it also seems as though this new form of betting was created to cater for the needs of those who had previously participated in the state lottery or major sweepstakes promoted by the newspapers, both of which had been curtailed as a result of pressure from the anti-gambling lobby. A further factor was the growth in the number of handicap races, always a medium for big betting, although whether these were a cause of the increase in betting, or were themselves created in response to the demand for more betting opportunities is not clear. As we have seen the Grand National itself became a handicap for financial reasons more than anything else.

But whatever the reasons, the growth in the number of betting houses, often linked to public houses and to prostitution, in the 1840s and 1850s was phenomenal, and was noticed by many commentators. Charles Dickens, writing in 1852, noted that "betting shops spring up in every street!" [1]. Writing at around the same time, Surtees too thought that formerly "there was not a tithe of the betting that there is now". It was his opinion that this was one of the main reasons why racing fostered such "an enormous amount of knavery and idleness", and he even proposed that the government reinstate "the good old lotteries", for "then, at all events, if a master was robbed in order that his servant might buy a ticket, he would have the satisfaction of knowing that the rogue had contributed something to the service of the state", instead of lining the pockets of the bookmakers. These Surtees regarded as "a growing and dangerous evil" [2].

Dickens reported that most bookmakers were self-made men, who had started out as waiters, butlers, small shopkeepers or cab drivers: "All these men began with small beginnings, and rose upon their capacity for, and knowledge of, figures". They could easily be distinguished from other racegoers through the newness of their clothes and hats, "evidently bought at fashionable shops", and by the "profuse quantity of watch-chain knick-knacks" that they wore. Dickens distinguished between the respectable bookmakers and the "welchers"; the latter "when he has taken money enough from his dupes, departs from the scene of his labours, and trusts to his luck, a dyed wig, or a pair of false whiskers, not to be recognised". If he did well a "welcher" would then "take a low public house, which becomes the resort of similar scoundrels" [3].

As a major urban centre, and one moreover that was close to the racecourses at Aintree, Chester and Manchester, it would be surprising if Liverpool had not been affected by these trends. In fact, it seems as though betting was especially prevelant in the town, something which many commentators, both at the time and since, have linked to the fact that many of Liverpool's traditional merchant activities, and in particular the cotton trade, were themselves a form of gambling. Dickens, writing in 1868, claimed that "Liverpool numbers its welchers by the hundred" [4].

A vivid picture of the betting activities that went on in many of Liverpool's pubs can be found in the writings of Hugh Shimmin. Shimmin was a crusading journalist who, like many other social reformers of the time, regarded betting and drink as major causes of working class poverty and destitution. His writings are thus unashamedly polemical in tone, but this is no reason to doubt the accuracy of his observations.

Without naming it, Shimmin described the principal betting house as having been in one of the main streets. At the front of the house was the bar, through which one passed to reach the betting room itself. This was about thirty feet long and twenty four feet wide and was lit by means of a skylight. In one corner there was a bookcase containing one hundred volumes of the *Turf register*, and the walls were covered with portraits of racehorses and celebrated jockeys. Over the fireplace was a green baize notice board which was used to display telegrams giving the latest state of the odds, and copies of the sporting papers were scattered around on the tables.

At this pub, as no doubt at many others, there was a close link between betting and prostitution, for one of the other doors led to the tap room, where, Shimmin revealed, "on almost any afternoon or evening, may be seen groups of women of the worst character, dressed out profusely in silks and satins, their heads decorated with feathers, their cheeks daubed with paint. They giggle and pass vulgar jokes amongst themselves whilst waiting for the gentlemen, who are now in the betting room, and who have promised to meet them here. It is no unusual thing to see a stylish young fellow, a clerk who has obtained a day's holiday or is 'off on sick leave', when he has dropped in for a 'good thing' take one of these 'passion flowers' to his arms [and] carry her to a 'Hansom' which is waiting at the door" [5].

Shimmin was at pains to point out that people from every class in life could be seen in the betting rooms, including, on a typical day, "broken-down merchants, clerks, foundrymen, one convicted dog-stealer, a 'gent' said to be 'worth a plum' in the shape of £20,000, cardrivers, cartowners, brewers and their draymen, counter-skippers [6], billiard players, [and] the fellow who 'does the music on his cheeks' for coppers in the low houses about the docks". The inclusion of billiard players in the list is significant, for they were well known as unemployed loiterers on the fringes of the criminal world, who made a living through playing for stakes in the back rooms of pubs. Interviewed by Shimmin, one of them was candid enough to say that "Work and I have fallen out many years ago... and the man who would offer me any sort of work would offer me the greatest insult". Aside from billiards, this man earned some money as an Irish comic singer, but also admitted that he had been involved in violent crime. Some billiard players later turned to bookmaking as a way of increasing their income.

Most bookmakers, however, doubled as publicans, although they rarely did it at their own houses as this was illegal. Shimmin has left us vivid portraits of some of the "heavy brigade", as the leading Liverpool bookmakers were known. One, nicknamed "the Beau Brummel of Liverpool bookmakers", was "a dapper, dressy little man [who] has on now a tweed suit, the coat rounded off well at the skirts, and buttoned tight across the chest, a cloth cap rakishly adjusted on his head, and his hands pressed into his side pockets. He kept a betting house, or bank, and when the act closed his bank he 'did the welcher trick', and invested the capital he held in a spirit vaults... He is a list keeper and lays the odds at his own house. From his card, which he kindly hands about, we find that he calls himself a 'commission agent'... Merchants, tradesmen, and what are generally looked upon as respectable men, keep, and in some instances court, his society. Not that they like him – very few do this – but sometimes he gets early lists or good tips."

The man who was regarded as the "leviathan", or the largest bookmaker in the town, seems to have been an even more unsavoury character: "He looks like an overgrown boy, talks very loud sometimes, and generally with a very dictatorial air. He frequently wears a cap, and his dress is very slovenly when he is 'knocking about the crib', which he now makes his headquarters... He is said to be anything but pleasant in his mode of conducting business, and his professional brethren speak of him as disagreeable. He gives no quarter and is terribly vindictive: woe betide the needy wretch who cannot 'stump up' on the 'settling day', for he is sure to expose him on all sides, and is not at all chaste in his choice of terms."

A third man, who was regarded as a rising star in his profession, had started out as an assistant in a grocery store, but was quoted as saying "I have cut the counter, and make a good deal more 'sugar' by betting than I ever did by serving it out". Like some other leading bookmakers, he was also "great" at billiards, and "seldom or never gets 'bested' in a match of his own making".

Bookmakers such as these frequented the better-known betting house pubs, and took bets from men of all classes and backgrounds. Nor were the sums of money involved negligible, for Shimmin records that some members of the betting ring were popularly supposed to make books worth up to £50,000, and individual bets of £25 (a "pony") appear to have been common.

Betting shops in the working class areas were altogether simpler and more homely. Shimmin describes one in "a very old portion of the town" thus:

"Here you will find a beerhouse, the sign of which is an evident allusion to the practices to be found within. A bill attracts the attention. This announces a monster sweep for the Chester cup, and bears on it the name of the proprietor of the house as the promoter of the 'sweep'. There are to be five hundred subscribers at one shilling each, and we are told the list is fast filling; ... and here are victims being sacrificed, or sacrificing themselves, for the chance of obtaining £5 for the winner, £3 for the second horse, £2 for the third, and £5 to be divided amongst the starters. Independent of the actual cash to be gained by the promoters of a 'sweep', there is to be taken into consideration the company that is by such means attracted to the house, and consequently the money spent and drink consumed during the time the list is filling. At this house all sorts of bets are offered and taken; 'fancy bets' prevail, and there is no restriction placed on the amount... Running, jumping, dog fighting, cards – offer bets on anything, you will find men here ready 'to take you'. The house is cleanly kept, and no doubt is much more comfortable than many of the places from which the sportsmen came, and where they will have to return, and call 'home'..."

To modern ears this all sounds harmless enough, but to Shimmin and others who thought like him, such places were but the first step on a road which could lead to total destitution and depravity. He drew a lurid picture of the area in which this pub was situated, with its "filthy houses, haggard and ragged women, [and] wretched children, amusing themselves in play which induces filthy habits, unattended, uncared for", and blamed this on the fathers "investing a tanner or two" at the betting shop, and the mothers pawning their clothes "to supply the cravings of the gin fiend".

This may have been an unduly simplistic view of the problems facing the poor, but it was one that was widely held, and the government came under increasing pressure to make betting houses illegal. The result was an Act of Parliament for the Suppression of Betting Houses in 1853 which outlawed betting houses, and empowered magistrates to search any premises suspected of being used in this way and to confiscate any material connected with racing or betting. The penalty for being convicted of running a betting house was set at six months imprisonment or a fine not exceeding £100.

This Act was a blatant piece of class legislation for neither Tattersalls nor on-course wagering between individuals was touched; in other words, owners and other members of the sporting aristocracy and gentry could carry on betting, but the poor could not. No doubt it was the political influence of the many members of the House of Lords who had an interest in the turf, which was the prime factor in preventing betting from being outlawed altogether. As it was, off-course betting was simply driven out from the pubs on to the streets, where it remained until 1960.

Or was it? There is ample evidence to show that, in Liverpool at least, the magistrates and the Watch Committee were curiously reluctant to use their new powers (perhaps because they themselves were members of the "light brigade" of punters?), and that betting houses continued to exist in the town for many years after 1853, tobacconists and stationery shops often acting as fronts for the bookmakers [7]. Shimmin's writings are themselves the best evidence of this, for his descriptions of betting houses in *Liverpool life* were written four years after the Act was passed, and as late as 1877 he was still attacking the Watch Committee for their inactivity in prosecuting illegal bookmaking [8].

By that time, however, most off-course betting, at least during the day time, was taking place on the streets rather than in pubs. The centre for this activity was Williamson Square, which was "crowded daily with the betting rabble of the town". It is clear that people from all classes of society availed themselves of the services that were on offer. Shopkeepers, office boys, shoe-blacks and carters were prominent amongst the crowd, but there were also "several young men, sons of highly-respected parents". Even more significantly, it was reported that "regular messengers are despatched almost daily during the season from select coteries around 'the Flags' to 'put the money on' in and around 'the Square' "; in other words Liverpool's merchant princes were just as eager to bet on horses as they were on the cotton market. So important was this trade to the bookies that some of them even set up stall on the Exchange Flags themselves, without fear of being molested by the police or the magistrates, who seem to have turned a blind eye to their activities in Liverpool's commercial heartland [9].

At night time the trade moved back inside the public houses, where it had always belonged. In the area around Williamson Square "the gaudy public houses... and some of the respectable-looking ones too, are nightly rendezvous for the betting fraternity; and not only can one go any evening to some of these and bet away to one's heart's content, but also, if you happen to win off certain bookmakers, you will find them next morning making use of a public-house bar-parlour to disburse their gambling losses – so closely are their sails trimmed to the legal wind" [10].

One of the pubs around Williamson Square which was known to be a haunt of bookmakers was the Rainbow, which was situated on the corner of Basnett Street and Houghton Street (George Henry Lee's now occupies the site). In 1888 Charles Millward, who was an associate of Shimmin's, reported that it had "become a haunt for a very low class of the 'genus' betting men. Gentlemen to whom honest labour has long been an unknown quantity, men who 'spin not, neither do they toil' were hurrying in and out of the place, and small groups of them held noisy altercations at the door and kept up a ceaseless din at the street corner. It... appeared to me more like a gathering of the scum of the city than an assemblage at a house which was once a respectable and well-conducted hotel" [11].

Despite having to operate in these less than propitious circumstances, some Liverpool book-makers thrived and were fairly open about their profession. Arthur Magnus, for example, ran a bookmaking business in the city for thirty years and advertised his services in the national sporting press. By 1896 he was even offering a telephone betting service, using the Rutland Club in Houghton Street as his base [12]. This is interesting in suggesting that many of his clients were well enough off to afford a telephone at this early date, and also that they lived some distance away. (Liverpool was connected by telephone to London by 1890.) But Magnus was also careful to conceal his bookmaking activities behind a more legitimate business. In *Gore's Directory* for 1895 there are two Arthur Magnuses listed [13]. One was a picture frame maker and glazier, and the other a wine and spirit merchant; in view of the close connection between betting and drink, it seems highly probable that it was the latter who doubled as a bookmaker.

It is thus abundantly clear that, forty years after the Act against off-course betting was passed, the law was being openly flouted in Liverpool, with the magistrates and the Town Council choosing to ignore what was going on, and the moralists and reformers with little to show for their lengthy and vociferous campaign.

Betting on the race course remained legal, although not always approved of, and then, as now, it was one of the main attractions of going racing: "it cannot be anything else for the throng is so great that the racing cannot be seen by one in twenty of those upon the course, and thousands do not take the trouble to clear out of the tents to witness the running" [14]. Even the police on duty were noted as habitués of the betting ring [15].

On the course a distinction was made between the "professional betting men of the higher class", who were situated in an inner ring in front of the grand stand and who served the owners and their aristocratic or wealthy friends, and those outside this privileged enclosure who served the poorer

The Betting Ring

sections of the crowd. At the Grand National meeting of 1871 these comprised "a double line of sinister-looking men mounted upon stools, their hats labelled, all calling out in chorus the terms upon which they are prepared to bet with all-comers... 'Come on gents – now is your opportunity – a fortune may be made in a few minutes'. Thus shout out scores of professional book-makers. The babel of tongues surpasses description". The bookmakers were unfavourably described as "men with pugilistic countenances and the eternal billycocks; men with the cunning of the fox, the roughness of the bear, and the spring of the tiger when pouncing on his prey; these men, by scores, ... prey upon the poorer section of the community" [16].

Nevertheless, life was not always easy for the bookmakers. It was noted, for instance, that two Liverpool bookmakers lost £2000 at the Lincoln and Grand National meetings in 1889 [17]. Nor were all of them dishonest. Midlands bookmaker Dyke Wilkinson recalled how, shortly after he had started out in business, he was left in the lurch by his partner at a Liverpool Autumn Meeting. Having taken some imprudent bets, and his partner having disappeared, he found himself surrounded by an angry crowd of punters waiting to be paid: "My knees knocked against each other, and every fibre of me trembled with fear as I heard the ominous cry. I knew too well what it meant if I failed to satisfy the demands of this hungry pack of wolves which crowded about me... I saw fierce eyes intent upon the satchel which hung from the broad strap around my neck; I knew there would be a struggle first for that, and then for me." Fortunately for him, his brother, also a bookmaker, came to his rescue with enough money to satisfy the crowd, but this was only after his coat had been nearly torn off his back and he was showing "other signs of ill-usage", despite the efforts of a couple of policemen who were trying to protect him [18].

Fortunately, there are also some happier stories of the Aintree betting ring in the nineteenth century. At the 1892 Grand National, for example, an Irishman was overheard to say "Och, I'll stick to the church and the clergy", and then went off to back The Primate, Cloister and Father O'Flynn! This was a good bet for him as Father O'Flynn came home the winner at a starting price of 20-1, with Cloister a close second [19].

Race course tipsters seem to have come into existence in the 1840s and were generally drawn from the ranks of the very poor. In his account of the 'Grand Aristocratic Steeple-Chase' in *Mr. Sponge's Sporting Tour,* Surtees tells how as soon as the race was announced the 'Peeping Toms', 'Sly Sams', 'Infallible Joes' and 'Wide-Awake Jems' emerged with their tips, but that "a gentleman who took the trouble of getting tips from half a dozen of them found that no two of them agreed in any particular". He goes on to suggest that some of them at least made a good living out of the sport, for one of them named Enoch Wriggle prospered to such an extent that "from scarcely having any shoes to his feet, he very soon set up a gig" [20].

How typical this was of the experience of real-life tipsters is hard to say. Certainly later in the century there was a feeling that they were not doing as well as they had (perhaps because of the development of the sporting press), and the comment of one of them that "I made my money out of horses, and I am ass enough to lose it in the same way" may well reflect the experience of many [21]. It was certainly the case with the first man known to have made his living selling his tips on the course at Aintree. He was known as "Liverpool Charlie" and he appears to have been active in the late 1870s. On race days he was to be found, "attired little better than a tramp", outside the Sefton Arms flourishing envelopes which he stated contained the names of certain winners, and claiming that he got his information straight from the jockeys' mouths. He charged 3d a time for his tips, and did good business as he soon acquired "quite a heap of copper coins" and "sundry bits of silver". He also supplemented his income by doing other odd jobs around the racecourse, such as holding a horse's head or carrying a bookmaker's joint off the course for him. However, by the end of the afternoon "Charlie" could usually be found back in the Sefton Arms treating his pals and rapidly disposing of all his newly acquired funds. In fact, he was said to be over-fond of a drink, and it was thought that this contributed to his early death [22].

Somewhat later, one of the tipsters at Aintree was a real Liverpool character. Photographed at the 1901 Summer meeting, he was known as "Old Bob" or "the Black tipster". His origins are unknown, but it seems likely that he came from the Southern states of America, and he started out in partnership with another black man called Louis who could also play

'Old Bob', the Black tipster, photographed at Aintree, 1901

the guitar. "Old Bob" was an imposing figure, tall and big-boned, with thick grizzled hair and a greying beard and moustache, but his attire was even more remarkable and would have made him stand out in any crowd: "On his head he wore a pith sun helmet. His body was covered with a soldier's red tunic, which being too small to button was laced across by string. On his breast, dangling as medals, were a number of cocoa tin lids, and from his broad leather belt hung at least two empty salmon tins. His trousers were extraordinary and were composed of shreds and patches of all colours. On his feet he wore coverings which had not the slightest resemblance to boots; indeed they looked like small cabins. To complete his ensemble he carried a large heavy stave encircled with brass rings".

Where he got his information from was never discovered, but his tips were said to be "more than less reliable". As he could neither read nor write, they were written out on slips of papers for him, first by Louis, and then after Louis left him to get a more secure job in a warehouse, by the landlord of a pub in London Road, where Bob was also able to get his food and drink. This arrangement worked well for a long time, but there is a sad end to the story. One day there was a new barman in the pub. This "callous and cruel" man took advantage of Bob's illiteracy, and instead of writing his tips on the slips of paper wrote some "vulgar or filthy phrases". Unaware of what had been done, Bob went out on the street to sell his tips as usual and found himself mobbed by angry punters. His popularity disappeared overnight and he was never taken seriously as a tipster again; he soon became destitute and ended his days in the workhouse on Brownlow Hill [23].

Notes and references

1. *Household Words*, Vol. 5, no. 118, 26 June 1852, p.333.
2. Surtees. Plain or ringlets?, ch.19.
3. *All the Year Round*, Vol. 20, no. 477, 13 June 1868, pp.13-16.
4. *All the Year Round*, Vol. 20, no. 477, 13 June 1868, p.15.
5. This and subsequent references from Shimmin. Liverpool life, pp.96-122.
6. Counter-skipper was a slang term for shop assistant.
7. *Liverpool Review*, 2 November 1889.
8. *Porcupine*, 24 March 1877, p.823.
9. *Porcupine*, 17 March 1877, p.810.
10. *Porcupine*, 17 March 1877, p.810.
11. Quoted in O'Connor. A pub on every corner. Vol. 1, p.63.

12. *Dexter's Turf Times*, 1 June 1896.
13. *Gore's Directory*, 1895, p.554.
14. *Porcupine*, 25 March 1871, pp.651-652.
15. *Porcupine*, 18 July 1863, pp.126-127.
16. *Porcupine*, 25 March 1871, pp.651-652.
17. *Liverpool Review*, 6 April 1889.
18. Wilkinson. A wasted life, pp.73-77.
19. *Liverpool Review*, 2 April 1892.
20. Surtees. Mr. Sponge's sporting tour, ch.67.
21. Nightingall. My racing adventures, p.234.
22. Snowy. The Stanley of the turf, pp.13-14.
23. *Liverpool Echo*, 30 March 1937.

11.

The Topham years I: To 1940

Once he had gained control of Aintree, "Wizard" Topham moved swiftly to recast the fixture list into a pattern which would endure almost unchanged right through to the early 1960s. This consisted of a mixed Spring Meeting, the centrepiece of which was the Grand National, the traditional flat Summer Meeting, and a mixed Autumn Meeting, of which the highlight came to be the Grand Sefton Chase and the Liverpool Autumn Cup. Topham also made Aintree profitable, something that none of his predecessors had managed; unlike Lynn or Etty he died a relatively wealthy man, being worth around £12,000 at his death [1]. Indeed, it was said of his last Spring Meeting, just before he died in 1873, that "in a pecuniary sense [he] must have had an almost unparalleled meeting" [2]. This was despite the fact that by 1872 the rent for the course had risen to £1300 per year [3].

Edward William Topham ('The Wizard')

It is worth remembering that this rent was only for the race course proper; the land beyond the Melling Road over which the Grand National and the other steeplechases were run remained let to other tenants who farmed the land and could sometimes be less than co-operative with the race course authorities. In 1872, Topham complained that some of them had been planting cabbages and potatoes "right in the track" by the canal side [4], and two years later his sons, who took over the lease after his death, wrote to Lord Sefton's steward to complain that "the steeple chase course is in a very dangerous state owing to the number of rabbit burrows both in the open ground and along the hedge sides" [5].

However, the farmers had a point too. When the course passed through their crops they received some compensation from Topham, but they received no payment at all to recompense them for the damage done by the vast hordes of spectators, some of them on horseback, who swarmed over their land to view the race. In 1864 it was reported that "Mr. Topham shows some consideration for the farmers in marking out 'the course' and putting up notices, and where wheat or clover fields have to be crossed by the running horses the farmer is recompensed. But outsiders have no right of way over the course and yet the damage done by them... to fields and fences called forth a strong expression of opinion on the part of the sufferers", and it was suggested that the farmers should adopt some form of self-protection [6].

Many of the owners also became concerned about the state of the steeplechase course during the 1860s and early 1870s. In February 1874 a letter signed by twenty four members of the National Hunt Committee was sent to the Tophams demanding a number of improvements. They claimed that the growing number of small, trappy fences, and the crowds of spectators closing in on the horses at the fences were making the race more dangerous, and they requested that the course be railed off at every fence and that the fences themselves be maintained to a proper standard. The letter was couched in the strongest terms and the Tophams were obliged to commit themselves to making the changes which had been demanded; by the time of the 1874 Grand National it was reported that "all the fences are now such as we might expect to meet with in an ordinary hunting country" [7].

In 1877 the Tophams, "finding it quite impracticable to alter the steeplechase course without seriously damaging the prestige of the Grand National", purchased some land adjoining Becher's Brook for £1100 which they hoped to resell to Lord Sefton [8], but this was no real solution to the problem, and matters came to a head in 1884 when the Tophams were concerned that one of the tenant farmers would try to obtain an injunction to prevent the steeplechases being held over his land. Lord Sefton was equally concerned to secure the future of the Grand National and the result was a series of complicated negotiations with the three or four tenants involved which led to the Tophams gaining control over the steeplechase course beyond the Melling Road as well as the race course proper. Thus the 1885 Grand National became the first to be run over a course completely laid to turf. That year also saw the whole of the course railed in for the first time [9].

Topham was also happy for racing of a rather more unorthodox type to take place at Aintree. In 1863, for example, there was a curious race between an elephant and some ponies, accompanied by some amateur pedestrians, on the course. This strange affair "excited some interest" at the time, but sadly the result is not recorded [10].

The facilities at the course continued to be improved. In 1872 a telegraph office was established, and the same year Tophams began discussions with Lord Sefton about building a new stand. This was after the surveyor, David Howarth, had reported the existing stands as being "dilapidated" [11]. Eventually a new stand and weighing room were erected in 1878 at a cost of £1331.10.9d, the annual rent for which was to be £140 over and above what the Tophams paid for the rest of the course [12].

"Wizard" Topham was also keen to attract more "Liverpool ladies" to the course, and to this end he planned to move the betting ring so that they would be less offended by the "noisy Welchers", as he privately called the bookmakers [13].

As the railway network developed and travel became easier, so Topham was able to attract larger crowds to Aintree. By 1874, for example, there were twenty five special trains to the Grand National from as far away as

A Scottish racegoer about to set out for Aintree, 1890s (A sketch outside the Adelphi Hotel)

Birmingham, Nottingham and Leeds, in addition to an intensive local service of forty eight trains out to Aintree from the Lancashire and Yorkshire Railway's Tithebarn Street terminus in Liverpool [14]. Travelling by train out to Aintree was not always a pleasant experience, however. In 1863 it was reported that "the carriages were as filthy, as fully crammed, as little looked after, and as successfully worked as on any previous occasion". Nor were this reporter's travelling companions much better: "Huge men, with unshaved and greasy faces, thrust their bodies half through the windows and hailed friends as they passed by, and pulled them into the carriage, notwithstanding the remonstrances of mild swells with lorgnette glasses slung across their tweed suits ... Then they pulled the women on their knees and the laughing and joking began in earnest".

The scene when one alighted from the train at Aintree was not much better, for there one was confronted by one-armed ballad singers, "the very free remarks of the girls in light muslin dresses and gaudy bonnets", and "the sickening aspect of the man who has lost both his arms and who drags his shirt off the stumps with his teeth to assure you that there's 'no deception' " [15].

Despite criticisms such as these, by the time of his death in 1873 Topham had not only raised the prestige of the National to new heights, he had also ensured that his own family's connection with it would be an enduring one. This achievement was neatly expressed in a contemporary poem:

"Arous'd once more from winter's nap
As trees respond to quickening sap,
Or spendthrifts start at bailiff's tap,
The Muse resumed her lay:
O Topham! great through all the land
With chase intrinsically grand
Undimmed by that of south band
Your hand;
Again 'tis Aintree's day." [16]

There was a price to be paid for this success, however. Having inherited a successful formula, later generations of Tophams proved unwilling or unable to tamper with it. At first this did not matter, but later it made it harder for them to face up to changing circumstances and challenges to Aintree's former unquestioned pre-eminence from elsewhere. The result was that Aintree became stuck in a kind of time warp. To go racing there in the late 1960s or early '70s was in many ways little different from how it would have been before the First World War, except that each year the stands, all of which dated from the 19th century, became a little shabbier.

In the late nineteenth century, however, all this lay far in the future. "Wizard" Topham was succeeded by his sons Christopher Reuben and Joseph Bell Topham, the latter acting as the handicapper for the Grand National. They continued to improve the facilities at Aintree and to make the National the undisputed highlight of the National Hunt season. It was during their time in control, for example, that the whole course was laid to turf and railed in for the first time. Following a serious fire in September 1892, which destroyed most of the stands and the adjacent buildings, including the offices and some of the stables [17], the stands were rebuilt into the form they were to retain until the 1980s. Remarkably, this fire was not allowed to disrupt the racing programme, for only six weeks later the November meeting took place as planned, and was "one of the best which has been held there for many years" [18]. It was during this meeting that the great Cloister carried 12st 7lbs to victory in the Grand Sefton Chase, a feat he was to repeat in the Grand National itself the following spring.

Cloister was one of the finest horses to win the National, and his record of one win and two seconds in the race tells only part of the story. On his first appearance in 1891, he probably should have won, but for the tactics of his jockey, Roddy Owen, who decided to challenge the leader, Come Away, on the inside. Harry Beasley, who was riding Come Away, retaliated

Race card for the Liverpool Spring Meeting, 1882

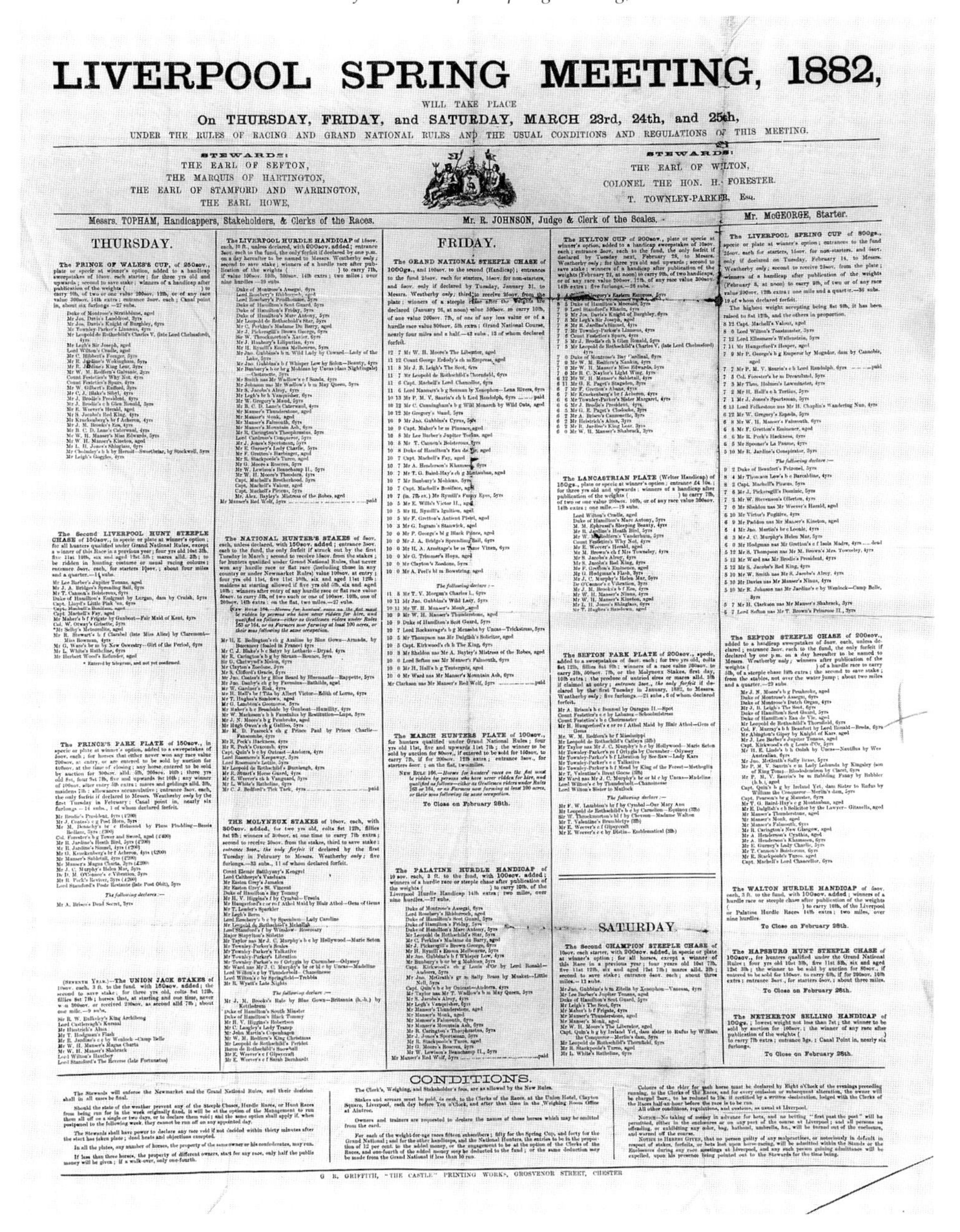

LIVERPOOL SPRING MEETING, 1882,

WILL TAKE PLACE

On THURSDAY, FRIDAY, and SATURDAY, MARCH 23rd, 24th, and 25th,

UNDER THE RULES OF RACING AND GRAND NATIONAL RULES AND THE USUAL CONDITIONS AND REGULATIONS OF THIS MEETING.

STEWARDS:
THE EARL OF SEFTON,
THE MARQUIS OF HARTINGTON,
THE EARL OF STAMFORD AND WARRINGTON,
THE EARL HOWE,

STEWARDS:
THE EARL OF WILTON,
COLONEL THE HON. H. FORESTER.
T. TOWNLEY-PARKER, Esq.

Messrs. TOPHAM, Handicappers, Stakeholders, & Clerks of the Races. Mr. R. JOHNSON, Judge & Clerk of the Scales. Mr. McGEORGE, Starter.

THURSDAY.

The PRINCE OF WALES'S CUP, of 25sov.

The Second LIVERPOOL HUNT STEEPLE CHASE of 150sov.

The PRINCE'S PARK PLATE of 150sov.

(SEVENTH YEAR.)—The UNION JACK STAKES of 10sov. each, with 150sov. added

The LIVERPOOL HURDLE HANDICAP of 15sov. each, with 200sov. added

The NATIONAL HUNTER'S STAKES of 5sov. each, with 150sov. added

THE MOLYNEUX STAKES of 10sov. each, with 300sov. added

FRIDAY.

The GRAND NATIONAL STEEPLE CHASE of 1000gs.

The MARCH HUNTERS PLATE of 100sov.

To Close on February 28th.

The PALATINE HURDLE HANDICAP of 10 sov. each, with 100sov. added

The HYLTON CUP of 200sov.

The LANCASTRIAN PLATE (Welter Handicap) of 150gs.

The SEFTON PARK PLATE of 200sov.

SATURDAY.

The Second CHAMPION STEEPLE CHASE of 15sov. each starter, with 200sov. added

The LIVERPOOL SPRING CUP of 800gs.

The SEFTON STEEPLE CHASE of 200sov.

The WALTON HURDLE HANDICAP of 5sov. each, with 100sov. added

To Close on February 28th.

The HAPSBURG HUNT STEEPLE CHASE of 100sov.

To Close on February 28th.

The NETHERTON SELLING HANDICAP of 100gs.

To Close on February 28th.

CONDITIONS.

G. R. GRIFFITH, "THE CASTLE" PRINTING WORKS, GROSVENOR STREET, CHESTER by hugging the rail himself and Cloister was unable to get through, eventually being beaten by just a length. Although he really had only himself to blame, Roddy Owen subsequently objected to the winner on grounds of jostling, but was overruled by the stewards, and the result was allowed to stand. In 1892, when the race was run in thick fog, Cloister started favourite, but was beaten by twenty lengths by Father O'Flynn to whom he was conceding 26lbs.

On firm going in 1893, even with 12st 7lbs on his back, but this time ridden by William Dollery, Cloister simply galloped his rivals into the ground. He led from start to finish and beat his nearest challenger, Aesop, by no less than forty lengths, in a then record time of 9 mins 32 secs, which was to stand for forty years. It was an awesome display of jumping, whose nearest modern equivalent has probably been that of Crisp in 1973. But

Cloister, winner of the 1893 Grand National

Crisp was carrying 7lbs less than Cloister, finished a tired horse, whereas Cloister appeared ready to go round again, and of course was beaten into second place by Red Rum. More recently, Lord Gyllene in 1997 also led from start to finish, but he had to carry only 10st, and beat a field that was probably inferior in quality to that of 1893 which also included two other National winners. He also won over a course that has been considerably modified, and by general consent made easier, since Cloister's day.

Sadly, Cloister never ran in another National. Both in 1894 and 1895 he was a firm ante-post favourite, but mysteriously went lame shortly before the race and had to be withdrawn. His trainer, Arthur Yates, thought that Cloister must have strained himself internally, possibly in the kidneys, during his win in 1893, and that this injury only reappeared when the horse was under great strain, but others, including his owner, Charles Duff,

Royal winner Ambush II, with Algy Anthony up, by William Clark

thought that he had been 'got at', and although nothing has ever been proved this does appear the more likely explanation, not least because on both occasions the bookmakers suddenly lengthened Cloister's odds before anyone else knew there was anything wrong. And although he was prevented from running in a National again, Cloister showed that he was still capable of jumping the Aintree fences successfully by winning the 1894 Grand Sefton at the November meeting. In its way this performance was as impressive as his National win, for, despite carrying the enormous weight of 13st 3lbs, Cloister once again led virtually from the start, and beat his nearest rival, Midshipmite, by twenty lengths [19].

It was during this period that Aintree received its first royal patronage. The Prince of Wales, later King Edward VII, attended the Grand National meeting for the first time in 1878. The weather was atrocious, with snow falling for much of the meeting, and that year's National was reported to be "one of the tamest on record", but this was not the fault of the Tophams who had "published a programme on a most liberal scale". The Prince travelled by special train direct from having watched the Lincoln, and stayed with Lord Sefton at Croxteth. For the Prince's visit to Aintree Lord Sefton's box had been enlarged by a "capacious gallery", together with extra luncheon and retiring rooms, and the furniture was "of the most elegant description". New telegraph poles had been erected for this meeting and the central one of these was surmounted by a crest of the Prince of Wales' feathers [20]. This was the start of the Prince's longstanding support of Aintree. He had his first runner in the National in 1884, and after many years of trying, he eventually saw his colours carried to success when Ambush II won in 1900.

This race was one of the most emotional ever run at Aintree, for the crowd was torn between wanting to see a royal victory, and wanting to see one of the all-time Aintree greats, Manifesto, win a third Grand National to add to his triumphs in 1897 and 1899. As they came to the last fence Ambush was in the lead but Manifesto was moving up from third to second and seemed poised to strike. As they came up the run-in, however, the weight Manifesto had to carry (12st 13lbs) began to tell and the Prince's horse held off the challenge. Manifesto was then eased and beaten a neck for second place by Barsac. One observer wrote "It is impossible to describe this tremendous race. No-one will ever describe it adequately. Men who saw it will know in their own minds what it was and what their feelings were when the grand old Manifesto made his supreme effort under 12st 13-lb and up to a hundred yards from the finish looked like getting there... The scene of Persimmon's Derby was nothing to that of today, and yet there were actually tears in men's eyes at the thought of Manifesto's defeat... I can write no more about it. There are some things about which it appears almost sacrilege to write in black and white" [21].

Manifesto, the horse Ambush II beat that day, was one of the greatest Aintree horses, and until the advent of Red Rum his record in the Grand National was unsurpassed. In full it runs as follows:

1895 (7 years old)	11st 2lb	Fourth to Wild Man of Borneo
1896 (8 years old)	11st 4lb	Knocked down at the first

Manifesto, one of the greatest Aintree horses

1897	(9 years old)	11st 3lb	Won by twenty lengths
1898			Did not run
1899	(11 years old)	12st 7lb	Won by five lengths
1900	(12 years old)	12st 13lb	Third to Ambush II
1901			Did not run
1902	(14 years old)	12st 8lb	Third to Shannon Lass
1903	(15 years old)	12st 3lb	Third to Drumcree
1904	(16 years old)	12st 1lb	Unplaced to Moifaa

Manifesto's second win in the National was a remarkable triumph, for at the Canal Turn on the first circuit he put in an enormous leap and landed on some loose hay which had been put down to protect the fence overnight and not been removed. Manifesto slipped on the loose surface and landed on his shoulder. His jockey, George Williamson later said "I saw one of his legs sticking straight up over my head in the air, the toe of my boot was on the ground, and both irons were gone, but I left everything to Manifesto and he recovered himself. I picked up the reins and went on" [22]. This display of coolness and bold jumping was symptomatic of Manifesto's performance that day; when he went into the lead after the last ditch the crowd began to cheer him home, and he received a great reception as he passed the post an easy five length winner, and the first dual winner since The Lamb in 1871.

Two years after Manifesto's second victory, and a year after Ambush II's win, there was one of those Nationals which produced an extraordinary story. In 1901 the race was run in a blinding snowstorm; indeed conditions were so bad that many of the leading jockeys petitioned the stewards to postpone it. The stewards, however, delayed only for about ten minutes and then told the jockeys they had to go. With visibilty almost non-existent and snow lying on the ground, few of the runners got round unscathed, one of the jockeys reporting afterwards that "It was like trying to find the North Pole without a compass". However one horse, Grudon, ridden by Arthur Nightingall, made light of the conditions. This was because his trainer, Bletsoe, seeing the conditions, had purchasd a large amount of butter just before the race, and stuffed Grudon's feet with it. This unorthodox tactic prevented the snow balling, and Grudon never put a foot wrong or slipped throughout the race, even though he was galloping through snow most of the time. He was always in the first two or three, and took up the running about a mile from home. From there on he was never seriously threatened, and despite making a mistake about 200 yards from the finish when he tried to jump the path that runs across the course at that point, he held on to win easily, beating Drumcree (who was to win his own National two years later) by four lengths. Grudon provided Arthur Nightingall with his third win in the National, as he had previously won on Ilex (1890) and Why Not (1894). Nightingall regarded Grudon as a beautiful jumper and thought it had been an "exhilarating spectacle when he was running at the head of his field during that memorable snow storm with his feet full of butter" [23].

In the early years of the new century Joseph Bell Topham was succeeded by his son Edward Anthony Christopher Topham. He was born in 1878 and controlled Aintree for twenty eight years, adding the role of Clerk of the Course to that of race course manager in 1912. He had the reputation of being very firm, but polite, reasonable and hard working, and it was said of him that "he loved the Grand National as if it were a son" [24], but it was during this period that inertia began to set in in the management of the course. Faced with mounting criticism, especially over the chaos of Tipperary Tim's National in 1928 when all but one of the forty two runners fell, Topham himself became disheartened, and, according to Mirabel Topham "got rather fed up and neglected the place" [25]. He was also said to have left matters "decidedly complicated" at his death in 1932 [26]. This included a court case in which a former clerk of the course sued Tophams for unfair dismissal. Tophams had to pay £3,500 in damages, but the official was not reinstated [27].

E.A.C. Topham should naturally have been succeeded by his brother, Arthur Ronald Topham, but he has been succinctly characterised as "a genial Peter Pan" [28], and he took no active part in the family business [29]. Instead, effective control passed to his wife Mirabel who by 1938 had become managing director of Tophams Ltd. Mrs. Topham was a formidable character, whose name, even today, nearly twenty years after her death, arouses strong and conflicting emotions. The racing journalist Clive Graham, who knew her well, thought that her charm of manner, her flair for newsworthiness and her inventiveness were all nullified by "a grasshopper-type of mind" which led to much misunderstanding and even litigation [30]. Her obituarist in *The Times* took this further, saying that she "lacked the tact and patience to win much-needed support, and was the hapless victim of her own self-inflicted wounds" [31]. On the other hand, her nephew, Jim Bidwell-Topham, said that she was "a wonderful person to work for, very fair and very straight... The Grand National was her life" [32]. Peter Beckwith-Smith, the Clerk of the Course from 1949 to 1957, whilst admitting that the stands were allowed to decay, said that "her diligence laid the foundation for the splendid condition of the turf" [33], and Reg Green, rather chivalrously, thinks that she "nurtured Aintree and the Grand National with the care and affection only a woman can provide" [34].

She was born in 1892, the daughter of Henry Hope Hillier, who described himself as an art craftsman. Later in life, Mrs. Topham described him as a talented artist but one who was more interested in the aesthetic side of art than in making money. Nevertheless, she had a happy childhood and said of her parents that they were "a honeymoon couple all their lives". As a young girl she claimed to have fenced, swam, cycled, rowed, walked miles and "danced the hours away", but, curiously in view of her later career, she said she never rode a horse except once when she had a part on horseback on the stage. There was a family connection with the theatre through Louis Hillier, the conductor and muscial director who later became general manager of the Criterion Theatre in London, and this became Mirabel's chosen career. Her first recorded appearance on the stage came on 29 May 1905 when, aged only thirteen, she played one of the playing card soldiers in an "unambitious" stage version of Lewis Carroll's "Alice", adapted by Nigel Playfair, which had one performance at the Court Theatre. Her younger sister Beatrix (Trixie) played the Dormouse in the same production, which was reported to have been "received with favour by an audience disposed to be entertained" [35]. Whether she later became a Gaiety Girl, as was sometimes claimed, is unclear, although her sister Trixie was certainly one at one time. Before the First World War she is known to have appeared in several light plays and musical comedies, including "Mrs. Ponderbury's Past" (Vaudeville, 1907), "The Chorus Lady" (Vaudeville, 1909), and a musical called "Are you there", with music by Leoncavallo and lyrics by Edgar Wallace (Prince of Wales', 1913); this last can hardly have been a conspicuous success as it ran for only twenty five performances. She also played once in a pantomime at Leeds (perhaps this was when she rode the horse).

At the beginning of the First World War both she and her sister were in a London show called "The Cinema Star" by Jack Hulbert, which had opened to enthusiastic reviews at the Shaftesbury Theatre on 4 June 1914. This had "melodious and catchy" music by Jean Gilbert, together with "that rare thing in modern musical comedy, a clear-cut, interesting and consequent plot" (which involved the hero and heroine being stuck in a lift between floors), with "some witty and well-tuned lyrics"; also commended were the "wealth and variety of the beautiful costumes worn by the ladies" [36]. Despite this, in the anti-German hysteria which broke out at the beginning of the war it was attacked by the press because of its German origins (it was an adaptation of "Kino Koeningen" by Georg Okonkowski and Julius Freund), and it was sent on tour to the provinces. During the week beginning 21 September it was at the Royal Court, Liverpool, where it was very well received, audiences being kept in "an effervescence of hilarity throughout the evening". Perhaps to counter the anti-German sentiments the show had encountered in London, the original overture was replaced by a medley of the national anthems of the Allies, which received enthusiastic standing ovations from the audience. All told, "The Cinema Star" week was quite a notable event [37]. According to Mirabel herself, it was at one of these performances that Arthur Topham first saw her. Initially he was attracted to her sister, but after going backstage he soon transferred his affections. He courted her for seven years before she agreed to marry him, saying afterwards "I don't make up my mind easily, but when I do it is the right decision". Her last appearance on the stage was in 1921, when, calling herself Hope Hillier, she was given a non-speaking part as one of the "ladies" in a production of J.M. Barrie's "Quality Street" at the Haymarket. Before the end of the run of the play she and Arthur Topham were married in April 1922 at the Catholic church of Our Lady of Grace in Chiswick High Road; it is noteworthy that Mirabel chose not to describe herself as an actress on her marriage certificate [38].

For the first ten years of her married life she appears to have had nothing to do with the running of Aintree, and although it took place a

THEATRE ROYAL, HAYMARKET.

Lessee and Manager - - FREDERICK HARRISON

Every Evening at 8.30

Matinées : Thursday and Saturday at 2.30

J. E. VEDRENNE's Production

QUALITY STREET

By J. M. BARRIE

Valentine Brown	LEON QUARTERMAINE
Ensign Blades	NIGEL BRUCE
Lieutenant Spicer	CECIL TROUNCER
Recruiting Sergeant	GORDON HARKER
A Waterloo Veteran	W. W. PALMER
Master Arthur Wellesley Tomson . .	ROBERT HENDERSON
Miss Susan Throssel	MARY JERROLD
Miss Willoughby	MARY BARTON
Miss Fanny Willoughby	MURIEL ALEXANDER
Miss Henrietta Turnbull	NANCYE KENYON
Miss Charlotte Parratt	DOROTHY RUNDELL
Patty	HILDA TREVELYAN
Isabella	RUTH MORGAN
Harriet	MARY LINCOLN
Miss Phœbe Throssel	FAY COMPTON

LADIES—Honor Clode, Grace Sepping, Sunday Wilshin, Marjorie Bamber, Hope Hillier, Kathleen Blake.

OFFICERS—Ralph Ledra, Donald Macardle, M. Hogan, Drew Carran, H. Irving.

The Scene is in England During the Napoleonic Wars.

ACT I.—The Blue and White Room in the House of Miss Susan and Miss Phœbe in Quality Street.

ACT II.—The Same—nine years after.

ACT III.—A Tent Pavilion, used as a Card and Retiring Room at the Officers' Ball—one week later.

ACT IV.—The Blue and White Room—two days after.

Theatre programme for J.M. Barrie's 'Quality Street', 1921
Mrs. Topham, as Hope Hillier, was one of the chorus of 'Ladies'

The box used by Royal Mail in 1937;
plaques above the doors in the stable block record the names of the National winners who have used the box

year after E.A.C. Topham's death, she does not seem to have been directly responsible for an important change which took place in 1933 and which at a stroke made Aintree hugely more profitable. This concerned entry to the course. It is not generally known that up until this time the Grand National, like the Derby, could be viewed for free if one went out in the country beyond the Melling Road, admission charges being payable only by those spectators who went on the race course proper. Thus a very large number of the huge crowds that thronged to Aintree made no contribution at all towards its costs. It is unclear whether he acted on behalf of the Tophams or not, but in 1933 Lord Sefton took steps to close and divert a public footpath which ran across the steeplechase course from the Melling Road to the railway sidings, and that year consequently saw the first "all-pay" National. There was some grumbling over this, but the decision does not seem to have been seriously challenged; nevertheless, it must have made a very significant difference to Tophams' profits [39].

In retrospect, the 1930s appear halcyon days for the National. Despite continuing criticism of the conditions, the prestige of the race remained high, and great horses, like Golden Miller, Reynoldstown and Kellsboro' Jack fought out thrilling contests before huge crowds. In 1937, for example, 60 main line race trains and 100 aeroplanes helped bring a crowd estimated at 250,000 to Aintree to see Royal Mail win in coronation year. Admission charges ranged from 1/- to 30/-, and with the annual rent to Lord Sefton remaining at £8,346, where it had been fixed in 1929, it is easy to see that it must have been a highly profitable event for the Tophams [40].

Improvements continued to be made to the course. In 1938 a new stand was built at the Canal Turn, [41] and the following year a new lounge bar and snack bar were established in the main stands, and electric fires and central heating installed in the County Stand "so that those on the roof will no longer be in danger of being enveloped in smoke from the chimneys" [42].

Further improvements were planned for 1940, but were put on hold because of the war [43], and by the time Aintree reopened its gates to the racegoing public six years later much would have changed, although in the post-war euphoria this was not immediately apparent.

Notes and references

1. Index of Wills, 1873, Vol. 11, p.422.
2. *Bell's Life*, 29 March 1873.
3. Letter from Topham to Halifax Wyatt, 7 August 1872, Molyneux Muniments (Croxteth Hall) DDM 55.
4. Letter from Topham to Halifax Wyatt, 31 October 1872, Molyneux Muniments (Croxteth Hall) DDM 55.
5. Letter from C. and J.B. Topham to Halifax Wyatt, 4 March 1874, Molyneux Muniments (Croxteth Hall) DDM 55.
6. *Porcupine*, 12 March 1864, p.397.
7. Seth-Smith. The history of steeplechasing, p.76; *Liverpool Mercury*, 25 March 1874.
8. Letter from C. and J.B. Topham to Halifax Wyatt, 18 April 1875, Molyneux Muniments (Croxteth Hall) DDM 55.
9. Smith. The Grand National, p.87.
10. *Notes and Queries*, 3rd series, vol. 3, 1863, p.209.

11. Letter from David Howarth to Halifax Wyatt, 8 April 1871, Molyneux Muniments (Croxteth Hall) DDM 55.
12. Letter from Halifax Wyatt to Tophams, 20 December 1878, Molyneux Muniments (Croxteth Hall) DDM 55.
13. Letter from Topham to Halifax Wyatt, 24 February 1872, Molyneux Muniments (Croxteth Hall) DDM 55.
14. *Liverpool Mercury*, 27 March 1874.
15. *Porcupine*, 18 July 1863, pp.126-127.
16. Scott. My life as soldier and sportsman, p.220.
17. *The Times*, 30 September 1892.
18. *The Times*, 14 November 1892.
19. Yates. Arthur Yates: trainer and gentleman rider, pp.229-246; Holland. Grand National, pp.46-49.
20. *Bell's Life*, 30 March 1878.
21. William Allison, quoted in Bird. A hundred Grand Nationals, p.154.
22. Quoted in Bird. A hundred Grand Nationals, p.151.
23. Nightingall. My racing adventures, pp.169-170; O'Leary. Grand National, pp.122-124.
24. *The Times*, 2 January 1933.
25. *The Times*, 7 October 1964.
26. Barton. Where the dream of "The Great Chase' was born.
27. *The Times*, 2 June 1980.
28. Barton. Where the dream of "The Great Chase' was born.
29. *The Times*, 5 November 1958.
30. Graham and Curling. The Grand National, p.55.
31. *The Times*, 2 June 1980.
32. Hughes and Watson. Long live the National, p.85.
33. Hughes and Watson. Long live the National, p.76.
34. Green. A race apart, p.348.
35. *The Stage*, 1 June 1905, p.14.
36. *The Stage*, 11 June 1914, pp.22-23.
37. *The Stage*, 24 September 1914, p.14.
38. Mrs. Topham's early life is shrouded in mystery and myth, even her birth certificate appearing to be missing from the registers. This account is largely drawn from articles in *Lancashire Life*, Vol. 4, no. 2 (March 1956), p.43, and Vol. 17 (September 1969), pp.46-49. In later life she embellished her stage career: the facts, as opposed to the fictions, can be traced in Wearing. The London stage (3 series covering 1900-1909, 1910-1919 and 1920-1924).
39. *Liverpool Daily Post*, 3 March 1933.
40. *Liverpool Evening Express*, 18 March 1937; *The Times*, 3 October 1964.
41. *Liverpool Daily Post*, 19 January 1938.
42. *Liverpool Daily Post*, 4 March 1939.
43. *The Times*, 12 March 1940.

12.

Aintree in Wartime

First World War

At first the war had little impact on racing, and although the seriousness of the situation on the Western Front began to come home to people as casualties mounted, the 1915 Grand National took place as usual, when, on a bright clear day, Ally Sloper won at 100-8 from a field of twenty runners. His owner, Lady Nelson, was the first woman to own a National winner. It was, however, a very different occasion to that of pre-war days. Under the heading "A Khaki Grand National", *The Times* reported that, although the attendance was good in the circumstances, with the crowd not much below average, it was "a Grand National shorn of all its spendour". In particular, it was the unusual composition of the crowd which attracted the reporters' attentions. Usually there was "a tremendous gathering of the working classes", but this year "the Liverpool lower middle classes and the working classes were doing their duty... They realized that for them this was no time to leave their work even for the Grand National". Strangely, it didn't seem to bother this correspondent at least that "the professional classes and businessmen of Liverpool bulked largely in the stands", and that their contribution to the war effort clearly didn't prevent them having a day out at the races. However, what was really striking about the crowd was the presence of so many men in uniform. On the stands there were almost as many army officers as civilians, whilst in the cheaper enclosures the rank and file of the army outnumbered the civilians. In fact, providing

Teaching Army Service Corps cadets to jump, May 1916

the troops with a morale-boosting day out was one of the principal justifications for running the National at all, when voices were beginning to be raised calling for the abandonment of racing altogether until after the end of the war [1].

This movement to ban racing became increasingly strident as the year progressed, and in December 1915 it was announced that the Liverpool Spring Meeting for 1916 had been abandoned [2]. In the event substitute races were run at Gatwick in 1916, 1917 and 1918, whilst the race course at Aintree was taken over by the War Office. It appears to have been used, most probably by the Royal Army Service Corps, for training cadets to ride. At the same time the stands were used as a staging post for wounded soldiers on their way to hospitals in Liverpool. They were transferred by lorry, and local people are said to have thrown cheap packets of Woodbine cigarettes into the lorries for the soldiers [3].

The Armistice in November 1918 was followed only a few days later by an announcement that there would be an early resumption of racing [4], and the next month it was confirmed that the Grand National would be run at Aintree the following spring [5]. The authorities must have had to work hard to get the course ready, for it was reported that during the military occupation many of the fences had "fallen to pieces". They were hastily rebuilt, but many of them were "not quite so wide as on the last occasion, while others were slightly wider" [6], and they were generally regarded as not as severe as normal [7]. (Interestingly, similar criticisms were made of the fences in 1946 at the first National after the Second World War). There were also some adminstrative problems. Topham was unable to make the handicap "owing to military duties" (he had been commissioned as a temporary 2nd Lieutenant in the Royal Army Service Corps in July 1917 [8]), so this task was undertaken by a Major Lee [9]. This was the first time since the race had become a handicap in 1843 that someone other than a member of the Topham family had been entrusted with this vital task. To mark the end of the war the trophy for the Grand National depicted St. George slaying the Dragon, whilst on the base were enamelled coats of arms of the Allied powers [10].

Starved of racing for the previous three years, an enormous crowd made its way out to Aintree to witness this first post-war National. The

Liverpool Courier's correspondent, who travelled out from Liverpool by train, said afterwards that "Shoulders, ribs, elbows and toes ache with memories of struggling humanity on every side. There are dim recollections of what seemed aeons and aeons spent in the midst of motionless, tight-packed people, becoming more and more congested as, after years of uneventful waiting, they slowly surged forward to the narrow entrance of a station platform". Nor were conditions much better on the course itself for "here was humanity, packed tightly within fences, all classes mixed in seemingly inextricable confusion, from the midst of which stentorian voices were yelling odds in an indistinguishable chorus". The bookmakers seem to have been particularly colourful that year: one of them flaunted a jockey's cap and a "motley-hued silk coat above a ragged pair of pantaloons", another wore a coaching hat of champagne silk, whilst a third was "a seedy wretch who resembles a cross between a hotel tout in a rather bad way of business and a superannuated billiard marker a little the worse for liquor" [11]. Visiting Aintree for the first time, Con O'Leary thought that the tipsters "sounded like sergeant-majors newly out of a job", and particularly noted "the wolfing around the shellfish stalls by fat men and slim girls... picture angels they looked, if not picture saints" [12]. Like all Nationals before the Second World War the race took place on a weekday, and there was undoubtedly a good deal of absenteeism that day. One local school even sent prefects to see if any of the boys were there. They found no boys, but three of the teachers, who had all come straight from their sick beds [13].

Despite snow showers earlier in the afternoon, the National was run in clear sunshine. The *Courier*'s man reported rather poetically that "the horses went away until in the dim far distance they seemed but toys and fluttering scraps of coloured cloth rising and falling in successive waves as fences came and went". Poethlyn, who had won the previous year's substitute event at Gatwick, triumphed under 12st 7lbs, only the fourth horse to do so. Because of this, he is sometimes compared to Cloister, Manifesto and Jerry M, the other three to have won with this weight, but the fact that the fences were easier than before the war makes this an unsatisfactory comparison.

As the vast crowd of "pickpockets and dukes, country farmers and stage-belles, merchants and office boys, matrons and flappers" left the course, the "frantic figure" of one of the bookmakers was seen "clambering over the adjacent hoardings, while behind him trickle across country a thin stream of obviously irate men". The "greatest fair of the year" was well and truly back in business [14].

Second World War

Remembering what had happened during the First World War, the government on the outbreak of war in September 1939 immediately announced the banning of all sporting fixtures. Although this order was soon rescinded, the military moved swiftly to occupy Aintree. By the end of the month the men of 136 Battery, 21st Light Anti-Aircraft Regiment, Royal Artillery, Territorial Army were billeted on the course. This unit had been formed in Birkenhead only the month before, and it reached Aintree by a rather circuitous route, by train through Runcorn and Wigan, presumably in order to maintain secrecy about its final destination. Conditions were primitive. On the first night the men were bedded down on straw in the main stands. Later they were moved into the stables, with five men to a box. The food was extremely poor, and washing facilities consisted of one outdoor cold tap for thirty men, although each week they were marched to Rice Lane Baths for a proper bath. Marching and drill were carried out on the hardstanding area in front of the stands and instruction on first aid was given in the weighing room. This unit was at Aintree for two or three weeks, before moving to Northwich to provide anti-aircraft defence for the I.C.I. works there [15].

The disappearance of these troops gave Mrs. Topham the chance to reclaim the race course, and during the last months of 1939 she fought to gain permission to stage the 1940 Grand National at Aintree. At one point it seemed as if a substitute race might be held at Newbury or Gatwick, as had happened in the First World War [16], but eventually all the relevant authorities, including crucially the Ministry of Transport, agreed that the race could go ahead at Aintree [17]. However the conditions of the race were altered to take account of the limited amount of steeplechasing that had been possible since the outbreak of war, and the race was made a £5000 plate instead of a sweepstakes [18].

Even during the "Phoney War", there were other more material changes to Aintree. In the spring of 1940 all available land within the boundaries of the race course was put under plough to help the "Dig for Victory" campaign. Fifty acres in the centre of the course were sown for wheat, forty for oats and twenty for potatoes. The course itself was left untouched, but was used for grazing sheep and cattle, who were later moved elsewhere to allow the Spring Meeting, including the Grand National, to take place [19].

Despite the War, the 1940 Grand National was accompanied by the usual social events as this poster from Liverpool's well-known Rialto Ballroom illustrates

The 1940 Grand National thus took place in unusual circumstances. Petrol rationing, aviation restrictions and a reduction in the number of special trains meant that the crowd was much lower than normal, and many of those attending, including several of the jockeys, were in uniform. Policemen on duty carried steel helmets, and four powerful loudspeakers were installed to broadcast emergency instructions in the event of air raids. Additional ambulances, fire pumps and three hundred air raid wardens were on hand to deal with any emergency, and additional water tanks, holding 40,000 gallons, were provided in case of fire fighting [20]. Fortunately, none of these precautions were put to the test as the day passed off without incident. Bogskar, owned and trained by Lord Stalbridge, and ridden by Mervyn Jones, was the winner of this wartime National. Two years later, Jones, a pilot-sergeant in the R.A.F., was killed in action.

Mrs. Topham received considerable praise for staging the National (it was seen as a morale booster), but in the aftermath of the fall of France and the British evacuation through Dunkirk, the whole situation changed, and there was no thought after then of continuing racing on other than the most minimal level. On 15 June 1940 it was announced that the Liverpool Summer Meeting had been abandoned [21], and the course was soon under military occupation again. Three bricklayers were hastily sent by the army to build several huts on the course, which were soon occupied by sailors from the French Navy. These men had had to leave France very suddenly as the Germans invaded, and had blown up an ammunition dump as they left. Consequently they had no weapons with them when they arrived in England, but they had nevertheless managed to bring some crates of wine with them which was stored under the main stand, prompting the sardonic comment from one of the bricklayers that they couldn't manage to bring any guns but they hadn't forgotten the vino [22].

The sailors may have had plenty of wine, but it soon became apparent that they had very little else. The camp had been erected so hastily that no provision had been made for any lighting, nor was there any food provided. When local people discovered what dire straits the sailors were in, they responded with the same generosity that their descendants were to show in the more recent crisis when the course had to be evacuated because of a bomb threat to the Grand National in 1997. Sailors were invited back to people's homes for meals, including such very English fare as rhubarb and custard, which few of them had seen before, and a large laundry basket was taken round to collect food for the troops still in the camp; despite wartime privations, people gave generously and this was soon full. In the same spirit candles were given out to provide some light in the camp, and in at least one case a local family bought a pair of shoes for one of the sailors when they saw that his own pair had lost their soles completely [23].

The French also began to frequent the local pubs, such as the Farmers Arms on Longmoor Lane, and friendships with local people quickly developed. Families "adopted" individual officers and men, who went round to their homes for meals every night [24].

Other detachments of French sailors were camped at Haydock Park, and on 30 June 1940 General De Gaulle travelled to Liverpool to appeal to

Ernest and Rodger Poilverd, two of the French Navy Officers, billeted at Aintree race course after the Fall of France, May 1940

both groups to join his Free French forces. However, at this time the attitude of the British authorities to the Free French was still somewhat ambivalent, it being argued in some quarters that the men would be regarded as rebels by the legal French government (which had capitulated) if they joined him. The men themselves were also divided over which course of action to follow, and perhaps this explains why, when De Gaulle arrived in Liverpool, he was told by the British admiral in command that he would not be allowed to speak to the men because this might be prejudicial to order. De Gaulle had to leave empty-handed on this occasion, but later many of the sailors at Aintree did enlist in the Free French forces, the others being repatriated to Vichy France [25].

After the French left, there were some Polish troops stationed on the race course [26], and it was also used as a reception camp for some of the British troops returning from France. These included a draft of Scots Guards, who had been rushed back from Marseilles when the situation in northern France began to deteriorate. In what was probably a fairly common experience, they stayed at Aintree only a few days before moving on to another camp in Ayrshire [27].

From 1942 onwards the race course was taken over by the Americans who used it as a transport depot. Over the next three years many thousands of American servicemen found themselves stationed there, and in the build up to D-Day especially, the whole of the area in front of the stands was used as a vast vehicle park. At one point the line of trucks stretched right up to and all along one side of the Melling Road. After the invasion had taken place the numbers were reduced as many of them were moved down to the south coast and then transported to France [28].

Finding themselves billeted at Aintree, especially during winter, could be depressing experience for some of the GIs, especially those who had never been away from home before. One eighteen year old remembered that he was "so cold, miserable and downright unhappy that first night that he cried". And although the Americans generally were well supplied, food could still sometimes be a problem. One transport driver, spending only his second night in England in the stables at Aintree, after spending the day driving up from Wiltshire, found that no rations had been provided and he "had to find a fish and chip shop to get anything to eat". Once again local people opened their homes to the troops in their midst, inviting many of them to share Christmas dinner with them, for instance. This could, however, also bring dividends, for unlike the French and the Poles, the Americans had access to luxuries unobtainable by most people in Britain at that time. One local woman later remembered a GI who "came with a gift for each member of the family... He gave my father a box of fifty cigars" [29].

Some of the troops stationed at Aintree were African Americans, and this caused problems, not so much with local people as with some of the white Americans, especially those who came from the segregated Southern states. There was a certain amount of pressure on local clubs and dance halls to ban all blacks, whether American or British, because white GIs

The 'Stars and Stripes' flies over Aintree during its wartime use as an American transport depot

objected to their presence, and although this was to some extent resisted, some institutions agreed to do so for fear of losing custom. But at the Aintree Institute, close to the race course, blacks were only barred after a shooting and stabbing incident involving drunk African American servicemen [30].

During the American occupation considerable changes were made to the race course. The box which had been used by Eremon, Jenkinstown and Poethlyn was converted into a barber's shop, additional windows were knocked out in some of the boxes used for billeting troops, nissen huts and workshops were erected in the carriage enclosures and sixty seven showers were installed in the Champagne Bar. A hard surface for army vehicles was laid over part of the flat course, but the steeplechase course was not touched, although it received little more than minimal attention; after the war, for example, it was discovered that rabbits had colonised much of the course, their burrows making the turf on the landing side of the fences unsafe [31].

Remarkably, over fifty years after the end of the war, some traces of the American occupation of the course can still be found. In the New Yard

Aintree's stable manager Derek Thompson points out the name of an American sergeant, 'Sgt Withnell', chalked on a door

many of the stable doors have the names of American GIs carved on them, and there is at least one door on which names written in chalk can still be clearly seen.

On VJ Day, 15 August 1945, the Americans at Aintree participated fully in the celebrations to mark the end of the war. One local girl later recalled that the whole area was "alive with trucks and jeeps driving through the streets laden with soldiers, civilians and children. Sirens and horns blowing, singing and shouting". A piano was brought out on to the street for her to play, whilst "a few GIs were strumming banjos" [32].

The end of the war did not bring an immediate end to the American occupation of Aintree, however. They were supposed to leave by November 1945, but a dockers' strike caused some delay, and in the end the final troops did not vacate the course until 21 February 1946 [33].They left behind them a major task of rehabilitation and reconstruction if Aintree was to be ready to stage the first post-war National in six weeks' time.

Notes and references

1. *The Times*, 27 March 1915.
2. *The Times*, 17 December 1915.
3. Harkins. Aintree past and present, p.90.
4. *Liverpool Courier*, 15 November 1918.
5. *Liverpool Courier*, 20 December 1918.
6. *Liverpool Courier*, 27 March 1919.
7. Bird. A hundred Grand Nationals, p.171.
8. *Army list*, December 1918, col. 1655f.
9. *Liverpool Courier*, 31 January 1919.
10. *Liverpool Courier*, 29 March 1919.
11. *Liverpool Courier*, 29 March 1919.
12. O'Leary. Grand National, p.4.
13. Shaw. My Liverpool, p.198.
14. *Liverpool Courier*, 29 March 1919.
15. Letter from G. Crozier to the author, 12 July 1998.
16. *The Times*, 7 December 1939.
17. *The Times*, 9 December 1939.
18. *The Times*, 15 December 1939.
19. *The Times*, 12 March 1940.
20. *Liverpool Daily Post*, 3 April 1940.
21. *The Times*, 15 June 1940.
22. Letter from J. Jones to the author, July 1998.
23. Letter from Margaret Brazendale to the author, 12 July 1998.

24. Letter from Helen Scorgie to the author, 16 July 1998.
25. De Gaulle. War memoirs. Vol. 1. The call to honour, 1940-1942, p.94.
26. Letter from Margaret Brazendale to the author, 12 July 1998.
27. Letter from S. McCormick to the author, 20 July 1998.
28. Letter from George Gardiner to the author, July 1998.
29. Longmate. The GI's, pp.74, 181.
30. Reynolds. Rich relations, p.312.
31. *Liverpool Evening Express*, 17 December 1945; *Liverpool Daily Post*, 22 February 1946.
32. Quoted in Longmate. The GI's, p.324.
33. *Liverpool Evening Express*, 17 December 1945; *Liverpool Daily Post*, 22 February 1946.

13.

The Topham years II: 1946-1973

As the Americans delayed their departure, there seemed a real danger that it would not be possible to get Aintree ready in time to stage the 1946 Grand National, and at one point it was even suggested that the race be transferred to Cheltenham [1]. That the course was restored to a condition fit to be used in a mere six weeks was possibly Mrs. Topham's finest achievement. She fought to get the necessary government permits to allow work to start and then harried the contractors and their men to get the job done on time. It was probably during this period that she gained the reputation of being "a ruthless dictator with a whiplash tongue" [2]. The Ministry of Works had given her a grant of £6000 towards restoring Aintree on condition that the Grand National was run, but when she applied for a further £6000 she was turned down on the grounds that housing needs in the area had a higher priority [3]. Perhaps this second application for government money was something of a bluff, for in the event Tophams were able to announce that the original £6000 was sufficient to ensure that all the essential public amenities would be available by the time of the meeting, although the accommodation and paddock facilities would still be limited. Perhaps most significantly, however, it was reported that the course itself and the jumps would be as they had been in pre-war days [4]. In fact, many of the jumps had to be rather hurridly constructed, and they were not built to the usual immaculate standards. Jim Bidwell-Topham later recalled "the clouds of dust that blew out of some of the fences as the horses jumped through them" [5].

Heroine and hero?
Mrs Mirabel Topham waves to three-times National winner Red Rum after he led the parade for the 1978 National

This Grand National, as in pre-war days, was run on the Friday of the meeting. It attracted a record crowd, estimated at around 300,000, but even so there were some harbingers for the future. The first day of the meeting, comprising some of the traditional flat races of the Liverpool Spring Meeting, attracted a smaller crowd than was expected [6], and even the great crowd for the National itself was "not quite so overwhelming as had been thought probable" [7]. The press also noted the substantial increase in admission prices. In 1940 a weekly County Stand badge had cost £6 6s, but in 1946 it was £10 10s, entry to the paddock had risen from £1 15s to £2 17s 6d, and the cost of going out in the country had risen from 1/- to 2/6d. Even so, Tophams claimed that their returns would be lower, owing to the increased cost of staging the meeting [8].

Nevertheless, in the immediate post-war years vast crowds, starved of racing during the war, flocked to Aintree and the future must have seemed bright. Encouraged by this in 1947 Tophams approached Lord Sefton about buying the course from him, arguing that they did not feel justified in making alterations and improvements to the course unless they had longer security of tenure (at that point the existing lease still had nineteen years to run). Like many large landowners at the time, Lord Sefton was suffering from cash flow problems – he had already sold the Kirkby estate to Liverpool Corporation for £375,000 – and so this approach was probably not unwelcome. In any event agreement was reached and the course was sold to Tophams for £275,000 in July 1949; the deal required an initial payment of £60,000, the balance to be paid in annual instalments, secured by a mortgage. Lord Sefton also inserted a clause in the conveyance which stated that the land could only be used for racing or for agricultural purposes. This, it was thought, would safeguard the future of the Grand National, although the future was to prove otherwise [9].

The introduction of the Topham Trophy, a new race over the Grand National course, seemed to suggest that Tophams were committed to promoting horse racing at Aintree, but unfortunately, the early years of their ownership were also marked by a series of disasters and fiascos, which combined to lower the prestige of the Grand National and to alienate public support. The first of these occurred in 1951 when the starter pressed his

'The Grand Crashional', the scene at the first fence in 1951

lever before many of the runners were ready. No attempt was made to recall those horses that had started whilst those jockeys who were still walking their horses around had to hastily turn their horses and set off in pursuit as best they could. This farce was compounded by disaster at the first fence where twelve horses, a third of the field, fell. Only three runners completed the course, and this fiasco was dubbed "The Grand Crashional" by a hostile press.

The following year there was once again mayhem at the first fence where ten horses out of a field of forty seven fell. However, even this disaster was overshadowed by Mrs. Topham's monumental blunder in replacing the B.B.C.'s radio commentary team with some of her own staff. As Brough Scott later wrote, her amateur broadcasters produced "a homemade commentary of the race which sounded as if it was broadcast from the Tower of Babel" [10], in which, amongst a catalogue of errors, the eventual winner, Teal, was announced as having fallen at the first.

In 1954 four horses were killed in the National, resulting in much adverse press coverage and calls for the course to be made easier or the conditions altered. The matter was even raised in the Horse of Lords. Opening the debate, which took place on 6 April 1954, Lord Ammon gave details of the numbers of horses who had been killed or failed to finish the course; to prevent any repetition of the "tremendous cruelty" involved, he suggested that Becher's and the Chair should be modified, that the distance of the race be reduced to three and a half miles, that the first fence be altered, and that something should be done "to humanise the race". He felt that "all that Tophams have been concerned about is the commercial angle". Lord Calverley was equally outspoken. He thought the Grand National was "a cruel spectacle" and called for the National Hunt Committee to "see that Tophams Limited run the race in a humane fashion or cancel the licence of the company to run the race"; they should moreover "inform the Aintree people that if they do not put their house in order the race will be transferred to Cheltenham". Front bench spokesmen managed to defuse the debate by saying that this was not an appropriate field for government action, but announcing that there were to be discussions between the Home Secretary and the National Hunt Committee, and no formal motion was passed [11].

The following year the National took place in atrocious conditions, which led to the water jump being omitted for the only time, and the Stewards were understandably nervous beforehand. The Clerk of the Course, Peter Beckwith-Smith, later recalled that Lord Sefton told the jockeys to ride sensibly according to the conditions, adding that "Any nonsense and this could be the end of the National" [12]. Fortunately, the race was completed without serious incident, with thirteen out of the thirty runners completing the course (the highest number since 1948), but more ominously it took place before the smallest crowd in living memory.

The 1956 National will forever be remembered for the collapse of Devon Loch, just yards from the finish. As with the 1993 void race, this bizarre and still unexplained event may well have raised interest in the National, but the following year Mrs. Topham chose to revert to the pre-War pattern of running it on a Friday rather than on a Saturday, as had become the custom since 1946. The result could have been foreseen, a crowd that even Mrs. Topham admitted was 30% down on the previous year [13].

In 1959 there was a further fatality, and only four horses finished, out of a field of thirty four, leading once again to calls for changes in the conditions of the race and the construction of the fences.

Eventually, changes were made in response to these criticisms. The conditions were altered so that no horse had to carry more than 12st. Perhaps more significantly, the construction of the fences was altered to make them more inviting to jump. Since 1961 the plain fences, including Becher's and Valentine's, have been sloped on the take off side. This has the effect of giving horses an extra two feet in which to gain sufficient height to clear the fences, whereas before this, when the fences were straight up, it was possible for horses to get far too close before taking off and have no chance of getting over. The open ditches, such as the Chair,

The sloping of the take-off side of the plain fences was introduced in 1961. Pictured at the Canal Turn is Gerry Scott who won the last of the Nationals over the 'upright' fences on Merryman II

The Chair and other open ditches have retained their original upright construction (pictured at the Chair is Bob Champion, winner of the 1981 National on Aldaniti)

however, have retained their original upright construction, the ditches giving the horses the space needed to jump them. These changes have undoubtedly reduced the number of fallers in the race and made it a fairer test of horse and rider, although ironically the greatest pile-up in the history of the race, when Foinavon won in 1967, occurred after the fences had been modified.

Throughout this period little money appeared to be invested in the course, prize money other than for the National itself was reduced, and the flat racing programme, once so prestigious, dwindled into insignificance. The huge crowds, estimated in the hundreds of thousands, who had packed the course for the National in the interwar years and in the immediate post-war period had effectively subsidised the rest of the racing programme at Liverpool, and as they declined so did the course's finances. Even the National, with the rise in status of the Cheltenham Festival, lost its former unquestioned pre-eminence. Before the war the National was generally worth around ten or eleven times as much to the winning owner as the Gold Cup. In 1947 it was still worth nine times as much, but by 1960 it was only worth two and a half times as much. It was thus perfectly possible for top class steeplechasers to win big prize money without going near Aintree at all, something that was simply not possible before the war, and it is perhaps significant that after Prince Regent in 1947, no other Gold Cup winner ran at Aintree until L'Escargot in 1972.

For all her energy and innovation Mrs. Topham appeared unable to halt the decline. She had many ideas but none of them seemed to work, and, in retrospect, some of them appear only half thought through. For example, she saw, as did many others, that there needed to be more steeplechasing at Aintree, but her solution was to establish the Mildmay course on which the fences were not regulation birch fences of the type found on park courses, but scaled down versions of the National fences. These never proved popular with owners or trainers, and indeed by the early 1970s they were only used for one race a year, the Mildmay Chase. Yet when, after Ladbrokes took over in 1976, the new Clerk of the Course, John Hughes, rebuilt the Mildmay Course with birch fences it proved an instant success, and some of the races run over this course at the Grand National meeting now rival the National itself in the attention they receive from serious racegoers.

The advent of race sponsorship was another area where Mrs. Topham saw clearly that there were major implications for Aintree and the Grand

Preparing the Grand National fences

National, but failed to follow them through sufficiently. Following the institution of the first sponsored race, the Whitbread Gold Cup at Sandown, in 1957, she moved swiftly to secure sponsorship for the National, and from 1958 to 1963 the Irish Hospitals Sweepstakes provided £5000 added money each year. In 1961 this was augmented by a further £5000 provided by Schweppes. This was repeated the following year, but in 1963 Schweppes chose to sponsor their own event, the Schweppes Gold Trophy Hurdle, instead. This was run at Aintree in its first year, but was then moved to Newbury where it became a highlight of the National Hunt season, and where, although now known as the Tote Gold Trophy, it is still run. For one year only Mrs. Topham secured the support of Vaux Breweries, who provided £5000 for the 1963 Grand National, but thereafter all these sponsorship deals were allowed to lapse, until a deal was made with B.P. who gave £10,000 added money in 1972. Nor was any attempt made to secure sponsorship for any of the supporting races, even though many of them were by this time televised.

Mrs. Topham's other major innovation was to introduce motor racing to Aintree. A circuit was built at a cost of £100,000 and opened in 1954. At the time there were rumours that Mrs. Topham planned to abandon horse racing and turn over Aintree solely to motor racing. Mrs. Topham responded immediately. "The Grand National", she said, "was christened by the Tophams and nursed by them for well over a century – such a union is not lightly or easily severed. Aintree is the home of the Grand National and nothing will be allowed to upset that connection" [14]. Ten years later, of course, she was to take a markedly different line. In the event the motor racing circuit rapidly became unsuitable for grand prix events as cars became faster and more powerful, and after only seven years the venture was abandoned [15].

Another innovation was evening racing. In 1957 the summer meeting was revived for the first time in seven years and was made an evening fixture in the hope of attracting a bigger crowd. Around 10-15,000 people turned up, but in other respects the event was a disappointment. The principal race, the Liverpool Summer Cup, attracted only four runners, and another race had only two. This lack of interest by owners and trainers was a sign of the times, and the experiment was not repeated [16].

By 1963 Mrs. Topham had decided that she had had enough and she started looking for a buyer for the course. After a series of secret discussions, she stunned the racing world by announcing on 1 July 1964 that she was selling Aintree to a property development company called Capital and Counties, who planned to build homes for 15,000 people on the site. Mrs. Topham claimed that "the Lancashire public did not support [Aintree] enough to make the fixtures a financial success", and that the demand in the area was for factories and houses. Rising costs and falling attendances were worse at Liverpol than at other courses, and since Tophams were determined that the Grand National should not become second rate she hoped that it might be staged at Ascot in future. To this end, she even suggested that some of the fences might be moved there. Leslie Marler of Capital and Counties added that he was sure the race would continue, "but homes come first" [17].

In the days that followed Doncaster and Newcastle were also mentioned as possible venues for the race, but as *The Times* correspondent noted "the new steeplechase wherever it is can only be a poor imitation of the Aintree Grand National" [18].

It is clear, however, that one of Mrs. Topham's principal aims at this time was to decouple the Grand National from Aintree, and, with this in mind, in March 1964 she had registered the race as a separate subsidiary company, wholly owned by Tophams. At the time this had been justified on the grounds of streamlining the organization and bringing it up to date [19], but once the news of the sale became known it immediately appeared in a much more sinister light.

Both at the time and subsequently, Mrs. Topham was vilified for her decision to sell Aintree to property developers, yet in the context of the time it was not as unusual as might at first sight appear. The early sixties was a time of considerable housing and industrial development, especially on the edges of the big cities, and Mrs. Topham was not the only race course owner to see that there was more money to be made in selling out than in continuing to promote horse racing. Hurst Park (1962), Manchester (1963) and Birmingham (1965) were all first rate courses that closed down at this time, and major races such as the Triumph Hurdle (which went from Hurst Park to Cheltenham) and the Manchester November Handicap (which went to Doncaster) had to be relocated. Had it not been for the uniqueness of the Grand National course, there is no doubt that Liverpool too would have closed down. Mrs. Topham's miscalculation was to believe that the National could, like these other races, be transferred elsewhere without losing everything that made it such a compelling spectacle.

Reaction from Aintree's traditional supporters to the news of the sale was immediate. Lord Derby was quoted as saying "This is the most staggering piece of news I have ever heard" [20]. Lord Sefton said "I hate the prospect of no racing at Aintree. I think it's an appalling loss to Liverpool. [The Grand National] may be run elsewhere, but I do not think there is anywhere suitable. I can see no alternative to it" [21]. He then sought a court injunction preventing the sale, arguing that it was in breach of covenants in the 1949 agreement that the land would only be used for horse racing or, in part, for agricultural purposes. He said that only a few months before he had refused a request from Mrs. Topham to release her from the restrictive covenants. She had referred to the financial difficulties in keeping the course going and said "We want to sell before it is too late", adding "I doubt if you appreciate all we have done to keep the Grand National flag flying at Aintree" [22].

The case was heard before Mr. Justice Stamp in October 1964 and received wide press coverage. Each side used the occasion as an opportunity to blame the other for Aintree's ills, and the dispute was given an added virulence through being to a large extent a class-conflict, and perhaps also one between sexes. Lord Sefton, for example, in his evidence, said that "there had been trouble at Aintree and he had tried in every way to help Mrs. Topham, but quite a lot of her troubles were of her own making". However, even by his own account, he was not very helpful when Mrs. Topham had come to tell him "with tears in her eyes" that she could not carry on, for he told her "that he was not going to discuss it and that she knew he did not discuss business matters with her". His principal concern seems to have been that the end of racing at Aintree "would alter his whole way of life".

Lord Sefton also sought to show that Aintree had been mismanaged by the Tophams. He said that a previous Clerk of the Course had made Aintree a going concern "in spite of the management", and that his successors had been "unable really to do their job owing to the restrictions put on them by the management" [23]. Lord Sefton gave no details of what these restrictions might be, but his general contention that Aintree had been badly managed was supported by his fellow peer, Lord Cadogan, who said that "his impression had always been that Aintree had been steadily run down since the war". Perhaps significantly, he added that "racing people felt they were not really wanted", and that "there seemed no enthusiasm to improve things at all". As a Steward of the National Hunt Committee he had received so many complaints that he had personally inspected the catering and other facilities and found that the amenities were "extremely bad" [24].

Lord Sefton in his evidence, no doubt unwittingly, showed that although he had sold Aintree to the Tophams, he still regarded them as some sort of tenants, and that he thought of the racecourse in some sense as his own personal fiefdom. Curiously, Mrs. Topham seemed also to subscribe, at least in part, to this view, for in her evidence she said that on race days she kept herself very much in the background, adding "Lord Sefton is the host". Mrs. Topham also said that when she first became involved in 1935 "the family considered Aintree would become derelict". In view of the huge crowds which attended the National then, this seems an unduly pessimistic view, and, in the light of later events, can perhaps be seen as a self-fulfilling prophecy. It is also hard to square with Mrs. Topham's enthusiasm to buy the course in 1949.

Mrs. Topham claimed that even with the advent of income from television rights, which by 1963 were worth £34,000, it was impossible to make Aintree a going concern. The net profit had fallen to £10,000 a year, the buildings were too old, and "the whole place was unacceptable to the public". It was her view that even if millions were spent on the course it could not be made to pay, and the National would be better off going to Ascot. Indeed, so fixed were her views that Aintree was beyond redemption that she seemed unwilling to let anyone else try to make a success of it, adding that "the whole place had become rather unpleasant with all the surrounding factories and built up atmosphere" [25].

Amongst all the mudslinging, one comment by Mrs. Topham's lawyer, G.H. Newsom, was overlooked. He said that "it was common ground to all of the witnesses and between the parties that the racecourse was very good, but that the stands were getting old. Tophams of course could not put up new stands without money" [26]. There are several points of interest in this statement. First, however bleak the situation, Mrs. Topham and her ground staff always maintained the course itself to the highest standards, and it is the course, not the stands, which determines the whole character of the National. Tradition cannot be transplanted and there can be little doubt that had the race moved elsewhere it would soon have lost its character and become little more than a long distance handicap. Secondly, it was certainly true that the profits Tophams were making by the 1960s were insufficient to allow large scale rebuilding, but although Lords Sefton and Cadogan were undoubtedly right to complain about the facilities, neither they nor anyone else seems to have been willing at this stage to put any money into improving them. They were quite content to let Tophams carry the can. Writing four years later, Vian Smith caught the ambivalence towards Aintree of many in the racing world at this time, when he said "For years owners and trainers had realised that Aintree was declining as the traditional home of steeplechasing. In public sometimes, and in private often, they had been critical, even despairing; giving their support to other meetings, helping to promote Cheltenham to a stature which rivalled Aintree. Yet they sought to defend it from summary change, just as those who never pass within a cathedral or contribute to its maintenance might rush to defend it from demolition" [27].

Mr. Justice Stamp ruled in favour of Lord Sefton. Mrs. Topham appealed; in May 1965 the Appeal Court also found in Lord Sefton's appeal, but Mrs. Topham appealed again, this time to the House of Lords, and by a majority decision of three to two the Law Lords found in her favour. Lord Sefton was faced with legal costs of £30,000 [28], whilst Mrs. Topham declared "I count it a moral victory. Tophams always understood that they were entitled to act as they did" [29].

It may have been a moral victory, but in some ways the legal verdict solved nothing, for, as had correctly been stated early on in the case, nothing could force Tophams to continue promoting horse racing at Aintree, whilst the local authorities had indicated that they would be unlikely to grant planning permission to any scheme which did not retain the majority of the site for sporting or recreational use. It was also clear, however, that no public money would be made available to buy the course.

Just days before the announcement of the House of Lords' verdict, Mrs. Topham stated her case again in a lengthy interview she gave to the *Liverpool Daily Post*. In this she stated that "in the recent past Liverpool has shown very little interest" in the Grand National, and she estimated the crowd in 1965 as having been "less than half 120,000" (which if true, it may be noted, was still larger than that in the mid-1990s, which the present executive regard as satisfactory). She went on to reveal that "It is not the case that we have *lost* money each year but we have not had the profits to spend on improvements, nor, even more important, for maintenance... I am not prepared to throw away thousands on the course if there is no prospect of getting it back" [30].

Faced with the situation where she was unable to sell the course because of the uncertainty over planning permission, Mrs. Topham had little choice but to soldier on, and in the summer of 1966 she announced that she would stage the Grand National the following year as a "sporting gesture" in order to maintain the continuity of the race. This would mean repainting the stands and bearing "heavy maintenance costs", but she was willing to do it "if it means the race will be saved" [31]. Perhaps this was the magnanimous gesture she presented it as, but she may also have been aware that any income from the course, however small, was better than none.

The 1967 Grand National was one of the most sensational in the history of the race, for this was the year that a loose horse, Popham Down, by running across in front of the 23rd fence, brought the entire field to a standstill, causing the biggest pile-up since Tipperary Tim's year in 1928. John Oaksey, riding Norther, was one of the first to be brought down, and he later described the scene as that of a defeated cavalry charge. Under the headline "National fell apart before my eyes", he wrote that "Horses were everywhere, heads and heels appearing through and above the shattered birch", adding that "If my description sounds incoherent, the only excuse is that that was precisely how it felt" [32]. The unconsidered Foinavon, ridden by John Buckingham and plodding along at the rear of the field, was the only horse to jump the fence unscathed, and by the time the next

The race card for the 1967 Grand National depicting an artist's impression of Captain Becher's fall at the world-renowned brook; the entry tickets are for the Canal Turn enclosure which had a close-up view of the famous pile-up at the twenty-third fence

horse, Honey End, got over, he was too far ahead to be caught. He came home a 15 length winner at odds of 100-1, with Ladbrokes announcing that they would not have to pay out on a single spring double. The fence after Becher's has been known as Foinavon's ever since.

Fortunately, there were no casualties, equine or human, and although there were subsequently calls for tighter entry qualifications and for more gaps in the inside running rail to encourage loose horses to run off the course, Tophams did not come in for the same degree of criticism as they had in the early 1950s. Possibly this was because the race was televised, enabling more people to see what had actually happened, although this was of small comfort to the crowds in the stands who, on a very wet day, were unable to see much of what was happening at the far end of the course – remarkably, there were at that time no televisions in the stands, let alone out on the course. But it may also represent the beginning of a trend for the National to be seen truly as Reg Green has called it, "a race apart", in which anything might happen. This trend could be seen most clearly a quarter of a century later in the aftermath of the infamous "void" National of 1993. One might have thought that all the adverse publicity generated by the latter would have led to a decrease in public interest the following year, but in fact quite the reverse happened, and the crowd in 1994 was actually larger. It almost seems as if some of them were turning up to see if something equally bizarre would happen again!

There is a curious link between the two disasters of 1967 and 1993, for the 1967 Grand National was started by flag after the starting gate mechanism had failed [33]. In that regard at least, Aintree's officials during Mrs. Topham's reign showed considerably more good sense than their successors in 1993, who persevered with the starting gate with disastrous consequences, when it was perfectly obvious to many in the stands that it would have been better to start the race by flag [34]. Had she still been alive, Mrs. Topham would surely have appreciated the irony that, after all the criticisms made of her management of the course, the greatest debacle in the history of the Grand National should have occurred after the Jockey Club, whose members had been amongst her fiercest critics, had taken over.

Although the future of Aintree and the Grand National remained very uncertain in the late '60s and early '70s, Mrs. Topham kept her word and

LIVERPOOL AUTUMN MEETING

THE CHRISTENING OF THE BROOK BY CAPT. BECHER, 1839.

28th OCTOBER, 1972

OFFICIAL PROGRAMME

10p

Printed for **Messrs. Tophams Limited,** by Withy Grove Press Ltd., Thomson House, Manchester M60 4BJ, with the Authority of the Clerk of the Course.

Mrs. Topham experimented with an autumn meeting in 1972

maintained the continuity of the race by staging the three day spring meeting each year until 1973. In 1972 she even reintroduced, for the first time since 1965, a one-day mixed autumn meeting with two races over the Grand National fences. No official attendance figures were released, but it was noted that "the rings appeared to be as full as they usually are on the first two days of the Grand National meeting" [35]. This may not have been enough to make the venture a success financially (and it is significant that there was no further autumn meeting for another twenty years), but it gave much encouragement for those who wanted Aintree to be saved with an expanded programme of steeplechasing. The first of the races over the National fences was the 2 mile 5 furlong B.P. Steeplechase, in which the Queen Mother's Inch Arran beat the former National winner Gay Trip. This was followed by the William Hill Grand National Trial over 2 miles 7½ furlongs, in which Glenkiln, trained at Southport by Ginger McCain and carrying the same colours of Noel Le Mare that Red Rum would make so famous, led throughout, and despite making a number of jumping errors was strong enough to maintain his advantage and beat the dual Gold Cup winner, L'Escargot, who was later to win the 1975 National, by 12 lengths. It was on the basis of this performance that many commentators preferred Glenkiln to his stablemate when it came to the National the following spring. On that occasion, however, Glenkiln's jumping errors let him down badly at the Chair, where he fell, and thereafter it would always be Red Rum who was the stable's star.

With such an uncertain future, there was only minimal investment in the course during this period. The facilities became even more run down and the public became increasingly disillusioned and stayed away. In 1971, for example, the first two days of the meeting were reported to be among the quietest ever. Hotels in Liverpool reported bookings 10% down on the previous year, and the police inspector in charge of traffic control said "Most of our men have been sat on their backsides during these first two days of the meeting... I have never known the traffic to be so light". There seemed to be no answer to what the papers called "the mystery of the missing crowds" [36].

It is hard to make a fair judgement of Mrs. Topham's stewardship of Aintree. She certainly deserves credit for having kept the National going, at a time when no-one else seemed very interested in doing so, but it is equally hard to escape the conclusion that many of her problems were of her own making. Nevertheless, after all the trials and tribulations of the preceding years, it was perhaps fitting that the last Grand National to be held under Tophams' auspices, in 1973, should have turned out to be one of the finest races of modern times, as Red Rum wore down the bold front-runner Crisp to snatch victory on the line and record the first of his historic three wins at Aintree. Despite the continuing uncertainty over the course's future, this was a race which restored Aintree's pride. It also saw the birth of an equine superstar in Red Rum, and there can be little doubt that Rummy's popularity played an important part in reviving public interest in the National at a time when it might easily have disappeared completely.

In November 1973, Mrs. Topham announced that, after negotiations which had lasted nineteen months, she had sold the course for £3 million to the Walton Group, a locally-based property development company,

Proposed plan for the redevelopment of Aintree, 1972, as shown in that year's Grand National race card

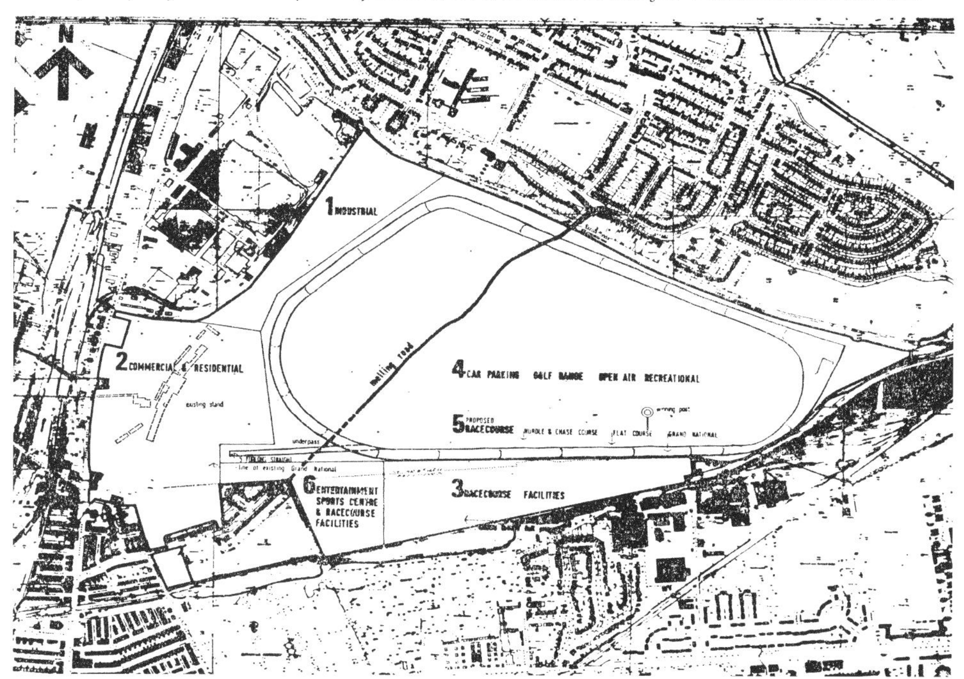

headed by Bill Davies. Part of the deal was an agreement that the Grand National would continue to be run for at least the next five years. At the press conference, Davies was expansive, announcing plans to rebuild the stands, possibly on the embankment beyond the Melling Road (a plan which had in fact first been floated by Mrs. Topham and publicised in the 1972 Grand National race card), increase the number of days' racing and reintroduce grand prix racing on the motor racing circuit. However, it was also clear that much if not all of this depended on his being granted planning permission to develop 40 acres of the site as a shopping complex [37]. Had his plan come off it would have meant radical changes to the course, involving the relocation of fences such as the Chair and the Water Jump, and the end of racing on the Mildmay course; in retrospect, one can only feel a certain amount of relief that it never came to fruition.

The situation that Bill Davies inherited was dire. In the words of *The Times'* racing correspondent, Michael Phillips, Aintree had become "little more than a relic of the past, [and] a monument of those pre-war days when there was no television to keep the crowds at home" [38]. What was badly needed was an administrator of genius, flair and courage, something that sadly became even more apparent during the next two years when Bill Davies ran the course himself. Unfortunately, he proved to be no more adept at public relations than Mrs. Topham had been, got on just as badly with the Jockey Club, and invested no more money in the course than Tophams had done, but attempted to make it more viable by raising the admission charges. In 1975 a County Stand badge for Grand National day cost £20, whilst to go out on the course was £2 [39]. A quarter of a century later these prices do not seem so unreasonable, but at the time they were regarded as unacceptable, and it has to be remembered that they represented major increases over what Mrs. Topham had charged, when, for example entry on to the course at the Canal Turn had been 10/- for a car and driver and only 4/- for each additional passenger [40]. The public stayed away in droves and the 1975 Grand National was watched by only 9,000 people, the smallest crowd on record [41].

Somewhat perversely in view of Aintree's fame as a steeplechasing course, one of Davies's principal ideas was to turn it into a major flat racing course, and he put forward plans to stage a £100,000 "Aintree Derby" at a new meeting to be held in the autumn. Racing's administrators were unenthusiastic and turned the idea down [42].

The flat racing meetings that Davies did hold could hardly have been further away from his publicly stated ambitions for the course. The programmes at the two summer meetings held in June and July 1975 were uninspiring and the prize money derisory, with only one race at the two day meeting in June worth more than £1000. Despite free car parking the public was, not surprisingly, unenthusiastic and the crowd at these meetings was almost certainly numbered in the hundreds rather than the thousands. It was almost painfully obvious that flat racing at Liverpool had reached the end of the line, and one racegoer must surely have expressed the thoughts of many when, after noting the "really rather small crowd", he reflected that "Liverpool would surely be better served by high standard steeplechase meetings in the winter than by more summer flat meetings" [43].

In May 1975 Davies announced the sale of the course to Patrick McCrae, an Irish property dealer, but the deal was never finalised. Negotiations over the future of the course dragged on, until the Jockey Club issued an ultimatum that unless agreement was reached by the 29th December the National would be transferred to Doncaster. At the last minute bookmakers Ladbrokes stepped in and, in a deal worth £1.6 million, agreed to lease the course from Davies, with an undertaking to run the National for the next seven years [44]. It was only after Ladbrokes had taken over and installed John Hughes as the Clerk of the Course that the situation improved. Flat racing was abandoned after 1976 and replaced by a programme of all jumping races, skillfully designed to complement the Cheltenham Festival, which soon proved popular with owners, trainers and the public alike. Sponsorship enabled the prize money of all the races to be substantially increased and far more effort was put into public relations to improve Aintree's by now sadly tarnished image. This included reducing the admission charges, so that, for example, a County Stand badge for Grand National day in 1976 was halved to £10 [45]. These policies were immediately successful. In 1976, the crowd on Grand National day was back to 42,000, and the following year 51,000 saw Red Rum gallop into the record books with his historic third victory in the race [46]. Although

The official souvenir race card for the 1977 National (top right) depicted horses running the wrong way round the course. Red Rum at the start (top left) for the 1977 National in which he achieved his record-breaking third victory. Red Rum races to victory (bottom left) ...and returns with the traditional police escort reserved for all National winners (bottom right)

Aintree's long-term future was not finally secured until the Jockey Club purchased the course in 1984, there can be little doubt that its present-day success owes as much to the work of John Hughes and his team during the Ladbroke era as to anyone else, and it was entirely appropriate that the Topham Trophy should have been renamed the John Hughes Memorial Trophy after his death in 1988.

Notes and references

1. *The Times*, 2 February 1946.
2. *Lancashire Life*, Vol. 4, no.2 (March 1956), p.43.
3. *The Times*, 5 February 1946.
4. *The Times*, 20 February 1946.
5. Hughes and Watson. Long live the National, pp.81-82.
6. *The Times*, 5 April 1946.
7. *The Times*, 6 April 1946.
8. *Liverpool Daily Post*, 4 April 1946.
9. *The Times*, 3 October 1964.
10. *Sunday Times*, 1 June 1980.
11. *Parliamentary Debates: Lords*, 1953-54, Vol. 186, cols. 1041-1054.
12. Hughes and Watson. Long live the National, pp.78-79.
13. *Liverpool Echo*, 10 May 1957.
14. *Liverpool Daily Post*, 22 March 1954.
15. *The Times*, 2 June 1980.
16. *Liverpool Daily Post*, 4 July 1957.
17. *The Times*, 2 July 1964, *Liverpool Daily Post*, 2 July 1964, *Liverpool Echo*, 2 July 1964.
18. *The Times*, 3 July 1964, 4 July 1964.
19. *Illustrated Liverpool News*, Vol. 6, no. 48 (March 1964), p.33.
20. *The Times*, 2 July 1964.
21. *Liverpool Echo*, 3 July 1964.
22. *The Times*, 4 July 1964.
23. *The Times*, 6 October 1964.
24. *The Times*, 7 October 1964.
25. *The Times*, 7 October 1964.
26. *The Times*, 9 October 1964.
27. Smith. The Grand National, p.193.
28. *Liverpool Daily Post*, 31 March 1966.
29. *Liverpool Echo*, 30 March 1966.
30. *Liverpool Daily Post*, 25 March 1966.
31. *Liverpool Echo*, 2 August 1966.
32. *Sunday Telegraph*, 9 April 1967.
33. *Sunday Telegraph*, 9 April 1967.
34. Author's personal diary, 3 April 1993.
35. *The Times*, 30 October 1972.
36. *Liverpool Daily Post*, 3 April 1971.
37. *The Times*, 20 November 1973.
38. *The Times*, 20 November 1973.
39. Prices as given in the 1975 spring meeting race cards.
40. Prices as given on 1968 entry tickets (author's collection).
41. Hughes and Watson. Long live the National, p.33.
42. For a succinct account of the period of Davies's ownership see King. The Grand National, pp.98-101.

43. Author's personal diary, 18 July 1975.
44. *The Times*, 23 December 1975.
45. Price as given on a 1976 badge (author's collection).
46. Watson. The world's greatest steeplechase, pp.10, 12.

14.

The Overseas Challenge

As its name implies, the Grand National was always intended as a race which would attract entries from all over the country, but it also did not take long before it began to attract horses from overseas as well. It is not surprising that the first of these should have come from Ireland, and, as we have seen, the first Irish winner came as early as 1838 when Alan McDonogh rode Sir William to victory. About the next Irish winner, Mathew (in some books his name is spelt Matthew, but this is the contemporary spelling) in 1847, there is a strange story. It seems that the evening before the race a lady "in the mesemeric state" declared that he would win the National, and "what she said in her sleep was the cause of many of her countrymen keeping themselves awake". As a result Mathew was backed down to 7-1 favourite. However, just before the start his price went out to 10 or 11-1. This was probably caused by his appearance in the paddock when he was seen to be "rather stilty on his hind legs... while his colour, a rather mealy brown, gave him a somewhat mean look". There was a close finish that year with several horses in with a chance at the last hurdle, but on the run-in Mathew drew ahead to win by a length. "A considerable amount of cash" returned to Ireland following his win, but since this was at the time of the potato famine in Ireland people were "well satisfied that it should find its way to a place where all classes cry out that they so very much want it" [1].

This story of the clairvoyant predicting the winner of the Grand National has been much embellished over the years, most notably in Con

O'Leary's book *Grand National*, published in 1945, but of its essential veracity there can be little doubt as it appears in the newspaper reports of the time.

Since Mathew's win there has been a whole string of Irish successes, of which the most notable is perhaps Vincent O'Brien's hat trick of winners in 1953, 1954 and 1955, with Early Mist, Royal Tan and Quare Times. However, at the time of writing there has been no Irish winner since L'Escargot over twenty years ago in 1975.

What is less well-known is that there is also a long tradition of interest from continental Europe, which now stretches back for over a hundred and thirty years. Steeplechasing began in France as early as 1830 and the Société Générale des Steeple-Chases was formed in 1863 with its headquarters at

Irish-trained L'Escargot (right) foils Red Rum's attempt to win three successive Grand Nationals; when L'Escargot ran in his first Grand National in 1972, he was the first Cheltenham Gold Cup winner to contest the race since Prince Regent in 1947

Vincennes. The first French-owned winner of the Grand National was The Huntsman in 1862, but since he was both bred and trained in this country and had already run twice in the race for English owners, his win cannot really be regarded as an unalloyed French victory. His jockey and trainer in 1862 was Harry Lamplugh, a Yorkshireman by birth, who, at the age of seventeen, had moved to France and set up as a jockey and trainer there, mainly for the De la Motte family at Chantilly. On three occasions, in 1856, 1857 and 1859, he brought over a French horse, Jean du Quesne, to challenge for the National, but the nearest he came to winning was in 1859 when, after jumping the last hurdle in the lead, he was caught on the run-in and beaten a short neck by Half Caste. After this, he became convinced his team would never realise their ambition unless they bought an English horse, so he went over to England and purchased The Huntsman for his employers, with the specific aim of winning the National with him [2]. Later Lamplugh managed the Duke of Hamilton's chasers in France, but he never really recovered after suffering a crashing fall in a race at Angers, and died relatively young in 1867, shortly after winning his second National with Cortolvin.

Lamplugh may have been unduly pessimistic about the ability of French horses to contest the National successfully, for it was only three years after The Huntsman's win, in 1865, that a French-bred horse won the race. This was Alcibiade, whose victory was the more remarkable because it was his first ever run in a steeplechase. He had, however, been throughly schooled in secret at home. The race developed into a duel between Alcibiade and Hall Court, and Alcibiade, ridden by Captain Coventry, won one of the closest finishes on record by a short head. Alcibiade had been so poorly supported that hardly a cheer was raised as he passed the post. One correspondent rather sourly referred to him as a "cast-off racing plater", but took some comfort from the fact that his victory "made us even with our friends on the other side of the Channel who beat us at Liverpool with our own cast-off (if such a heavy-priced horse as Huntsman can be called one) three years ago" [3]. He ran five more times in the Grand National, finishing third in 1868, fourth in 1869, and eighth in 1870; he fell in 1866 and failed to finish on his last appearance in 1871. In fact, after his victory at Aintree he never won another race.

Alcibiade was followed by the mare Astrolabe, owned by Baron Finot, who ran in 1867 and 1868. In 1867 she was given top weight of 12st 7lbs, without having won a steeplechase in this country, but despite this one correspondent thought that she would "like the country amazingly and it would be nothing astonishing to see the top weight pull through" [4]. But in the race she was brought down by Havelock at the Canal Turn, and despite having been remounted "returned the contrary way" a long time after the rest of the runners [5]. The following year she was described as "long the French cross country crack" and was given 12st to carry, but in the heavy going she was unable to make any impact on the race, and finished a distant fifth, after pulling up at Becher's second time round [6].

Following this there were a good number of French-bred runners throughout the last quarter of the 19th century, most of whom made little

The 1909 winner Lutteur III (Georges Parfrement up)

impact. In fact, the French had to wait until 1909 for their first, and so far only, undisputed victory in the race. This came with Lutteur III, who was owned by James Hennessy, and was initially trained by Georges Batchelor in France. His first win was in a steeplechase at Enghien, and he then won five chases in a row at Auteuil and was only beaten a neck in another, so that by the age of four he had become the most successful and talked-about French chaser for many years. He was then brought over to England as a five year old to be prepared for the Grand National. Based at Harry Escott's yard near Lewes, his first run in England in the Champion Chase at Hurst Park was little short of sensational, for he took on a field of older and much more experienced horses at level weights and beat them easily. His win in the National was almost equally effortless. Held up on the first circuit, he then cruised through the field and took up the running with a mile to go, finally crossing the line two lengths ahead of Judas. He was the last five year old, and one of a mere handful of entire horses, to win.

Lutteur III ran on two other occasions in the National. In 1911 he got stuck on top of the fence after Becher's, and in 1914 he finished third [7].

Lutteur III's jockey, Georges Parfrement, remains the only Frenchman to have ridden the winner of the Grand National. He had many other good wins, in both England and France, and was killed in a fall at Enghien in 1923, only a month after winning the Imperial Cup at Sandown.

Curiously, French interest in the National waned after Lutteur III's victory, and it is only recently that runners from France have reappeared at Aintree. However in 1994 trainer Francois Doumen entered The Fellow, a top-class horse who had already won the King George VI Chase at Kempton and the Cheltenham Gold Cup. The latter win had come less than a month before the National, and with only 11st 4lbs, The Fellow seemed to have an outstanding chance and was backed down to joint third favourite. At the beginning of the second circuit he was well up with the leaders, but then as he began to tire his jumping became less fluent, and, after nearly falling at Becher's, he came down at the Canal Turn when placed fourth.

Doumen returned to Aintree in 1998, this time running Ciel de Brion, ridden by his son Thierry. Starting at 16-1, he fell at the 26th when well in contention.

Encore Un Peu, who was runner-up to Rough Quest in 1996, came close to being the first French-bred winner of the National since Lutteur III. He was, however, trained in England by Martin Pipe.

It was not long after the first French horses appeared at Aintree that entries from central and eastern Europe, and especially the lands comprising the Austro-Hungarian Empire, also began to appear. The first of these, Buszke (Hungarian for 'glorious'), was a Hungarian gelding owned by Count Károlyi, who was entered for the 1868 Grand National after cantering to victory in the big steeplechase at Baden-Baden in the summer of 1867. This was over a course which in some ways was even more testing than Aintree's as it ran through "a wood, the hop gardens, the public garden, potato and cabbage patches and a cornfield" [8]. However, as the best of his opponents in that race had fallen, and as the second-placed horse, Jack of Trumps, was giving him 9 lbs, the correspondent of *Bell's Life* was probably right to say of this victory that "there is nothing decisive there". Moreover, in his four other starts Buszke only managed to win once. He was given top weight of 12 st in the National, and, partly as a consequence of this, attracted little support in the betting market.

Count Károlyi came to Aintree to see his horse run, and both he and Buszke's jockey, fellow Hungarian aristocrat Count Szapáry, stayed at Croxteth Hall as Lord Sefton's guests for the duration of the meeting. Buszke was one of the last two away at the start, but then steadily worked his way up the field, and was well-placed in the van by the time they jumped the water. However, the going was heavy that year and Buszke must have been tiring by the time he pulled up at Becher's second time round, especially as the ground immediately before the fence had been left as plough. He was far from disgraced, but it was to be some time before the next challenger from eastern Europe appeared [9].

Count Ivan Szapáry was born in 1835 and was a younger brother of Count Gyula Szapáry who wrote several works on horse breeding and later held a number of government positions. In the mid 19th century it was said that "The Hungarian is as fond of a horse as an Irishman, and understands him as well as a Yorkshireman". In Hungary horses were mainly bred for racing and riding, and "Gentleman riders of the first class" were numerous [10]. Ivan Szapáry was one of these, and he also, in 1869, drew up a new code of rules for horse racing in Hungary [11]. He never returned to have a second attempt at Aintree.

However, the next aristocratic owner and jockey from Austria-Hungary to take an interest in the race, Count, later Prince Charles Kinsky, was to enjoy an outstanding success, winning on his mare Zoedone in 1883. Kinsky was born in 1858 [12] into a family who had been prominent in Bohemia for centuries. Both of his parents were devoted to riding and hunting, and since his father's master of horse was an Englishman, Rowland Reynolds, it is not surprising that Kinsky grew up an Anglophile too; in later life he recalled that "it became my constant dream as a boy to go [to England], and see it all for myself – to hunt and ride races - and above all win the Grand National! I had quite made up my mind as to that, and the idea never left me until the day I *did* win it" [13].

Kinsky came to England for the first time in 1878 to hunt with the Pytchley from Cottesbrook, and in 1881 he was appointed to a post in the Austrian Embassy in London, which he continued to hold off and on for the next fifteen years. All this time he was not only indulging his love of hunting, but also riding in steeplechases, not just in England, but also in Germany, France and even India. One of his best wins came on a mare called Contegne in the first big steeplechase to be held at Pressburg (now Bratislava).

Kinsky was one of that circle of young, horse-loving aristocrats, who attached themselves to the beautiful but unstable Empress Elizabeth, wife of the Austrian Emperor Franz Josef. The Empress's most recent biographer draws parallels between her life and that of Princess Diana, but, unlike Diana, she was an accomplished horsewoman, who adored both hunting and steeplechasing. On one occasion, when she was staying on the Isle of Wight, a steeplechase meeting was organized specially for her, and Empress, the winner of the 1880 Grand National, was named after her. In 1881 she spent the season hunting in Cheshire, staying at Combermere Abbey, near Wrenbury. It was from there that she went, with Kinsky amongst others, to see the Grand National. They travelled by special train from Wrenbury to Edge Hill, where Lord Sefton had provided a coach to take her to the course. The weather was terrible, with a mixture of snow and rain falling throughout the morning, and a wind "sufficiently keen to cut the edge of a knife", but there was "a loud round of cheering" as the Empress arrived and was conducted by Lord Sefton to a luncheon room that had been specially constructed for the occasion. After lunch, with the Austrian standard flying over the grandstand, the Empress was able to see Woodbrook, trained by her friend Ben Linde in Ireland and ridden by Tommy Beasley, gallop through the heavy ground to win by four lengths [14].

It was whilst hunting in Cheshire that Kinsky first saw Zoedone, and he bought her the following year, after she had finished third in the 1882 National. In the 1883 Grand National she gave Kinsky an almost perfect ride. For much of the first circuit the favourite, Zitella, was in the lead, but as they came back on to the race course Zoedone took closer order and was only a length behind at the water jump. She took the lead on the second circuit and was well clear by Valentine's as Zitella struggled in the heavy ground. Zoedone eventually finished ten lengths ahead of Black Prince, with the favourite a long way back in fifth place. Kinsky thus became the

Count Kinsky on Zoedone

first foreigner to ride the winner. In his native country he became a hero; the Austrian sports writer J. Kunitz-Albertinsky wrote that "Count Karl Kinsky's English victory is the proudest and most brilliant to be gained by a steeplechase rider", and the following ditty was heard in the streets of Vienna:

"Count Kinsky and his Zoedone
Are in a class all of their own." [15]

The following year Kinsky and Zoedone were again first back on to the race course, but this time Zoedone had to carry 12st 2lbs (16lbs more), and in the heavy going it was too much. She was overtaken and finished a gallant fourth.

In 1885 Zoedone was a heavily-backed second favourite for the National, and was coupled in many bets with the Lincoln winner Bendigo. Kinsky received several anonymous warnings that the mare would be got at, and he therefore arranged that she would be saddled in her box and then taken straight out on to the course where he would mount her. Unfortunately, the very thing they wanted to avoid happened. When Kinsky went out to join his horse, there was a great crowd of people around her, and no doubt it was then that she was poisoned. As Kinsky mounted he noticed a spot of blood on her nostril, and soon he realised that his worst fears had been realised. Zoedone fell heavily at the preliminary hurdle on the way to the start, and Kinsky only decided to continue because so many people had backed the horse. On the first circuit Zoedone ran "like a dead thing", jumping with none of her usual fluency; then at Becher's the second time round she suddenly made an extraordinary vertical leap and crashed down in terrible pain. Kinsky was almost equally distressed, one woman in the crowd reporting that "None of us will ever forget the way he looked, for everyone knew how he loved that mare" [16]. Zoedone later recovered but never ran in a race again.

Zoedone's trainer was W.H.P. 'Jenks' Jenkins, who was one of the great steeplechasing characters of the time. The returns for the 1869 Grand National show that in eighth place was a horse called The Robber ridden by Mr. P. Merton for Mr. Doncaster. 'Mr. Merton' was in fact Jenkins, an undergraduate at Merton College, Oxford at the time, who, since the University authorities frowned on student involvement in steeplechasing, used his college's name as a pseudonym when riding; and 'Mr. Doncaster' was a fellow undergraduate named J.J. Atkinson. Jenkins later became a succesful trainer, but Zoedone was his only success in the Grand National [17].

Kinsky continued to ride in England for some time after Zoedone's last run in the National. He became an honorary member of the Jockey Club and was elected to the National Hunt Committee. However, the First World War was a personal tragedy for him. He had to return to his own country, now at war with England, where he volunteered to serve with the cavalry on the Russian front, to avoid having to fight his former friends. After he had left England there was an unpleasant rumour to the effect that he had ordered his groom to poison his hunters to prevent them being commandeered by the British military and used in the war effort against his homeland. In fact, he had asked that if they were commandeered they could be allocated to his friends, and this is what happened, four of his horses being used to carry two British generals, both of whom were old friends of his [18]. He died in Vienna on 11 December 1919 [19], saddened by the collapse and break-up of Austria-Hungary at the end of the war, and his being unable to return to England [20].

In 1889 another of the Empress Elizabeth's circle, Count Nicholas Esterházy, entered his German-bred mare Et Cetera for the National. In his younger days he had ridden in many steeplechases himself, and was the jockey who rode the dual National winner The Lamb in the 1872 Grosser Preis von Baden-Baden, in the course of which The Lamb broke a leg and had to be destroyed. Et Cetera had finished first in the big Manchester Steeplechase in December 1888, but was later disqualified on the grounds of the correct foreign and veterinary certificates not having been lodged with Weatherby's. She came to Aintree with the reputation of never having fallen, but on this occasion fell at the third fence.

The next challenge from eastern Europe came in 1931 when Captain Rudolph Popler rode Gyi Lovam! Although both Popler and Gyi Lovam! came from Czechoslovakia, the horse's name was Hungarian, and it means simply 'Gee up, my horse!'. Gyi Lovam! was a nine year old when he ran at Aintree and had already won the Velka Pardubicka in 1927 and been placed third on another occasion. Popler had won the Pardubicka twice and aimed to become only the second rider to do the Pardubicka-Grand National double, the first having been George Williamson who won the Pardubicka twice in 1890 and 1893 and the National on Manifesto in 1899.

Gyi Lovam! and Popler arrived in England in March 1931 and were based at the Bangor on Dee stable of Stanley Harrison, who had become friendly with Popler whilst riding in Bohemia himself. Gyi Lovam! was 100-1 for the National and never really made any impact during the race. At the end of the first circuit he was last of the twenty nine runners remaining from the forty three starters, and he was still near the rear of the field when falling at Becher's on the second circuit. Popler planned to return to Aintree to renew his challenge, but before he could do so he was killed in a fall at Pardubice the following season [21].

It was fifty five years before another horse from Czechoslovakia was entered in the National, but then there were four runners in nine years. In 1986 the challenger was Essex, an eight year old Hungarian bred horse, who was both trained and ridden by Vaclav Chaloupka. Essex won three of his seven chases in Czechoslovakia, although he fell in the 1985 Velka Parbubicka whilst in the lead halfway round; according to Chaloupka "he became too impatient later on". In an interview before the National Chaloupka said that Essex "goes ahead right from the start, and hates horses in front of him", adding that "he's very difficult to control". It was therefore not altogether surprising that, after blazing a trail in the early part of the race, he failed to complete the course, being pulled up at the Chair, after part of his tack had broken, and well behind the leaders at the time. Nevertheless, this sporting challenge, which involved Chaloupka driving across Europe for four days, complete with horse box, caught the imagination of the public, and it inspired the other Czech challenges that followed [22].

The following year the 1986 winner of the Velka Pardubicka, Valencio, was entered for the National. In this case the horse was brought to England some time before the Grand National meeting, and was trained by B.J. Wise at Polegate. On his British debut at Newton Abbot he was pulled up, and in the National itself, ridden by Roger Rowell, he fared little better, falling at the 25th.

In 1991 Vaclav Chaloupka returned to Aintree, this time to ride Fraze, trained by Vaclav Sebesta at Benesov, thirty five miles from Prague. Fraze came to England having won ten of her twelve starts over fences in Czechoslovakia, and having been beaten by only a neck in the 1990 Velka Pardubicka. This year the journey from Czechoslovakia to Aintree took three days, and Fraze was accompanied by trainer, jockey, interpreter, and two drivers who also doubled as cooks. They arrived in England three weeks before the National, and Chaloupka reported Fraze as being "a good horse with great jumping ability"; unlike Essex, he thought she would settle well and not attempt to dictate the pace. Despite carrying top weight, and having no experience of racing in England, Fraze attracted considerable support and it was reported that some 400 Czechs had travelled over to Aintree to see her run. Nevertheless, starting at 100-1, she fared no better than Essex in the race and was pulled up [23].

Quirinus, winner of the 1992 Velka Pardubicka, was entered for the the void National of 1993, and returned to contest the 1994 running. Owned by a farming cooperative and trained in Slovakia, he was again allotted top weight, and was already tailed off when he fell at the Chair.

To date, there have been no further runners from the Czech Republic or the other lands of the former Austro-Hungarian Empire. Perhaps this is not so surprising when it is remembered that although the Velka Pardubicka is popularly known as the Czech Grand National, the two courses are quite dissimilar, Aintree being a big galloping course with fences that have to be jumped, whilst the Czech track is much sharper, with fences that can be brushed through.

No account of the Eastern Europe challenge would be complete without mention of the Russians, who, at the height of the Cold War, entered three horses for the 1961 National. The deal was arranged by Nikolaevich Dolmatov, the director of a Moscow race course, and Moussia Soskin, a Russian merchant banker. In January they visited Aintree to look over the course and reported that their horses had been training on a course similar to Aintree at Rostov [24]. The Russians' enthusiasm was boosted by a visit of the B.B.C.'s racing correspondent, Peter Bromley, who, three weeks before the race, visited Moscow and showed the jockeys and trainers a film of the previous year's running. He said afterwards that "At the end of the film show everyone stood up and cheered. It was the most marvellous thing they had ever seen".

Sadly, the Russians' preparations for the race did not match their enthusiasm. On arrival in England, at the end of a 2000 mile journey by train and ship, their saddles and bridles were seen to be made of poor quality leather, and their reins appeared too short to cope with the big Aintree fences. Their cause suffered a further blow when their best horse, Epigraf II, was declared unfit to run. Even so, when they walked the course before the race they said "We are not worried", and professed to be more concerned about the open ditches than the big drop fences such as Becher's [25].

1961. Russian entry Grifel parts company with his rider Vladimir Prakhov at Becher's...

...but is soon remounted

Given top weight of 12st, both the two Russian horses left in the race, Grifel and Reljef, started at 100-1. Neither completed the course. Grifel's jockey, Vladimir Prakhov, was pulled out of the saddle by the reins at Becher's first time round. John Oaksey, who was riding Taxidermist that year, fell at the same fence, and he later recalled that "out of the crowd sprang the Russian Chef d'Equipe, who grabbed Prakhov, and heedless of my cries of 'Nyet, nyet' (the only Russian I know), Prakhov was loaded up again and set off for the seventh. He then pulled up and returned, saying something to the team manager. We all assumed, it being in the days of the Cold war, that he was saying to the manager, who we assumed worked for the KGB, something to the effect of 'Go and jump in the Mersey'. We later found out that he had said 'Comrade Colonel, please may I have my whip'. Prakhov eventually pulled Grifel up at the water, having at least completed one circuit of the course. Reljef did not get so far, unseating his rider, Boris Ponomarenko, at Valentine's. Afterwards the Russians were taken on a tour of the countryside and treated to a picnic by Lake Windermere. Prakhov, who won the Velka Pardubicka twice, later became a successful trainer for the Army Sports Club in Moscow [26].

In 1986 the then Clerk of the Course, John Hughes, said he was hoping the Russians would come again [27] but this has not happened so far. In 1991 Russian trainer Makmud Tokov hoped to run two horses but in the event the financial and logistical problems proved unsurmountable [28].

The Spanish challenge is synonymous with one man, the Duque of Alburquerque. Born in 1918, he, like Count Kinsky sixty years before, dreamed of winning the National from childhood. When he was eight years old he saw a newsreel film of the race. "I saw this beautiful race", he said later, "the greatest test of horse and rider in the world. I said then that I would win it one day".

Sadly, that boyhood dream was never to be fulfilled, but it was not for want of trying. In all the Duque had seven rides in the National, but he only completed the course once, when coming eighth on Nereo in 1974. The Spanish Civil war and then the Second World War meant that his first ride at Aintree did not come until 1952 when he was already 33. On this occasion he rode Brown Jack III, who he had bought specially for the purpose and who was trained by Peter Cazalet at Fairlawne in Kent. This was the year when ten horses fell at the first, but Brown Jack III was not among them. However he did not get much further, for he fell at Becher's first time round, leaving the Duque with two crushed vertebrae; for the first, but by no means the last, time his quest for National glory ended in Liverpool's Walton Hospital. In 1963 he rode Jonjo and fell at the 21st, in 1965, on Groomsman, he fell at the 9th and broke his leg, and in 1966, on L'Empereur, he pulled up at the 26th.

However, the Duque's name will always be most associated with Nereo, a horse he bred himself, and then sent to Fred Winter to be trained for the National. In 1973 he had high hopes of doing well, but his stirrup leather broke and he had to pull up at the Canal Turn. Undaunted, he returned again the following year to try again. Considering that only weeks before the National he had sixteen screws removed from a previously-smashed leg, and that he then broke a collar-bone at Newbury just a week before Aintree, it was an extraordinary achievement for a man of 55 to ride at all. That he managed to finish eighth in these circumstances was in its own way a triumph almost as great as if he had won, and the broad smile on his face as he crossed the line told its own story. "I rode Nereo like a sack of potatoes", he is reported to have said. "With some help he would not have been far away and he definitely deserves another chance".

The Duque of Alburquerque and Nereo (left) about to land the Dick McCreery Cup at Sandown from Matchboard; the Duque and Nereo teamed up several times in the National

Sadly, that other chance ended in disaster. In 1976 Nereo fell heavily at the 13th. The Duque was unconscious for two days afterwards and was severely concussed. He had broken two vertebrae, seven ribs and his right thigh. It was not, therefore, surprising, except perhaps to the Duque himself, that the following year the licensing stewards and their medical adviser refused to grant him a permit to ride. For the Duque it was the end of his quest, but Nereo ran on two further occasions, falling in 1977, but finishing 14th in 1978.

Over the years the Duque became a great Aintree character, with some bookmakers offering 66-1 against his getting round. It is worth remembering, however, that he was a first-rate amateur rider, who won many races in Spain, and completed the course in the Velka Pardubicka. His misfortune was that he did not acquire a good Aintree horse until he was too old to have a real chance of winning [29].

The only other Spaniard to ride in the race has been the amateur Jose Simo who rode Gallic Prince in 1990. Gallic Prince was leased for the day by the Spanish airline, Iberia, and was trained by Philip Hobbs. Starting at 100-1, he completed the course and was a far from disgraced 13th of twenty finishers.

In this century it has been the Americans who have dominated the overseas challenge for Aintree's great prize [30]. Racing over jumps in North America appears to have started in the 1840s. There were military steeplechases in Ontario in 1842 and 1843, and the following year the first races over fences in the United States took place at Hoboken, New Jersey. There were also steeplechase meetings at Fauquier White Sulphur Springs, Virginia, from 1846 to 1849, but it was not until after the Civil War that steeplechasing became firmly established in America, with the most important early meetings being held at Paterson, New Jersey from 1865. What is now regarded as America's premier steeplechase, the Maryland Hunt Cup was founded in 1894 [31].

American-bred runners began to appear at Aintree as early as the 1880s but the first to win the National was Rubio in 1908, who was bred in California by James Ali Ben Haggin at his Rancho del Paso near Sacramento. As a yearling he was shipped to England and sold at Newmarket to Major Frank Douglas-Pennant in 1899 for the knock-down price of 15 guineas. Kept first as a hunter, Rubio progressed to steeplechasing in 1903, but, after winning three races, he broke down and it seemed as if his racing career was over. Instead, on the advice of a vet, he was lent to the owner of the Prospect Arms Hotel (now the Saracens Head) at Towcester with instructions that he should be used to pull the hotel bus to and from the local railway station twice a day. For three years Rubio performed this humble duty, but the vet's advice was wise, for in the course of that time he became sound again, and by the autumn of 1906 he was able to go back into training. He ran in seven races during 1907, winning two of them at Newbury and Towcester. However, his most significant race was the Grand Sefton at Liverpool in November 1907, in which he was third, for it was this performance which persuaded his owner to enter him for the National the following spring.

Rubio (Bryan Bletsoe up), the first American-bred winner of the Grand National

The 1908 National was run in very heavy going. Rubio was an unconsidered 66-1 outsider, but he was well up with the leaders from the start and was in the lead as they jumped the water. He was still in the lead at second Becher's, but after Valentine's began to be challenged by his better-fancied stable companion Mattie MacGregor. Rubio's jockey, Bryan Bletsoe said afterwards, "Rubio was going very well, and he kept jumping away from Mattie. I knew three fences from home that I had only to stand up to win", and so it proved. The two stable companions were well clear of the rest of the field coming to the last, but Rubio jumped it much the better and went on to win by ten lengths. The Lawyer III was a further six lengths back in third and King Edward VII's horse Flaxman was fourth.

Rubio's victory was later commemorated in verse, and the magnificent trophy that he won can be seen at the Royal Green Jackets Museum in

Winchester. He ran again the following year, but fell and was immediately retired from racing [32].

The first success for an American owner came in 1923 with Sergeant Murphy. He had been bought by carpet trader John Sanford and given to his son Stephen who was then an undergraduate at Cambridge. Sergeant Murphy was 13 when he won the National, and he remains the oldest winner in the history of the race; remarkably he was to run again in 1924 when he finished fifth and in 1925 when he was tenth at the grand old age of 15. This was the start of a period of considerable interest in the National from wealthy American owners, and it was rare in the 1920s and '30s for there not to be an American-owned horse in the field.

Of these, Billy Barton, who ran in Tipperary Tim's year, 1928, is in many ways the most interesting, for he was not only American-owned and American-bred, he was also the champion American steeplechaser of his day, having won the Maryland Hunt Cup, the Virginia Gold Cup and the American National twice. This was the year in which Easter Hero became stuck on top of the Canal Turn, putting twenty runners out of the race, and by the end of the first circuit only nine horses were left in the race. Billy Barton went clear at second Valentine's, and by the last Tipperary Tim was his only rival left standing. An American victory seemed virtually certain, as Billy Barton had only to jump it to win, but he fell leaving Tipperary Tim to win a sensational race. Billy Barton was remounted to finish second. In 1929 he returned to Aintree for a second attempt, only to fall; later he was honoured by a statue at the entrance to Laurel Park race course in the United States.

Billy Barton was owned by Howard Bruce, whose grandson, Charlie Fenwick, would win the race fifty-two years later on Ben Nevis.

The same year there was another American horse in the field, Burgoright, who had won the 1925 Maryland Hunt Cup. He was not fully fit at the time of the race and was probably not a serious contender; in any case he was put out of the race in the pile up at the Canal Turn.

In 1933 there were two horses with an American interest. The winner, Kellsboro' Jack, was owned by an American, Mrs. Ambrose Clark, but a more genuine American entry was the 1932 Maryland Hunt Cup winner,

Trouble Maker, who was ridden by the American amateur jockey Noel Laing and finished fifteenth.

A further American triumph came with Battleship's win in 1938, for Battleship not only had an American owner, Mrs. Marion duPont Scott (who had also owned Trouble Maker), he was also American-bred and had won the 1934 American Grand National. He was then sent over to England to be trained for the National by Reg Hobbs at Lambourn. The 1938 Grand National was one of the most exciting on record, for, having made several jumping errors early on and nearly fallen at the third last, Battleship came to challenge the long time leader Royal Danieli after the last. The two horses fought it out stride for stride up the long run-in right to the line, and there was then an agonising wait until the judge declared that Battleship had won by a head. Battleship's jockey, Bruce Hobbs, the trainer's son, was only 17 at the time, and remains the youngest winning rider of the race, and Battleship was the last stallion to win. Afterwards he was a successful sire in the United States, and died in 1958.

Not all American attempts were so successful. In 1952, the triple winner of the Maryland Hunt Cup, Pine Pep, was sent to England to be trained for the National. He was entered for the Grand Sefton at Aintree's autumn meeting in order to qualify for the National itself by finishing in the first three; he finished fifth, and that night his owner, William Clothier, sat up all night in his hotel writing a book, which he had privately printed, on "The story of a great horse and a foolish undertaking" [33]. In the light of the subsequent victories by Jay Trump and Ben Nevis, both winners of the Maryland Hunt Cup, one is tempted to think he should have shown greater perseverance.

Rubio had been bred in America, but was owned and trained in England, Battleship was American-bred and owned, but was ridden to victory by an Englishman, but in 1965 there was the, so far, unique achievement of victory for an American jockey, Tommy Smith on an American owned and bred horse, Jay Trump.

Tommy Smith came from a family who had been involved in foxhunting and steeplechasing in America for three generations. His grandfather, Harry Worcester Smith was a wealthy Massachusetts cotton manufacturer who in 1910 sold his factories, machines and patents for six million dollars and devoted the rest of his life to hunting and steeplechasing. Two years later he shipped his string of seventeen horses, accompanied by seven Black grooms, to Ireland for the hunting season, and he was still going out hunting when he was seventy-five in 1940. In his younger days he was also a noted amateur steeplechase rider, and on one occasion, in 1896, took part in a recreation of Henry Alken's famous "Moonlight Steeplechase". The original race probably never took place, but this one certainly did, and Harry Worcester Smith, riding in nightshirt and overalls, was the winner. Tommy's father, Crompton Smith, was also a noted steeplechase rider, so it is no surprise that Tommy first went hunting, strapped in a basket saddle, when he was six months old, and was hunting on his own pony by the age of four.

Significantly for the future, Tommy was also brought up, like Count Kinsky and the Duque of Alburquerque, with the dream of winning the Aintree Grand National. A picture of the Grand National hung over a fireplace in Harry Worcester Smith's home, and at Tommy's christening he held the infant up to the painting and recited Will Ogilvie's stirring poem "Aintree calls!".

With such a background it seems almost inevitable that Tommy Smith should have become a leading amateur jockey over fences in the United States. Jay Trump, on the other hand, came from a far less glamorous background. He was discovered by Smith as a three year old at a minor race course at Charles Town, West Virginia, where he was still a maiden after eight starts on the flat in cheap selling races. Smith purchased him for $2,000 on behalf of his patron, Mary Stephenson, a family friend, and schooled him for jumping so successfully that he won nine races out of twelve starts in 1962-64. These included the Maryland Hunt Cups of 1963 and 1964, the first won in a new record time, and the remarkable achievement of winning all three of Maryland's premier steeplechases, My Lady's Manor and the Maryland Grand National, as well as the Hunt Cup, within a period of less than three weeks in the spring of 1964. As Mrs. Stephenson received the challenge trophy for the Hunt Cup she said "Jay Trump's done everything there is to do in America. Why not try him at Aintree?" Tommy Smith was eager to accept the challenge, and in July 1964

Jay Trump was brought to England and sent to be trained by Fred Winter at Lambourn.

Tommy Smith also travelled over to England, to be taught how to ride in English steeplechases by Fred Winter. He and Jay Trump won their first race in England, the Autumn Trial Chase at Sandown in October, which qualified Jay Trump to be handicapped for the National. After winning a second race at Windsor, he was then entered for the King George VI Chase at Kempton on Boxing Day. The weather was atrocious that year and the field was reduced to just two runners, Jay Trump and Frenchman's Cove. The conditions didn't suit Jay Trump and, after hitting the third last fence, he was beaten an easy fifteen lengths. In the New Year he was entered for the Harwell Chase at Newbury, which he won comfortably. Following this victory he became a 14-1 favourite for the National, but then Fred Winter's horses began to go down with the cough, and although Jay Trump was moved to another yard to isolate him, he began to drift in the betting, going out to 25-1. On the day of the Grand National itself he was priced at 100-6, whilst Freddie started favourite at 7-2. It was these two horses which were to dominate the closing stages of the race.

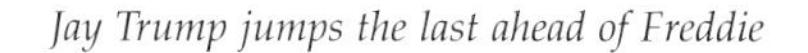

Jay Trump jumps the last ahead of Freddie

Jay Trump (Tommy Smith up)

Perhaps the most remarkable feature of Tommy Smith's winning ride on Jay Trump was the way he followed Fred Winter's instructions to the letter, keeping to the inside thoughout, just as Fred Winter had done himself when winning on Kilmore three years before. Having moved up steadily through the field on the second circuit, as they crossed the Melling Road for the final time only Freddie was in front of them. The two horses jumped the last together, and then Jay Trump drew slightly ahead to jump the last in the lead. But Freddie never gave in and the result was in doubt until virtually the final few strides, with Jay Trump holding on to win one of the most exciting finishes in Aintree's history by just three quarters of a length.

When Jay Trump returned to Lambourn he received a hero's welcome and found Fred Winter's stable decorated with a large American flag. He and Tommy Smith then returned to America and a similarly enthusiastic reception. Nor were they finished then, for, after a period hunting, Jay Trump was put back into training, and won a third Maryland Hunt Cup in 1966 [34].

Three years later there was an American triumph of a different kind when sixty-eight year old grandfather Tim Durant, riding Highlandie, became the oldest jockey to complete the course. Durant was a somewhat colourful character. Having made and lost a fortune on the New York Stock Exchange, he moved to California in the 1930s, where he became a bit-part film actor, riding horses in many films, founded the West Hunt Club, Los Angeles, and acted as Charlie Chaplin's financial advisor. Having ridden in timber races all his adult life, in his sixties he formed an ambition to ride in the Grand National, and during the 1965-66 season he attached himself to Roddy Armytage's stable and bought Ariel III, the winner of the Liverpool Foxhunters the previous year. On this horse he completed the course in the Becher Chase at the Liverpool November meeting, and then began to prepare for the Grand National the following spring. Unfortunately, just before the race Ariel developed tendon trouble; a substitute was found in King Pin, but, after completing two thirds of the course, the partnership had to pull up.

Tim Durant and Highlandie

The following year Durant was back on Ariel III, who refused at the nineteenth fence, thus departing from the race before the mayhem at the twenty-third which only Foinavon negotiated successfully, but in 1968, now riding Highlandie, who he had purchased only a few weeks before the race, it was third time lucky; despite falling at Becher's Durant gallantly remounted and finished fifteenth of sixteen finishers. By this time, like the Duque of Alburquerque, he had become something of an Aintree institution and the crowd gave him a great ovation as he passed the post. He had taken a bet of £500 to complete the course and generously gave the proceeds to the Injured Jockeys Fund.

Having achieved his ambition, and become something of a celebrity in doing so, Tim Durant never rode at Aintree again, but he continued riding in the United States until well into his seventies. He died when aged eighty five in Beverly Hills [35].

The next American success came with Charlie Fenwick and Ben Nevis in 1980. Like Jay Trump, Ben Nevis was a dual winner of the Maryland Hunt Cup, but unlike him was English-bred, having been purchased in this country by Fenwick's father-in-law, Redmond Stewart, Jnr. In America he had a spectacular career over timber, winning twelve races and breaking the course record for the Maryland Hunt Cup. It was then decided to send him to England to try for the 1979 Grand National. He was based at Tim

Ben Nevis and Charlie Fenwick are the toast of Letcombe Bassett on their return from Grand National glory

Forster's yard, and Fenwick, his wife and their three children moved to England to prepare for the race. That year, however, their quest was to be in vain, for Ben Nevis showed little form in races in England, and then in the National itself he was brought down by a loose horse at the Chair.

Fenwick decided to try again the following year. This time his family stayed in America, and he himself became a long distance commuter, flying over seven times to ride Ben Nevis in his preparation races. Once again he showed little form, and he was allowed to start at 40-1 in the National itself. That year the going was very heavy. Ben Nevis was left in front a long way from home and stayed on well to win easily by twenty lengths; only three other horses completed the course. It was not a classic race, but that hardly mattered to the winning connections. "To have it all come together after the disaster the first year", Fenwick later said, "made it the high point of my career".

Japanese involvement in the National has so far been minimal, Fujino-O, a 100/1-shot who completed a circuit before refusing at the Chair in 1966, is the only Japanese horse to challenge for the National. Jockey Tsuyoshi Tanaka rode The Committee in 1995, only to fall at the first fence.

It was not long after the first American runners appeared that the first horses from New Zealand also began to be entered. The first of these was Levanter who was fifth in the 1900 National and fourth the following year. He paved the way for the giant Moifaa who won the race in 1904. In his native country Moifaa won nine of his thirteen races, including New Zealand's principal steeplechase, the Great Northern at Ellerslie, in 1901. He was then bought by Spencer Gollan with the specific aim of winning the Grand National and shipped to England.

There is a romantic story about Moifaa's journey to England from New Zealand, which has it that, after being shipwrecked off the Irish coast, he swam to safety on a small island, where some fishermen found him a few days later. This story appears in D.H. Munroe's 1931 history of the Grand National, in which it is said to have been current then in America, but unknown in England [36], and it has been repeated many times since, often with embellishments, one even stating that Moifaa had swum a distance of fifty miles. A version of the story by Michael Hardwick, which appears in a book called *Strange mysteries from the sea*, has Moifaa abandoned on the deck of the sinking ship "sneering defiance at the sea whose level was rising swiftly to the level of those great shoulders. His expression seemed to defy death..." [37].

Sadly for the romantics, recent research by Richard and Bridget Larn suggests that the story is untrue, although what appears to have happened is almost as strange. They claim that shortly before Moifaa travelled to England, two other steeplechasers, Chesney and Kiora, were also travelling to Liverpool by the SS *Thermopylae* from Melbourne. As this ship was turning into Table Bay at the Cape of Good Hope on 12 January 1899 she struck a reef. All the passengers and crew abandoned ship but the two horses were left on board. On reaching shore, their trainer, Joe Bloomfield, told a Cape policeman called Evans of the animals' plight, and Evans then swam out

The 1904 winner Moifaa

to the ship and brought Chesney back with him, a feat of some courage. However, he was too exhausted to try again to rescue the second horse, and it was assumed that Kiora had drowned. But the next day Kiora was found on a shallow reef some distance away, having escaped from the wreck and swum to safety himself. Both horses were then nursed back to health and resumed their journey to England. Like Moifaa, Kiora ran in the 1904 Grand National, but fell at the third fence. Meanwhile, Moifaa, in the lead from the start, powered his way over the Aintree fences and simply out-galloped the rest of the field to win comfortably by eight lengths. The Larns' conclusion is that somehow the press got mixed up the New Zealand winner with the New Zealand-sounding Kiora, and the shipwreck story became attributed to the wrong horse. The fact that Moifaa's sire was named Natator, which means 'swimmer', may well have played a part in encouraging this confusion [38].

Immediately after the race Moifaa was purchased for King Edward VII by Lord Marcus Beresford. He ran carrying the royal colours in the 1905 National only to fall at Becher's. He then became the king's favourite hack, and at his funeral in 1910 Moifaa followed the gun carriage carrying the coffin, his master's boots reversed in the stirrups as is customary at state funerals.

More recently, in the 1990s New Zealand horses have enjoyed an excellent record in the race, providing two winners in Seagram (1991) and Lord Gyllene (1997). However, perhaps the most famous challenger from the southern hemisphere was a loser. No-one who saw it, will ever forget the epic front running performance of the Australian gelding Crisp in 1973. Despite carrying top weight, he was over twenty lengths in front of the rest of the field for much of the race and jumped Aintree's big fences as if they were hurdles. In one of the most exciting finishes ever seen at Aintree he was just caught on the line by Red Rum, both of them beating the course record by almost twenty seconds. Red Rum was to go on to become the Grand National's finest hero, but, as John Oaksey wrote at the time, through his magnificent failure Crisp "earned a sort of immortality wherever men admire brave horses" [39].

Red Rum (left) wears down the gallant Crisp in the last few strides of the 1973 Grand National

One problem that overseas runners in recent years have faced is that, unless they have some English form, they have been automatically allocated top weight. This has clearly been a major disadvantage, and in December 1998 the British Horseracing Board announced that henceforth the handicapper will have the discretion to allocate weight, rather than automatic top weight, to foreign horses who have qualified for the National by finishing in the first three in the Maryland Hunt Cup, Virginia Gold Cup, Velka Pardubicka or Grand Steeplechase de Paris [40]. This very welcome decision will hopefully result in more foreign horses being entered for the National with a realistic chance of winning.

Notes and references

1. *Bell's Life*, 7 March 1847.
2. Yates. Arthur Yates: trainer and gentleman rider, pp.68-69.
3. *Bell's Life*, 11 March 1865.
4. *Bell's Life*, 2 March 1867.
5. *Bell's Life*, 9 March 1867.
6. *Bell's Life*, 7 March 1868.
7. Holland. Grand National, pp.66-70.
8. Yates. Arthur Yates: trainer and gentleman rider, p.114.
9. *Bell's Life*, 8 February 1868, 29 February 1868, 7 March 1868.
10. Smith. The book of the horse, pp.214, 251.
11. Budapest Lexicon. Vol.2, p.39.
12. In a letter quoted in Richardson and Mason's *Gentlemen riders past and present* Kinsky stated he was born in 1859, but the standard *Oesterreichisches Biographisches Lexicon*

1815-1950 gives his date of birth as 29 November 1858.

13. Richardson and Mason. Gentlemen riders past and present, p.372.
14. *Bell's Life*, 26 March 1881; Welcome. The sporting empress, p.177.
15. Fugger. The glory of the Habsburgs, pp.150-151.
16. Smith. The Grand National, pp.87-88.
17. Bird. A hundred Grand Nationals, p.115; Richardson and Mason. Gentlemen riders past and present, pp.182-185.
18. *The Times*, 16 December 1919.
19. Oesterreichisches Biographisches Lexicon.
20. Smyly. Encyclopaedia of steeplechasing, pp.138-139.
21. Article by Guy Butchers in the 1986 Grand National race card.
22. *Liverpool Echo. The grand double souvenir issue*, 1 April 1986, p.3.
23. *Liverpool Echo. Grand National supplement*, 2 April 1991, p.12.
24. *Liverpool Echo*, 12 January 1961.
25. *Liverpool Daily Post*, 16 March 1961.
26. Article by Marcus Armytage, 'The eastern challenge', in the 1991 Aintree Official Souvenir Magazine, pp.29-31.; *Liverpool Echo. Grand National special*, 30 March 1998, p.10. Hughes and Watson. Long live the National, pp.86-87.
27. *Liverpool Echo. The grand double souvenir issue*, 1 April 1986, p.3.
28. Article by Marcus Armytage, 'The eastern challenge', in the 1991 Aintree Official Souvenir Magazine, p.31.
29. Article by John Oaksey, 'A grand old iron duke', in the 1995 Martell Grand National Official Guide, pp.35-37; Hughes and Watson. Long live the National, pp.114-119.
30. For an overview of the American challenge see the article by Ross Peddicord, 'A transatlantic love affair' in *150 years of the Aintree legend*, pp.63-67.
31. Longrigg. The history of horse racing, pp.221, 231-233.
32. *Liverpool Echo. Grand National special*, 30 March 1998, p.25; Bird. A hundred Grand Nationals, pp.162-163; Holland. Grand National, pp.60-65.
33. McIlvaine. The will to win, p.115.
34. A full account of Tommy Smith and Jay Trump can be found in McIlvaine. The will to win.
35. Holland. Grand National, pp.138-143.
36. Munroe. The Grand National, p.81.
37. Canning. Strange mysteries of the sea, pp.456-460.
38. Aintree '92: the official guide, pp.29-32.
39. *Sunday Telegraph*, 1 April 1973.
40. Aintree web page: http://www.demon.co.uk/racenews/aintree/page11.html.

15.

The past to the future

In the years since the Jockey Club gained control of Aintree, the course has undergone a major redevelopment, and it is now, in the words of the current executive, "enjoying its most successful period in modern times" [1].

The stands, so often the target of complaints during the latter years of the Topham era, have been almost entirely rebuilt. A major fire in the

The Aintree stands as they looked for most of the century

The same view in 1998, showing the new Princess Royal stand in the background

old stands in 1985 proved to be a blessing in disguise as it provided the opportunity to rebuild the oldest part of the County Stand in time for the 1986 Grand National. This was followed by the new Queen Mother Stand, which was opened on the site of the old Tattersalls Stand in 1991. Sympathetically designed to fit in with the older buildings next to it, this stand was an immediate success, and, with its striking clock tower and high pitched gables, rapidly became an attractive feature of the course. At the time, the then Clerk of the Course, John Parrett, spoke eloquently of the importance of the rear of the stand, which overlooks the paddock. "People don't look too closely at the front of a racecourse grandstand, because they're too busy being involved in the racing", he said, "I believe the back of the stand will become a strong feature of the course, which is why we had to avoid building something that looked like a squash court". Parrett pointed out that buildings are important to a top-class sporting venue, and he expressed the hope that in time people would remember the new stand at Aintree in the same way they do the twin towers at Wembley or the Centre Court at Wimbledon [2]. In this view he was surely right, and it is therefore all the more regrettable that the architects of the more modern Princess Royal Stand, opened in 1998, appear to have ignored this approach altogether, and produced instead a wholly unmemorable and featureless building, which is both overpowering and completely out of character with its neighbours. Moreover, although the view from the top of this new stand is breathtaking, those spectators on the lower seated area have a very poor view indeed, as their sightlines are partly blocked by the crowds standing on the adjoining Aintree mound.

The course too has seen some significant changes. In the 1987 National Dark Ivy, one of the fancied runners, was killed in a crashing fall at Becher's, and this was followed two years later by the deaths of Seeandem and Brown Trix at the same fence. These horrific accidents led to much criticism in the press and even calls for the race to be banned. The response was to redesign Becher's in such a way as to maintain its essential features, including the drop on landing, whilst making it safer for both horses and riders. The measures adopted were to widen the course immediately beyond the fence, allowing horses to jump straight ahead rather than on a turn, moving the spectators and photographers further back so as to lessen the chance of their distracting the horses, raising the level of the brook by 30 inches, and building up the ground on the landing side of the fence to remove the slope which often caught horses out; the combined effect of these last two measures was to reduce the risk of horses stumbling on landing and sliding back into the ditch, where in the past some had become stuck [3].

The Queen Mother opened the stand named in her honour at the 1991 Grand National meeting

Despite these measures, which are generally regarded as having achieved their aims, safety remains an issue. The 1998 Grand National, in which three horses died, was run in very heavy conditions, and this led subsequently to some acrimonious exchanges between the Aintree executive and leading trainer Jenny Pitman. As a result a series of additional safety measures were announced in November 1998, including the introduction of a special panel with the power to veto entries on the basis of previous form. It will also assess the suitability of horses for the race, even though they may qualify under the existing criteria. Responding to Jenny Pitman's criticisms of the state of the ground, measures have also been introduced to ensure that the course can be walked in race condition on the morning of the race, and specialist advice on ways of repairing the ground in wet conditions are being sought [4]. All these are eminently sensible steps, which should enable the National to remain the compelling spectacle it has always been, whilst minimising the risks. However, it is not only in the Grand National itself that fatalities can occur, and the death of Bold Account, who was 3 stones out of the handicap, after a fall at the Chair in the 1998 Becher Chase leads one to wonder whether these measures should not be applied to all races over the National fences.

Other changes to the National may also be on the way. In a move to increase the number of better class horses in the race, the age restriction is to be lowered from seven to six [5], and, perhaps more significantly, discussions have begun on changing the way in which the weights are allocated. This would involve constructing a one-off handicap, with account being taken of the length of the race, rather than simply weighting horses according to their British Horseracing Board rating as at present. This would, it is claimed, correct the current unbalanced nature of the handicap, in which often only a small number of the runners carry their correct weight. In 1998, for example, no fewer than 30 out of the 37 runners were technically out of the handicap. The problem is compounded by horses being weighted on their form over distances significantly shorter than the Grand National's 4½ miles, for the weight per length allowance, when based on runs over shorter distances, becomes magnified over the longer trip and gives horses in the 10 st. to 10 st. 7 lbs. section of the handicap a big advantage over runners at the top of the handicap. A one-off handicap could take account of these factors and make the race more competitive as a result [6].

That changes such as these are being discussed is surely a healthy sign, for, despite all the tradition that surrounds it, the Grand National has always been subject to change. The size of the fences, for example, has been a matter for debate since the earliest days, when many campaigned for the removal of the stone wall. In the 1860s there were complaints that the fences were too small, one correspondent writing that "it almost requires a microscope" to see them [7]. It was as a result of comments like this that the Chair fence was raised from 3′ 6″ to its present 5′ 2″ and the open ditch added in front of it in 1862. However, by the beginning of this century, possibly as a result of the development of the park courses, they came in for criticism as too big and "impossible" to jump. This brought a sharp retort from Arthur Yates, the trainer of Cloister, who roundly stated that "the fault does not lie in the conditions of the race or the supposed impossible fences, but to a great extent in the present-day methods of training", and he concluded that "The Grand National has stood the test of time for over eighty years, and it seems a pity because a few half-schooled horses go to post and come to grief that the Blue Riband of Steeplechasing should be subjected to so much unnecessary and I am afraid frequently ignorant condemnation" [8], words which, although written over seventy years ago, seem equally apposite today.

Yates' point about schooling is an important one. For many years horses in the Grand National have had little opportunity to experience the fences before the race itself, and the news that Aintree-style schooling fences are to be erected at the main training centres at Lambourn, Middleham and Newmarket is therefore very welcome [9].

The changes to the course and the conditions which have been introduced in recent years are a recognition that in order to survive and to retain its popularity with owners, trainers and the general public alike the Grand National cannot remain as it was fifty or even twenty years ago. That it remains such an exciting spectacle, whilst at the same time becoming safer and attracting a higher class of entry than was generally the case a generation ago, seems to indicate that they have been generally successful.

Second Becher's, 1990
It's the end of leader Uncle Merlin's challenge as he lands awkwardly, leaving Mr Frisk in a long lead

The last decade has seen many notable races for the Grand National, as well as the debacle of the void race in 1993 and the I.R.A. bomb alert of 1997. Two in particular stand out in the memory. The first of these was in 1990 when Mr. Frisk, ridden by Marcus Armytage, smashed the course record held by Red Rum and brought it below 9 minutes for the first time. The National attracted a high class field that year, including Whitbread winner Brown Windsor, Hennessy winner Ghofar, and, from America, the Maryland Hunt Cup winner Uncle Merlin, as well as West Tip, who had won the National itself in 1986. Conditions were good, and as the runners came back onto the race course for the first time, the majority of the field was still quite closely bunched. In the lead Uncle Merlin was giving a superb display of jumping, reminiscent at times of Crisp's performance in 1973, and in the run towards Becher's the second time an American victory seemed a real possibility. There, however, the race was completely transformed as Uncle Merlin unseated his rider, leaving Mr. Frisk in the lead a long way clear of the rest. He maintained that advantage for about the next mile, but as he came to the last he was being strongly challenged by Durham Edition, ridden by Chris Grant. The two horses jumped the last almost together, and it was from there to the Elbow that Durham Edition looked at his most dangerous. However, Marcus Armytage on Mr. Frisk always had a little more in hand and stayed on well to win an exciting finish, the final margin of victory being just three quarters of a length. At his best Mr. Frisk was a very good horse indeed, and later the same month he showed his class by winning the Whitbread at Sandown, becoming the first horse to achieve that particular double in the same season.

Equally memorable was Rough Quest's win in 1996, the first by a favourite since Grittar in 1982. Rough Quest's victory was especially notable as he had finished second to Imperial Call in the Cheltenham Gold Cup only sixteen days before. He also had the reputation for downing tools once he was in front, so Mick Fitzgerald rode a patient race on him, not taking the lead until catching Encore Un Peu at the Elbow and then staying on to win by one and a quarter lengths. Mick Fitzgerald's comment afterwards that "This was the best twelve minutes of my life. Sex is an anti-climax after this!" has since passed into Aintree folklore and become the definitive description of what it must feel like to ride the winner of the Grand National.

Much of Aintree's recent success is, of course, due to sponsorship. Seagram's involvement was largely responsible for saving the race from possible extinction in 1984, and they received a fitting reward (and surely a sponsor's dream) in the last year of their sponsorship when a horse called Seagram won the 1991 National. From 1992 the sponsorship of the Grand National, and indeed the entire three day meeting, has been taken over by Seagram's subsidiary, Martell. Seemingly unperturbed by the events of 1993 and 1997 (Patrick Martell merely commented "I think we got a little more excitement than we bargained for"), Martell recently signed a new six year contract worth over £4.5 million to sponsor the meeting until 2004. This is the biggest sponsorship deal in British racing history [10].

Sponsorship on this scale means that the prize money at Aintree has never been higher. In 1998 the total amount of added money over the three day meeting was £925,000, an 11% increase over the year before. The Grand National itself was increased by £50,000 from £250,000 to £300,000; over the three years from 1995 to 1998 its value increased by a remarkable 90% [11]. To put these figures into perspective it is worth noting that the added money for the National in 1972 was £30,000, a mere tenth of what is on offer today.

Crowds evacuating the course after the bomb warning in 1997

Sponsorship has also enabled successive Clerks of the Course to build up the rest of the meeting, so that it now contains no fewer than four Grade 1 and six Grade 2 races. These have now become well-established, and it is probably fair to say that for many of racing's professionals they are as much of an attraction at the meeting as the Grand National itself. Certainly no-one who saw the epic battle in 1995 for the Mumm Melling Chase can have doubted that they had witnessed the finest race of the meeting, and perhaps the finest race of the decade over the Mildmay Course. In this race four of the leading contenders, Nakir, Viking Flagship, Deep Sensation and Martha's Son, all jumped the penultimate fence together. Nakir was the first to crack as Deep Sensation slipped through on the inside to take a fractional lead at the last, but on the run in Viking Flagship wore him down inch by inch, whilst Martha's Son also put in a strong challenge on the stand side. It went right to the line, where Viking Flagship snatched a dramatic victory to beat Deep Sensation by the shortest of short heads. The setting may have been less spectacular, but this win was in some ways even more impressive than Viking Flagship's victory in the Queen Mother Champion Chase at

One of the great races over the Mildmay fences, the 1995 Melling Chase. Eventual winner Viking Flagship is sandwiched between Martha's Son (nearest camera) and Deep Sensation at the last

Cheltenham a few weeks before. Viking Flagship was to win the Melling Chase again the following year, but Martha's Son got his revenge when he came from behind to win the 1997 running, beating Viking Flagship into third place on that occasion.

The principal hurdle race at the meeting is the Martell Aintree Hurdle (formerly the Templegate Hurdle), which tests Champion hurdlers over half a mile further than at Cheltenham. In recent years the outstanding performance in this race has been that of Morley Street who won it four times in succession between 1990 and 1993. However, in the late 1970s the popular Irish Champion hurdler Monksfield dominated the race to almost the same extent, winning three consecutive runnings. His first win, when he dead-heated with Night Nurse in 1977, remains for many people the finest hurdle race ever run at Aintree. In this race Night Nurse set out to make all the running, but made a bad mistake at the last hurdle on the far side, which enabled Monksfield to draw almost level. Then Night Nurse made a further mistake at the third last, and from there to the line there

Monksfield (left) forces a dead-head with Night Nurse in the 1977 Templegate Hurdle

was never more than a head between the two horses. They jumped the last absolutely together, and from there until the line neither runner was able to gain an advantage; in the last few strides Monksfield just got his nose in front, but then right on the line Night Nurse surged back, and a dead heat between these two outstanding Champion hurdlers was for almost everyone the perfect result.

Racing of this quality draws the crowds, and it is noticeable that, up until 1998, there has been a crowd of over 50,000 on Grand National day every year since 1977. More remarkably, the crowd on the first two days of the meeting, which twenty years ago was often derisory, has increased dramatically. In 1998 there were record crowds on both the Thursday (14,623) and the Friday (30,523, an 11% increase over the year before). However, on Grand National day itself, there was a remarkable 18% fall from 56,628 to 46,182, the lowest figure since 1976. In public, the Aintree authorities put a brave face on this, Charles Barnett, the Clerk of the Course commenting "I am very pleased with the crowd figure, which is much as we expected because of reductions in capacity in the County area... we are ahead of budget" [12]. This statement glosses over the fact that although the County Stand's capacity may have been reduced, this was more than compensated for by the opening of the new Princess Royal Stand, which Barnett himself claimed would "dramatically increase our high-level viewing to over 5,000" [13]. And although it is good to know that Aintree were ahead of budget, the day itself lost something of the big-race atmosphere that only a large crowd can provide.

It may be that the disappointing attendance on Grand National day in 1998 is a statistical blip, caused partly by people's recollections of the inconvience they suffered when the course had to be evacuated the year before, and partly by the very tight security surrounding the 1998 event which led, amongst other measures, to only very restricted parking facilities being available at the course. Some people may have simply decided that the difficulties of getting to the course and the long queues to pass through security at the entrances were too much effort, and that it would be easier to watch the race on television at home. This is a difficult balance for the authorities to get right, but it certainly seemed to many racegoers in 1998 that the security measures were intruding rather too much on their pleasure on what above all should be an enjoyable day out.

Crowds at race meetings today are generally far less unruly than they were a hundred years ago, and public disorder is now associated more with football than with horse racing. Nevertheless, the local Liverpudlian element, with its sharp Scouse wit, gives the crowd at Aintree an "edge", which is not generally found at other race meetings. There was a good example of this at the Monday Grand National in 1997, after the race had had to be postponed because of the I.R.A. bomb threat on the Saturday, when the then Prime Minister, John Major, decided to take time out of the General Election campaign and attend as a gesture of support. This was almost certainly the first time an incumbent Prime Minister has been to the Grand National, and there was a ripple of appreciative applause as he entered the paddock before the race. By the end of the afternoon, however, a crowd chanting "Three more weeks!" had gathered below the balcony on which he was standing. To his credit, he took it in good part, perhaps already aware that he was going to lose the election, and that their words were only too prophetic [14].

After a twenty year gap, the executive took the welcome decision to reintroduce an autumn meeting in 1992, the centrepiece of which was the Becher Chase, run over 3 miles 3 furlongs over the Grand National course. The weather was atrocious, with heavy rain falling throughout the afternoon, and visibility so poor that it was virtually impossible to see anything of what was happening beyond the Melling Road other than on the television, yet a large and enthusiastic crowd turned up to see a fine win by veteran chaser Kildimo. Since then the meeting has become firmly established in the calendar, yet it has failed to develop as successfully as Aintree's management must have initially hoped for. In particular, the attempt to extend it into a two-day fixture met with a very lukewarm response from the public and sponsors alike, and, after a few years persevering with this format, in 1998 it reverted to being a one-day meeting only. That year the Becher Chase received a notable fillip when it was won for the first time by a Grand National winner, Earth Summit, who jumped the fences as impeccably as he had the previous spring and recorded an easy 16 length victory over Samlee.

Horse racing, both on the flat and over the jumps, has changed enormously over the last 160 years, and many races which were then the summit of every owner's dream no longer have the same prestige. It is, therefore, all the more remarkable that the Grand National should have not just survived but maintained its position as the richest steeplechase in the calendar and as a spectacle which now, through television, attracts a worldwide audience estimated at 500 million [15]. William Lynn would surely approve.

Notes and references

1. 1998 Martell Grand National and Aintree media guide, p.8.
2. 1991 Aintree Official Souvenir Magazine, pp.21-23.
3. 1990 Aintree Official Souvenir Magazine, pp.16-17.
4. Aintree web page: http://www.demon.co.uk/racenews/aintree/page4.html.
5. Aintree web page: http://www.demon.co.uk/racenews/aintree/page8.html.

6. *The Times*, 26 November 1998.
7. Quoted in Willoughby de Broke. Steeplechasing, p.31.
8. Yates. Arthur Yates: trainer and gentleman rider, p.119.
9. Aintree web page: http://www.demon.co.uk/racenews/aintree/page4.html.
10. 1998 Martell Grand National and Aintree media guide, p.6.
11. 1998 Martell Grand National and Aintree media guide, pp.2-3.
12. Aintree web page: http://www.aintree.co.uk/quotes98.htm.
13. 1998 Martell Grand National and Aintree media guide, p.94.
14. Author's personal diary, 7 April 1997.
15. 1998 Martell Grand National and Aintree media guide, p.80.

16.

The Grand National, Aintree: 1836-1998

The following table of race results provides the owner, the name of the winner, the jockey, the starting price, the value of the race to the winner, the names of the placed horses and the number of runners. Grateful acknowledgement is made to John Randall whose earlier work established the definitive results of many of the 19th century returns.

1836 Mr. Sirdefield's ch g **The Duke** a, ridden by Capt. Becher 3/1 £170
2. Polyanthus 3. Cockahoop. 10 ran

1837 Mr. Sirdefield's ch g **The Duke** a, ridden by Mr. H. Potts 6/1 £150
2. The Disowned 3. Zanga. 4ran

1838 Mr. McDonogh's ch h **Sir William** a, ridden by Owner 2/1 £55
2. Scamp 3. The Duke. 3 ran

1839 John Elmore's br g **Lottery** 9yr, ridden by Jem Mason 5/1 fav. £590
2. Seventy-four 3. Paulina. 17 ran

1840 Mr Villebois's b g **Jerry** a, ridden by Mr. B. Bretherton 12/1 £630
2. Arthur 3. Valentine 13 ran

1841 2nd Earl of Craven's b g **Charity** 11yr H. N. Powell 14/1 £430
2. Cigar 3. Peter Simple. 11 ran

1842 John Elmore's b g **Gaylad** 8yr, ridden by Tom Olliver 7/1 £515
2. Seventy-four 3. Peter Simple. 15 ran

1843 6th Earl of Chesterfield's b g **Vanguard** a, ridden by Tom Olliver 12/1 £565
2. Nimrod 3. Dragsman. 16 ran

1844 Mr Quartermaine's ch g **Discount** a, ridden by H. Crickmere 5/1 jt-fav. £535
2. The Returned 3. Tom Tug. 15 ran

1845 William Loft's br g **Cure-all** a, ridden by Owner unquoted £585
2. Peter Simple 3. The Exquisite. 15 ran

1846 Mr Adam's b g **Pioneer** 6yr, ridden by W. Taylor unquoted £695
2. Culverthorpe 3. Switcher. 22 ran
1847 John Courtenay's b g **Mathew** 9yr, ridden by Denny Wynne 10/1 jt-fav. £840
2. St Leger 3. Jerry. 28 ran
1848 Josey Little's br g **Chandler** 12yr, ridden by Owner 12/1 £1,015
2. The Curate 3. British Yeoman. 29 ran
1849 Finch Mason's b g **Peter Simple** 11yr, ridden by Tom Cunningham 20/1 £825
2. The Knight of Gwynne 3. Prince George. 24 ran
1850 Joseph Osborne's b g **Abd-el-Kader** 8yr, ridden by Chris Green unquoted £950
2. The Knight of Gwynne 3. Sir John. 32 ran
1851 Joseph Osborne's b g **Abd-el-Kader** 9yr, ridden by T. Abbott 7/1 £750
2. Maria Day 3. Sir John. 21 ran
1852 J. P. Mason's b m **Miss Mowbray** Mr. Alec Goodman 12/1 £790
2. Maurice Daley 3. Sir Peter Laurie. 24 ran
1853 Josey Little's b g **Peter Simple** 15yr, ridden by Tom Olliver 9/1 £750
2. Miss Mowbray 3. Oscar. 21 ran
1854 William Moseley's b g **Bourton** a, ridden by Tasker 4/1 fav. £795
2. Spring 3. Crabbs. 20 ran
1855 Mr Dunn's b.h. **Wanderer** a, ridden by J. Hanlon 25/1 £730
2. Freetrader 3. Maurice Daley. 20 ran
1856 W. Barnett's br h **Freetrader** 7yr, ridden by George Stevens 25/1 £720
2. Minerva 3. Minos. 21 ran
1857 George Hodgman's b g **Emigrant** a, ridden by Charlie Boyce 10/1 £945
2. Weathercock 3. Treachery. 28 ran
1858 Christopher Capel's b g **Little Charley** 10yr, ridden by William Archer 100/6 £730
2. Weathercock 3. Xanthus. 16 ran
1859 Mr Willoughby's br h **Half Caste** 6yr, ridden by Chris Green 7/1 £820
2. Jean du Quesne 3. Huntsman. 20 ran
1860 Christopher Capel's b m **Anatis** 10yr, ridden by Mr. Tommy Pickernell 7/2 fav. £720
2. Huntsman 3. Xanthus. 19 ran
1861 J. Bennett's br m **Jealousy** 7yr, ridden by Joe Kendall 5/1 £985
2. The Dane 3. Old Ben Roe. 24 ran
1862 Vicomte de Namur's b h **Huntsman** 9yr, ridden by Harry Lamplugh 3/1 fav. £910
2. Bridegroom 3. Romeo. 13 ran
1863 9th Earl of Coventry's ch m **Emblem** 7yr, ridden by George Stevens 4/1 £855
2. Arbury 3. Yaller Gal. 16ran
1864 9th Earl of Coventry's ch m **Emblematic** 6yr, ridden by George Stevens 10/1 £1,035
2. Arbury 3. Chester. 25 ran
1865 Cherry Angell's ch h **Alcibiade** 5yr, ridden by Captain Bee Coventry 100/6 £1,105
2. Hall Court 3. Emblematic. 23 ran
1866 Edward Studd's b/br g **Salamander** 7yr, ridden by Mr. Alec Goodman 40/1 £1,600
2. Cortolvin 3. Creole. 30 ran
1867 12th Duke of Hamilton's br g **Cortolvin** 8yr, John Page 16/1 £1,660
2. Fan 3. Shangarry. 23 ran

1868 6th Earl Poulett's gr h **The Lamb** 6yr, ridden by Mr. George Ede 9/1 £1,570
2. Pearl Diver 3. Alcibiade. 21 ran
1869 John Weyman's br h **The Colonel** 6yr, ridden by George Stevens 100/7 £1,760
2. Hall Court 3. Gardener. 22 ran
1870 Executors of John Weyman's br h **The Colonel** 7yr,
ridden by George Stevens 7/2 fav. £1,465
2. The Doctor 3. Primrose. 23 ran
1871 6th Earl Poulett's gr h **The Lamb** 9yr, ridden by Mr. Tommy Pickernell 11/2 £1,665
2. Despatch 3. Scarrington. 25 ran
1872 E. Brayley's ch m **Casse Tête** 7yr, ridden by John Page 20/1 £1,455
2. Scarrington 3. Despatch. 25 ran
1873 James Machell's b h **Disturbance** 6yr, ridden by Mr. Maunsell Richardson 20/1 £1,960
2. Ryshworth 3. Columbine. 28 ran
1874 James Machell's ch h **Reugny** 6yr, ridden by Mr. Maunsell Richardson 5/1 fav. £1,890
2. Chimney Sweep 3. Merlin. 22 ran
1875 Hubert Bird's b g **Pathfinder** 8yr, ridden by Mr. Tommy Pickernell 100/6 £1,940
2. Dainty 3. La Veine. 19 ran
1876 James Machell's bl g **Regal** 5yr, ridden by Joe Cannon 25/1 £1,485
2. Congress 3. Shifnal. 19 ran
1877 Fred Hobson's ch h **Austerlitz** 5yr, ridden by Owner 15/1 £1,290
2. Congress 3. The Liberator. 16 ran
1878 John Nightingall's br h **Shifnal** 9yr, ridden by Jack Jones 7/1 £1,665
2. Martha 3. Pride of Kildare. 12 ran
1879 Garrett Moore's b/br g **The Liberator** 10yr, ridden by Owner 5/1 £1,695
2. Jackal 3. Martha. 18 ran
1880 P. Ducrot's ch m **Empress** 5yr, ridden by Mr. Tommy Beasley 8/1 £1,145
2. The Liberator 3. Downpatrick. 14 ran
1881 T. W. Kirkwood's ch g **Woodbrook** 7yr, ridden by Mr. Tommy Beasley 11/2 jt-fav. £925
2. Regal 3. Thornfield. 13 ran
1882 3rd Baron Manners's b g **Seaman** 6yr, ridden by Owner 10/1 £1,000
2. Cyrus 3. Zoëdone. 12 ran
1883 Graf Karl Kinsky's ch m **Zoëdone** 6yr, ridden by Owner 100/7 £925
2. Black Prince 3. Mohican. 10 ran
1884 H. F. Boyd's br g **Voluptuary** 6yr, ridden by Mr. Ted Wilson 10/1 £1,035
2. Frigate 3. Roquefort. 15 ran
1885 Arthur Cooper's br g **Roquefort** 6yr, ridden by Mr. Ted Wilson 100/30 fav. £1,035
2. Frigate 3. Black Prince. 19 ran
1886 A. J. Douglas's b g **Old Joe** 7yr, ridden by Tom Skelton 25/1 £1,380
2. Too Good 3. Gamecock. 23 ran
1887 E. Jay's b g **Gamecock** 8yr, ridden by Bill Daniels 20/1 £1,206
2. Savoyard 3. Johnny Longtail. 16 ran
1888 Ned Baird's bl g **Playfair** 7yr, ridden by George Mawson 40/1 £1,175
2. Frigate 3. Ballot Box. 20 ran
1889 Mat Maher's b m **Frigate** 11yr, ridden by Mr. Tommy Beasley 8/1 £1,234
2. Why Not 3. M.P. 20 ran

1890 George Masterman's ch g **Ilex** 6yr, ridden by Arthur Nightingall 4/1 fav. £1,680
2. Pan 3. M.P. 16 ran
1891 William Jameson's b g **Come Away** 7yr, ridden by Mr. Harry Beasley 4/1 fav. £1,680
2. Cloister 3. Ilex. 21 ran
1892 Gordon Wilson's b g **Father O'Flynn** 7yr, ridden by Capt. Roddy Owen 20/1 £1,680
2. Cloister 3. Ilex. 25 ran
1893 Charles Duff's b g **Cloister** 9yr, ridden by Bill Dollery 9/2 fav. £1,975
2. Aesop 3. Why Not. 15 ran
1894 C. H. Fenwick's b g **Why Not** 13yr, ridden by Arthur Nightingall 5/1 jt-fav. £1,975
2. Lady Ellen 3. Wild Man from Borneo. 14 ran
1895 John Widger's ch g **Wild Man from Borneo** 7yr, ridden by Mr. Joe Widger 10/1 £1,975
2. Cathal 3. Van der Berg. 19 ran
1896 William Hall Walker's b g **The Soarer** 7yr, ridden by Mr. David Campbell 40/1 £1,975
2. Father O'Flynn 3. Biscuit. 28 ran
1897 Harry Dyass's b g **Manifesto** 9yr, ridden by Terry Kavanagh 6/1 fav. £1,975
2. Filbert 3. Ford of Fyne. 28 ran
1898 C. G. Adam's b g **Drogheda** 6yr, ridden by John Gourley 25/1 £1,975
2. Cathal 3. Gauntlet. 25 ran
1899 John Bulteel's b g **Manifesto** 11yr, ridden by George Williamson 5/1 £1,975
2. Ford of Fyne 3. Elliman. 10 ran
1900 HRH Prince of Wales's br g **Ambush** 6yr, ridden by Algy Anthony 4/1 £1,975
2. Barsac 3. Manifesto. 16 ran
1901 Bernard Bletsoe's b h **Grudon** 11yr, ridden by Arthur Nightingall 9/1 £1,975
2. Drumcree 3. Buffalo Bill. 24 ran
1902 Ambrose Gorham's b/br m **Shannon Lass** 7yr, ridden by David Read 20/1 £2,000
2. Matthew 3. Manifesto. 21 ran
1903 John Morrison's b g **Drumcree** 9yr, ridden by Percy Woodland 13/2 fav. £2,000
2. Detail 3. Manifesto. 23 ran
1904 Spencer Gollan's br g **Moifaa** 8yr, ridden by Arthur Birch 25/1 £2,000
2. Kirkland 3. The Gunner. 26 ran
1905 Frank Bibby's ch g **Kirkland** 9yr, ridden by Tich Mason 6/1 £2,025
2. Napper Tandy 3. Buckaway. 27 ran
1906 Prinz Franz von Hatzfeldt's ch g **Ascetic's Silver** 9yr,
ridden by Aubrey Hastings 20/1 £2,175
2. Red Lad 3. Aunt May. 23 ran
1907 Stanley Howard's b g **Eremon** 7yr, ridden by Alf Newey 8/1 £2,400
2. Tom West 3. Patlander. 23 ran
1908 Frank Douglas-Pennant's ch g **Rubio** 10yr, ridden by Henry Bletsoe 66/1 £2,400
2. Mattie Macgregor 3. The Lawyer. 24 ran
1909 James Hennessy's ch g **Lutteur** 5yr, ridden by Georges Parfrement 100/9 jt-fav. £2,400
2. Judas 3. Caubeen. 32 ran
1910 Stanley Howard's b g **Jenkinstown** 9yr, ridden by Bob Chadwick 100/8 £2,400
2. Jerry M. 3. Odor. 25 ran
1911 Frank Bibby's b g **Glenside** 9yr, ridden by Mr. Jack Anthony 20/1 £2,500
2. Rathnally 3. Shady Girl. 26 ran

1912 Sir Charles Assheton-Smith's b g **Jerry M.** 9yr, ridden by Ernie Piggott 4/1 jt-fav. £3,200
2. Bloodstone 3. Axle Pin. 24 ran
1913 Sir Charles Assheton-Smith's b g **Covertcoat** 7yr, ridden by Percy Woodland 100/9 £3,170
2. Irish Mail 3. Carsey. 22 ran
1914 Tom Tyler's b g **Sunloch** 8yr, ridden by William Smith 100/6 £3,515
2. Trianon 3. Lutteur. 20 ran
1915 Lady Nelson's b/br g **Ally Sloper** 6yr, ridden by Mr. Jack Anthony 100/8 £3,515
2. Jacobus 3. Father Confessor. 20 ran
3 war-time substitute races were run at Gatwick:
1916 Vermouth 1917 Ballymacad 1918 Poethlyn
1919 Mrs Gwladys Peel's b g **Poethlyn** 9yr, ridden by Ernie Piggott 11/4 fav. £3,590
2. Ballyboggan 3. Pollen. 22 ran
1920 Thomas Gerrard's br g **Troytown** 7yr, ridden by Mr. Jack Anthony 6/1 £4,425
2. The Turk 3. The Bore. 24 ran
1921 Malcolm McAlpine's b g **Shaun Spadah** 10yr, ridden by Dick Rees 100/9 £7,060
2. The Bore 3. All White. 35 ran
1922 Hugh Kershaw's b g **Music Hall** 9yr, ridden by Bilbie Rees 100/9 £7,075
2. Drifter 3. Taffytus. 32 ran
1923 Stephen Sanford's ch g **Sergeant Murphy** 13yr,
ridden by Capt. Tuppy Bennet 100/6 £7,850
2. Shaun Spadah 3. Conjuror. 28 ran
1924 12th Earl of Airlie's ch g **Master Robert** 11yr, ridden by Bob Trudgill 25/1 £8,240
2. Fly Mask 3. Silvo. 30 ran
1925 David Goold's ch g **Double Chance** 9yr, ridden by Major Jack Wilson 100/9 £8,120
2. Old Tay Bridge 3. Fly Mask. 33 ran
1926 Charlie Schwartz's ch g **Jack Horner** 9yr, ridden by Billy Watkinson 25/1 £7,635
2. Old Tay Bridge 3. Bright's Boy. 30 ran
1927 Mrs Mary Partridge's ch g **Sprig** 10yr, ridden by Ted Leader 8/1 fav. £8,215
2. Bovril 3. Bright's Boy. 37 ran
1928 Harold Kenyon's br g **Tipperary Tim** 10yr, ridden by Mr. Bill Dutton 100/1 £11,255
2. Billy Barton, only 2 finished. 42 ran
1929 Mrs M. A. Gemmell's ch g **Gregalach** 7yr, ridden by Bob Everett 100/1 £13,000
2. Easter Hero 3. Richmond. 66 ran
1930 Walter Midwood's ch g **Shaun Goilin** 10yr, ridden by Tommy Cullinan 100/8 £9,805
2. Melleray's Belle 3. Sir Lindsay. 41 ran
1931 Cecil Taylor's b g **Grakle** 9yr, ridden by Bob Lyall 100/6 £9,385
2. Gregalach 3. Annandale. 43 ran
1932 William Parsonage's br g **Forbra** 7yr, ridden by Tim Hamey 50/1 £8,165
2. Egremont 3. Shaun Goilin. 36 ran
1933 Mrs Florence Clark's b g **Kellsboro' Jack** 7yr, ridden by Dudley Williams 25/1 £7,345
2. Really True 3. Slater. 34 ran
1934 Miss Dorothy Paget's b g **Golden Miller** 7yr, ridden by Gerry Wilson 8/1 £7,265
2. Delaneige 3. Thomond. 30 ran

1935 Noel Furlong's bl/br g **Reynoldstown** 8yr, ridden by Mr Frank Furlong 22/1 £6,545
2. Blue Prince 3. Thomond. 27 ran
1936 Noel Furlong's bl/br g **Reynoldstown** 9yr, ridden by Mr Fulke Walwyn 10/1 £7,095
2. Ego 3. Bachelor Prince. 35 ran
1937 Hugh Lloyd Thomas's bl g **Royal Mail** 8yr, ridden by Evan Williams 100/6 £6,645
2. Cooleen 3. Pucka Belle. 33 ran
1938 Mrs Marion Scott's ch h **Battleship** 11yr, ridden by Bruce Hobbs 40/1 £7,598
2. Royal Danieli 3. Workman. 36 ran
1939 Sir Alexander Maguire's br g **Workman** 9yr, ridden by Tim Hyde 100/8 £7,284
2. MacMoffat 3. Kilstar. 37 ran
1940 2nd Baron Stalbridge's br g **Bogskar** 7yr, ridden by Mervyn Jones 25/1 £4,225
2. MacMoffat 3. Gold Arrow. 30 ran
1941 to 1945 no race
1946 John Morant's b g **Lovely Cottage** 9yr, ridden by Capt. Bobby Petre 25/1 £8,805
2. Jack Finlay 3. Prince Regent. 34 ran
1947 Jack McDowell's br g **Caughoo** 8yr, ridden by Eddie Dempsey 100/1 £10,007
2. Lough Conn 3. Kami. 57 ran
1948 John Procter's b m **Sheila's Cottage** 9yr, ridden by Arthur Thompson 50/1 £9,103
2. First of the Dandies 3. Cromwell. 43 ran
1949 Fearnie Williamson's b g **Russian Hero** 9yr, ridden by Leo McMorrow 66/1 £9,528
2. Roimond 3. Royal Mount. 43 ran
1950 Mrs Lurline Brotherton's b g **Freebooter** 9yr, ridden by Jimmy Power 10/1 jt-fav. £9,314
2. Wot No Sun 3. Acthon Major. 49 ran
1951 Jeffrey Royle's b m **Nickel Coin** 9yr, ridden by Johnny Bullock 40/1 £8,815
2. Royal Tan 3. Derrinstown. 36 ran
1952 Harry Lane's b g **Teal** 10yr, ridden by Arthur Thompson 100/7 £9,268
2. Legal Joy 3. Wot No Sun. 47 ran
1953 Joe Griffin's ch g **Early Mist** 8yr, ridden by Bryan Marshall 20/1 £9,330
2. Mont Tremblant 3. Irish Lizard. 31 ran
1954 Joe Griffin's ch g **Royal Tan** 10yr, ridden by Bryan Marshall 8/1 £8,571
2. Tudor Line 3. Irish Lizard. 29 ran
1955 Mrs Cecily Welman's b g **Quare Times** 9yr, ridden by Pat Taaffe 100/9 £8,934
2. Tudor Line 3. Carey's Cottage. 30 ran
1956 Mrs Stella Carver's b/br g **E.S.B.** 10yr, ridden by Dave Dick 100/7 £8,695
2. Gentle Moya 3. Royal Tan. 29 ran
1957 Mrs Geoffrey Kohn's ch g **Sundew** 11yr, ridden by Fred Winter 20/1 £8,868
2. Wyndburgh 3. Tiberetta. 35 ran
1958 David Coughlan's b g **Mr What** 8yr, ridden by Arthur Freeman 18/1 £13,719
2. Tiberetta 3. Green Drill. 31 ran
1959 John Bigg's b g **Oxo** 8yr, ridden by Michael Scudamore 8/1 £13,646
2. Wyndburgh 3. Mr What. 34 ran
1960 Miss Winifred Wallace's b g **Merryman** 9yr, ridden by Gerry Scott 13/2 fav. £13,134
2. Badanloch 3. Clear Profit. 26 ran
1961 Jeremy Vaughan's gr g **Nicolaus Silver** 9yr, ridden by Bobby Beasley 28/1 £20,020
2. Merryman 3. O'Malley Point. 23 ran

1962 Nat Cohen's b g **Kilmore** 12yr, ridden by Fred Winter 28/1 £20,238
2. Wyndburgh 3. Mr What. 32 ran
1963 Pierre Raymond's ch g **Ayala** 9yr, Pat Buckley 66/1 £21,315
2. Carrickbeg 3. Hawa's Song. 47 ran
1964 Jack Goodman's b g **Team Spirit** 12yr, ridden by Willie Robinson 18/1 £20,280
2. Purple Silk 3. Peacetown. 33 ran
1965 Mrs Mary Stephenson's b g **Jay Trump** 8yr, ridden by Mr Tommy Smith 100/6 £22,041
2. Freddie 3. Mr Jones. 47 ran
1966 Stuart Levy's ch g **Anglo** 8yr, ridden by Tim Norman 50/1 £22,334
2. Freddie 3. Forest Prince. 47 ran
1967 Cyril Watkins's br g **Foinavon** 9yr, ridden by John Buckingham 100/1 £17,630
2. Honey End 3. Red Alligator. 44 ran
1968 John Manners's ch g **Red Alligator** 9yr, ridden by Brian Fletcher 100/7 £17,848
2. Moidore's Token 3. Different Class. 45 ran
1969 Tom McKoy's br g **Highland Wedding** 12yr, ridden by Eddie Harty 100/9 £17,849
2. Steel Bridge 3. Rondetto. 30 ran
1970 Tony Chambers's b g **Gay Trip** 8yr, ridden by Pat Taaffe 15/1 £14,804
2. Vulture 3. Miss Hunter. 28 ran
1971 Fred Pontin's br g **Specify** 9yr, ridden by John Cook 28/1 £15,500
2. Black Secret 3. Astbury. 38 ran
1972 Tim Forster's ch g **Well To Do** 9yr, ridden by Graham Thorner 14/1 £25,765
2. Gay Trip 3. Black Secret and General Symons. 42 ran
1973 Noel Le Mare's b g **Red Rum** 8yr, Brian Fletcher 9/1 jt-fav. £25,486
2. Crisp 3. L'Escargot. 38 ran
1974 Noel Le Mare's b g **Red Rum** 9yr, ridden by Brian Fletcher 11/1 £25,102
2. L'Escargot 3. Charles Dickens. 42 ran
1975 Raymond Guest's ch g **L'Escargot** 12yr, ridden by Tommy Carberry 13/2 £38,005
2. Red Rum 3. Spanish Steps. 31 ran
1976 Pierre Raymond's ch g **Rag Trade** 10yr, ridden by John Burke 14/1 £37,420
2. Red Rum 3. Eyecatcher. 32 ran
1977 Noel Le Mare's b g **Red Rum** 12yr, ridden by Tommy Stack 9/1 £41,140
2. Churchtown Boy 3. Eyecatcher. 42 ran
1978 Mrs Fiona Whitaker's b g **Lucius** 9yr, ridden by Bob Davies 14/1 £39,092
2. Sebastian 3. Drumroan. 37 ran
1979 John Douglas's br g **Rubstic** 10yr, ridden by Maurice Barnes 25/1 £40,506
2. Zongalero 3. Rough and Tumble. 34 ran
1980 Redmond Stewart's ch g **Ben Nevis** 12yr, ridden by Mr. Charlie Fenwick 40/1 £45,595
2.Rough and Tumble 3. The Pilgarlic. 30 ran
1981 Nick Embiricos's ch g **Aldaniti** 11yr, ridden by Bob Champion 10/1 £51,324
2. Spartan Missile 3. Royal Mail. 39 ran
1982 Frank Gilman's b g **Grittar** 9yr, ridden by Mr. Dick Saunders 7/1 fav. £52,507
2. Hard Outlook 3. Loving Words. 39 ran
1983 Brian Burrough's ch g **Corbière** 8yr, ridden by Ben de Haan 13/1 £52,949
2. Greasepaint 3. Yer Man. 41 ran

1984 Richard Shaw's b g **Hallo Dandy** 10yr, ridden by Neale Doughty 13/1 £54,769
2. Greasepaint 3. Corbière. 40 ran

1985 Anne, Duchess of Westminster's br g **Last Suspect** 11yr,
ridden by Hywel Davies 50/1 £54,314
2. Mr Snugfit 3. Corbière. 40 ran

1986 P. Luff's b g **West Tip** 9yr, ridden by R. Dunwoody 15/2 £57,254
2. Young Driver 3. Classified. 40 ran

1987 J. Joel's ch g **Maori Venture** 11yr, ridden by S. Knight 28/1 £64,710
2. The Tsarevich 3. Lean Ar Aghaidh. 40 ran

1988 Miss J. Reed's b g **Rhyme 'N' Reason** 9yr, ridden by B. Powell 10/1 £68,740
2. Durham Edition 3. Monanore. 40 ran

1989 E. Harvey's b g **Little Polveir** 12yr, ridden by J. Frost 28/1 £66,840
2. West Tip 3. The Thinker. 40 ran

1990 Mrs. H. J. Duffey's ch g **Mr Frisk** 11yr, ridden by Mr. M. Armytage 16/1 £70,871
2. Durham Edition 3. Rinus. 38 ran

1991 Sir Eric Parker's ch g **Seagram** 11yr, ridden by N. Hawke 12/1 £90,970
2. Garrison Savannah 3. Auntie Dot. 40 ran

1992 Mrs David Thompson's br g **Party Politics** 8yr, ridden by C. Llewellyn 14/1 £112,091
2. Romany King 3. Laura's Beau. 40 ran

1993 **Race Void**

1994 Freddie Starr's b/br g **Miinnehoma** 11yr, ridden by R. Dunwoody 16/1 £115,606
2. Just So 3. Moorcroft Boy. 36 ran

1995 G. and L. Johnson's ch g **Royal Athlete** 12yr, ridden by J. F. Titley 40/1 £118,854
2. Party Politics 3. Over The Deel. 35 ran

1996 A. T. A. Wates's b g **Rough Quest** 10yr, ridden by M. A. Fitzgerald 7/1 £142,534
2. Encore Un Peu 3. Superior Finish. 27 ran

1997 Stanley Clarke's b g **Lord Gyllene** 9yr, ridden by A. Dobbin 14/1 £178,146
2. Suny Bay 3. Camelot Knight. 36 ran

1998 The Summit Partnership's b g **Earth Summit** 10yr, ridden by C. Llewellyn 7/1 £212,569
2. Suny Bay 3. Samlee. 37 ran

Triple winner

Red Rum (1973 1974 1977)

Double winners

The Duke (1836 1837), Abd-el-Kader (1850 1851), Peter Simple (1849 1853), The Colonel (1869 1870), The Lamb (1868 1871), Manifesto (1897 1899), Reynoldstown (1935 1936 his only 2 starts in the Grand National), Poethlyn (1919) had won a war-time substitute race at Gatwick the previous year

Finished alone without mishap

Glenside (1911), Shaun Spadah (1921), Tipperary Tim (1928) and Foinavon (1967) were the only ones not to fall or otherwise be put out of the race, though in each case at least one other horse eventually completed the course

In 1928 at least half the runners were stopped at the Canal Turn on the first circuit when Easter Hero fell into the ditch in front of the fence. In 1967 a pile-up was caused at the 23rd fence by a loose horse, Popham Down, and Foinavon, who had been towards the rear, was alone in clearing the fence at his first attempt

Oldest

15 years—Peter Simple (1853)

13 years—Why Not (1894), Sergeant Murphy (1923)

Youngest

5 years—Alcibiade (1865), Regal (1876), Austerlitz (1877), Empress (1880), Lutteur (1909)

Longest odds

100/1—Tipperary Tim (1928), Gregalach (1929), Caughoo (1947), Foinavon (1967)

66/1—Rubio (1908), Russian Hero (1949), Ayala (1963)

Cure-all (1845), Pioneer (1846) and Abd-el-Kader (1850) were not quoted in the betting

Shortest odds

2/1—Sir William (1838)

11/4—Poethlyn (1919)

3/1—The Duke (1836), Huntsman (1862)

100/30—Roquefort (1885)

Trained in Scotland

Rubstic (1979)

Trained in Wales

Kirkland (1905)

Trained in Ireland

Sir William (1838), Mathew (1847), Wanderer (1855), The Liberator (1879), Empress (1880), Woodbrook (1881), Frigate (1889), Come Away (1891), Ambush (1900), Troytown (1920), Workman (1939), Caughoo (1947), Early Mist (1953), Royal Tan (1954), Quare Times (1955), Mr What (1958), L'Escargot (1975)

Trained in France

Huntsman (1862), Cortolvin (1867)

Bred in France

Alcibiade (1865), Reugny (1874), Lutteur (1909)

Bred in USA

Rubio (1908), Battleship (1938), Jay Trump (1965)

Bred in New Zealand

Moifaa (1904)

Also won Grand Steeple-Chase de Paris

Jerry M. (1912) won France's premier steeplechase in 1910 and Troytown (1920) did so in 1919

Also won American Grand National

Battleship (1938) won the Grand National at Belmont Park, New York in 1934

Also won Maryland Hunt Cup

Jay Trump (1965) won America's premier timber race in 1963, 1964 and 1966, and Ben Nevis (1980) did so in 1977 and 1978

Placed second three times without winning

Wyndburgh (1957 1959 1962)

Placed second twice without winning

Seventy-four (1839 1842), The Knight of Gwynne (1849 1850), Weathercock (1857 1858),

Arbury (1863 1864), Hall Court (1865 1969), Congress (1876 1877), Cathal (1895 1898), Old Tay Bridge (1925 1926), MacMoffat (1939 1940), Tudor Line (1954 1955), Freddie (1965 1966), Greasepaint (1983 1984), Suny Bay (1997 1998)

Most appearances

8 times—Manifesto (1895 fourth, 1896 fell, 1897 won, 1899 won, 1900 third, 1902 third, 1903 third, 1904 ninth)

7 times—Hall Court (1865-1870 1872), The Liberator (1876 1877 1879-1882 1886), Frigate (1884-1890), Gamecock (1885-1891), Why Not (1889-1891, 1893-1896), All White (1919-1922 1924 1925 1927)

Most often in first 3

5 times—Manifesto (1897 1899 1900 1902 1903), Red Rum (1973 1974 1975 1976 1977)

4 times—Frigate (1884 1885 1888 1889)

3 times—The Duke (1836 1837 and 1838), Peter Simple (1841 1842 1845), Huntsman (1859 1860 1862), The Liberator (1877 1879 1880), Ilex (1890 1891 1892), Cloister (1891 1892 1893), Why Not (1889 1893 1894), Royal Tan (1951 1954 1956), Wyndburgh (1957 1959 1962), Mr What (1958 1959 1962), L'Escargot (1973 1974 1975), Corbière (1983 1984 1985)

Most successful owners

3 wins—James Machell (1873 1874 1876), Sir Charles Assheton-Smith, formerly Charles Duff (1893 1912 1913), Noel Le Mare (1973 1974 1977)

Most successful trainers

4 wins—Fred Rimell (1956 1961 1970 1976)

3 wins—William Holman (1856 1858 1860), William Moore (1894 1896 1899), Aubrey Hastings (1906 1915 1924), Tom Coulthwaite (1907 1910 1931), Vincent O'Brien (1953 1954 1955), Neville Crump (1948 1952 1960), Donald McCain (1973 1974 1977), Tim Forster (1972 1980 1985)

Most successful jockeys

5 wins—George Stevens (1856 1863 1864 1869 1870)

3 wins—Tom Olliver (1842 1843 1853), Mr Tommy Pickernell (1860 1871 1875), Mr Tommy Beasley (1880 1881 1889), Arthur Nightingall (1890 1894 1901), Mr Jack Anthony (1911 1915 1920), Brian Fletcher (1968 1973 1974)

Successful as both jockey and trainer

Algy Anthony rode Ambush (1900) and trained Troytown (1920)

Fulke Walwyn rode Reynoldstown (1936) and trained Team Spirit (1964)

Fred Winter rode Sundew (1957) and Kilmore (1962) and trained Jay Trump (1965) and Anglo (1966)

Appendix

The Steeple-Chase

(A poem written to commemorate Cure All's victory
in the 1845 Grand National)

Away! away! though no horn is sounding!
Ride on! ride on! though no prey is bounding!
There's life in the field, there's sport in the wind,
Though no hound doth speak, and no Courser find:-
Away! away! ere the noon see the sun,
A chase shall be tried and a race must be run!

Away! away! see yon fiery gray,
Impatient to bear his load;
Away! away! there's a mettlesome bay
That is hot – without a goad:
Gallant riders are on them, exceeded by none
That a chase has e'er tried or a race e'er run.

Away! away! o'er rut, furze, brake and lawn,
Horses and riders together are gone,
They traverse the plain, and they mount the hill:
O'er each there is rattle and rivalry still;
They top the rough leap, they clear the broad dyke,

Cure-All, winner of the 1845 Grand National

And where danger lies they dare it alike:
No slack'ning of rein, no halting of pace
Are now, midst the heat of that Steeple-Chase.

Still on! still on! like rushing wind,
They dash and leave pursuit behind;
Swifter than vessel on the seas,
When she sails gaily with the breeze,
And cleaves with prow the liquid way,
As hawk the air to pounce her prey:
'Twas a stirring sight, that bright dawn to see
Those gallant steeds stride o'er fence and lea.

See, see, they've conquer'd plough-land and wood,
And now – what! will they tempt the flood
That, at the base of yonder hill,
Shows dull, and deep, and dark, and still?
They will – they will – what fear have they
Of weed or water, depth or spray?
If Caesar cross'd the Rubicon,
Ere fields were dar'd, and fights were won;
If fond Leander swam the stream,
When moon lent not her generous beam;
Shall not the Hunter dangers court,
To revel in his darling sport,
And, in his pastimes, conquer more,
Than king or lover did before?
That flood is rode at, but not past,
That bold dark steed to earth is cast;
The false bank crumbl'd 'neath his tread,
Or bonnier had the rider sped:
Yet now, and though on damp earth lain,
His wrist still bears the buckled rein;
But never again on saddle-tree,
Shall his rider mount for victory,
For see the horse drags his weary length,
And his pain-heaved loins are void of strength;
He has ta'en his last leap, his task is done,
And Kelly slips off, for his course is run:
Poor CLANSMAN sinks before myriad eyes,

His spine is broken – no more he'll rise!
Yet on and onward the leaders flew,
Again they turn and the goal's in view!

See Exquisite leading the panting throng,
As into the straight-run they steam it along;
I'll bet you a poney – no, I'd rather not -
For depend on't there's one that will physic the lot:
See CURE-ALL, th' unknown, he shows a-head;
Hurrah for "the Fielders", the favourite's sped -
'Tis the "dark-un's" chance and the "knowing-coves"
Are out this time – and as I'm alive! -
The "outsider"'s the hero of forty-five!

Dismount, dismount, the gallop is ended,
And cheers, blithe cheers, have the welkin rended;
For "Cure-all" has carried the laurel away,
May he Cure-all our woes at a future day,
And a-Loft flies the banner, and well have all done
Who joined that stiff chase, and that fast course run;
And again with spirits and pluck "like bricks",
May they run the "Grand Steeple" of "Forty-six"!

Bibliography

1. Primary sources

Census returns for 1841 and 1851. (Liverpool Central Libraries)
East Sussex baptism index, 1790-1812. (East Sussex County Record Office, Lewes)
John Johnson Collection of Printed Ephemera. (Bodleian Library, Oxford)
Molyneux Muniments. (Croxteth Hall, Merseyside)
Molyneux Muniments. (Lancashire County Record Office, Preston)
Index of Wills. (Principal Registry (Family Division), London)

2. Books and Pamphlets

150 years of the Aintree legend: official commemorative review. (Newbury, Kingsclere Publications, 1988)

Aintree Racecourse. 1998 Martell Grand National and Aintree media guide. (S.l., Aintree Racecourse and Martell Cognac, 1998)

Altcar Coursing Club. The coursing calendar; containing a complete account of the courses ran at the Altcar Club meetings, from its commencement in 1825, to the present season, 1839. (London, Simpkin, Marshall & Co., 1839)

Anstruther, Ian. The knight and the umbrella: an account of the Eglinton Tournament, 1839. (London, Geoffrey Bles, 1963)

Ashton, John. The history of gambling in England. (London, Duckworth, 1898)

Aspinall, Henry Kelsall. Birkenhead and its surroundings. (Liverpool, Liverpool Booksellers' Co., 1903)

Aspinall, James. Liverpool a few years since; by an old stager.2nd. ed. (Liverpool, Adam Holden, 1869)

Ayres, Michael and Newbon, Gary. Over the sticks: the sport of National Hunt racing. (Newton Abbot, David and Charles, 1971)

Barton, A.M. Where the dream of 'The Great Chase' was born. (S.l., s.n., 1964)

Bayles, F.H. The race courses atlas of Great Britain and Ireland. (London, Henry Faux, 1903)

Bevan, R.M. The Roodee: 450 years of racing in Chester. (Northwich, Cheshire Country Publishing, 1989)

Bevan, William. Prostitution in the borough of Liverpool. (Liverpool, B. Smith, 1843)

Billett, Michael. A history of English country sports. (London, Robert Hale, 1994)

Bird, T.H. A hundred Grand Nationals. (London, Country Life, 1937)

Birrell, Augustine. Some early recollections of Liverpool. (Liverpool, Henry Young & Sons, 1924)

Blaine, Delabere P. An encyclopaedia of rural sports. New ed. (London, Longman, Brown, Green, and Longmans, 1852)

Blair, Frederick G. Some notes on the history of Crosby races in the 16th, 17th and 18th centuries. [Paper read to the Crosby Historical Society ca. 1955; a copy is held by Crosby Library]

Blanning, Charles and Prescott, Sir Mark. The Waterloo Cup: the first 150 years. (Winchester, Heath House Press, 1987)

Blew, William C.A. A history of steeple-chasing. (London, John C. Nimmo, 1901)

Blundell, Nicholas. The great diurnall of Nicholas Blundell of Little Crosby, Lancashire; transcribed and annotated by Frank Tyrer. 3 vols. (Liverpool, Record Society of Lancashire and Cheshire, 1968-1972) *Record Society of Lancashire and Cheshire*, vols. 110, 112, 114.

Blundell, William. A Cavalier's note book, being the notes, anecdotes and observations of William Blundell; edited by T. Ellison Gibson. (London, Longmans, Green, 1880) *Crosby Records.*

Broadbent, R.J. Annals of the Liverpool stage from the earliest period to the present time. (Liverpool, Edward Howell, 1908)

Brooke, Richard. Liverpool as it was during the last quarter of the eighteenth century, 1775 to 1800. (Liverpool, J. Mawdsley, 1853)

Budapest lexikon. (Budapest, Akadémiai Kiadó, 1993)

Canning, John [ed.]. Strange mysteries of the sea: fifty true tales from the deep. (London, Chancellor Press, 1992)

Chandler, George. Liverpool. (London, Batsford, 1957)

Chapman, Henry Cleaver. The American stranger's guide to London and Liverpool at table. (London, Longman, Green, Longman & Roberts, 1859)

Chesney, Kellow. The Victorian underworld. (London, Maurice Temple Smith, 1970)

Chinn, Carl. Better betting with a decent feller: bookmaking, betting and the British working class, 1750-1990.(London, Harvester, 1991)

Clapson, Mark. A bit of a flutter: popular gambling and English society, 1823-1961. (Manchester, Manchester University Press, 1992)

Close, F. The evil consequences of attending the race course exposed in a sermon. (Cheltenham, Griffith and Cunningham, Chronicle Office, 1827)

Conran, Elizabeth. John Bowes: mystery man of the British turf. (Barnard Castle, Bowes Museum, 1985)

Conybeare, William John. Perversion, or the causes and consequences of infidelity. (London, Smith, Elder & Co., 1856)

Cox, Millard. Derby: the life and times of the 12th Earl of Derby. (London, J.A. Allen, 1974)

Craik, Dinah Maria. A life for a life. (London, Hurst and Blackett, 1859)

Curling, B.W.R. British racecourses. (London, Witherby, 1951)

De Gaulle, Charles. War memoirs. Vol. 1. The call to honour, 1940-1942. (London, Collins, 1955)

Dixon, Henry Hall ('The Druid'). Scott and Sebright. (London, Vinton, 1862)

Dixon, William Willmott ('Thormanby'). Famous racing men. (London, James Hogg, 1882)

Dixon, William Willmott ('Thormanby'). Kings of the turf. (London, Hutchinson, 1898)

Dixon, William Willmott ('Thormanby'). Sporting stories. (London, Mills and Boon, 1909)

Dixon, William Willmott. ('Thormanby'). Tales of the turf and the chase.(London, James Hogg, ca.1882)

Dowling, francis. Fights for the championship; and celebrated prize battles. (London, *Bell's Life* Office, 1855)

Egan, Pierce. Pierce Egan's book of sports, and mirror of life. (London, T.T. & J. Tegg, 1832)

Eliot, Elizabeth. Portrait of a sport: the story of steeplechasing. (London, Longmans, Green, 1957)

Enfield, William. An essay towards the history of Leverpool. (Warrington, 1773)

Faucher, Leon. Études sur l'Angleterre. (Brussels, Wouters Frères, 1845)

Fence by fence guide: the Martell Grand National. (Leigh, P.G. Publications, 1997)
Finch, John. Statistics of Vauxhall ward, Liverpool, shewing the actual condition of five thousand families. (Liverpool, Joshua Walmsley, 1842)
Formby, John. An account of the Liverpool races, established in the year 1827, with observations on the conduct of the committee formed in July 1828. (Liverpool, published by the principal booksellers, 1828)
Foster, Joseph. Pedigrees of the county families of England. Vol. 1. Lancashire. (London, Head, Hole & Co., 1873)
Fugger, *Princess* Nora. The glory of the Habsburgs: the memoirs of Princess Fugger. (London, Harrap, 1932)
Gash, Norman. Robert Surtees and early Victorian society. (Oxford, Clarendon Press, 1993)
Gill, James. Racecourses of Great Britain. (London, Barrie & Jenkins, 1975)
Goodlake, Thomas. The courser's manual or stud-book. (Liverpool, Harris & Co., 1828)
Gore's Directory, 1895: annals of Liverpool [reprinted as: An everyday history of Liverpool. (Liverpool, Scouse Press, ca. 1971)]
Graham, Clive and Curling, Bill. The Grand National: an illustrated history of the greatest steeplechase in the world. (London, Barrie & Jenkins, 1972)
Green, Reg. National heroes: the Aintree legend. (Edinburgh, Mainstream, 1997)
Green, Reg. Over Becher's Brook: an A-Z of the Grand National. (Chorley, Sport in Word, 1997)
Green, Reg. A race apart: the history of the Grand National. (London, Hodder & Stoughton, 1988)
Gregson, John Stanley. Gimcrackiana, or fugitive pieces on Manchester men and manners ten years ago. (Manchester, Wilmot Henry Jones, 1833)
Greville, Charles C.F. Memoirs. Part 2. A journal of the reign of Queen Victoria from 1837 to 1852. Vol. 1. (London, Longmans, Green, 1885)
Harkins, Joan. Aintree past and present. (Aintree, Aintree Parish Council, 1995)
Head, Sir George. A tour through the manufacturing districts of England in the summer of 1835. (London, John Murray, 1836)
Herbert, Ivor and Smyly, Patricia. The winter kings: great steeplechasers Lottery to Desert Orchid.(London, Pelham Books, 1989)
Hiley, Richard W. Memories of half a century. (London, Longmans, Green, 1899)
Holland, Anne. Grand National: the official celebration of 150 years. (London, Queen Anne Press, 1988)
Holt, Richard. Sport and the British: a modern history. (Oxford, Clarendon Press, 1989)
Hoult, James. West Derby and Old Swan: historical and topographical. (Liverpool, J. Donald, 1911)
Hughes, John and Watson, Peter. Long live the National. (London, Michael Joseph, 1983)
Isham, Warren. The mud cabin, or the character and tendency of British institutions. (New York, Appleton, 1853)
King, Peter. The Grand National: anybody's race. (London, Quartet, 1983)
Kirkpatrick, J.C. A brief outline of the Liverpool Racecourse and the Grand National. (London, Reid-Hamilton, 1952)
Lamb, Charles L. The story of Crosby. (Liverpool, the author, 1936)

Liverpool Town Books. Vol.2, 1571-1603; edited by J.A. Twemlow. (Liverpool, Liverpool University Press, 1935)
Lofthouse, Jessica. Lancashire villages. (London, Robert Hale, 1973)
Longmate, Norman. The G.I.'s: the Americans in Britain 1942-1945. (London, Hutchinson, 1975)
Longrigg, Roger. The history of horse racing. (London, Macmillan, 1972)
Mason, Finch. Heroes and heroines of the Grand National. (London, Biographical Press, 1907)
Mason, Finch. Sporting recollections of hunting, shooting, steeplechasing, racing, cricketing, &c. &c. (London, Fores, 1885)
McIlvaine, Jane. The will to win: the true story of Tommy Smith and Jay Trump. (Garden City, N.Y., Doubleday, 1966)
Midwinter, Eric. Old Liverpool. (Newton Abbot, David and Charles, 1971)
Munroe, David Hoadly. The Grand National, 1839-1930. (New York, Huntington Press, 1931)
Munting, Roger. Hedges and hurdles: a social and economic history of National Hunt racing. (London, J.A. Allen, 1987)
National Museums and Galleries on Merseyside. Grand National: 150 years of Aintree's steeplechase. (Liverpool, N.M.G.M., 1989)
Nevill, Ralph. Sporting days and sporting ways. (London, Duckworth, 1910)
Nightingall, Arthur. My racing adventures. (London, T. Werner Laurie, 1907)
O'Connor, Freddy. A pub on every corner. Vol. 1. Liverpool city centre. (Liverpool, Bluecoat Press, 1995)
O'Leary, Con. Grand National. (London, Salisbury Square, 1945)
Our mercantile marine: ships and sailors, by an ex-officer. (Congleton, Arthur Rothery, 1872)
Owen, Hugh. The Lowther family. (Chichester, Phillimore, 1990)
Paget, Guy and Irvine, Lionel. The flying parson and Dick Christian. (Leicester, Edgar Backus, 1934)
Picton, James A. Memorials of Liverpool, historical and topographical. 2nd. ed. (Liverpool, G.G. Walmsley, 1903)
Pitt, Chris. A long time gone. (Halifax, Portway Press, 1996)
Pye, J.K. A Grand National commentary. (London, J.A. Allen, 1971)
Reynolds, David. Rich relations: the American occupation of Britain, 1942-1945. (London, Harper Collins, 1995)
Richardson, John Maunsell and Mason, Finch. Gentlemen riders past and present. (London, Vinton, 1909)
Rowlands, John K. Lydiate and Maghull in times past. (Chorley, Countryside Publications, 1986)
Scott, J. Robson. My life as soldier and sportsman. (London, Grant Richards, 1921)
Select Committee on Inquiry into Drunkenness. Report. *British Parliamentary Papers*, 1834, vol. VIII.
Seth-Smith, Michael [and others]. The history of steeplechasing. (London, Michael Joseph, 1966)
Seth-Smith, Michael. Lord Paramount of the turf: Lord George Bentinck, 1802-1848. (London, Faber & Faber, 1971)
Shaw, Frank. My Liverpool. (London, Wolfe, 1971)

Shimmin, Hugh. Liverpool life: its pleasures, practices and pastimes. 2 vols. (Liverpool, Egerton Smith, 1857)
Shimmin, Hugh. Low life and moral improvement in mid-Victorian England: Liverpool through the journalism of Hugh Shimmin; edited by John K. Walton and Alastair Wilcox. (Leicester, Leicester University Press, 1991)
Smith, Egerton. The elysium of animals: a dream. (London, J. Nisbet, 1836)
Smith, Sidney. The book of the horse. (London, Cassell Petter & Galpin, 1875)
Smith, Vian. The Grand National: a history of the world's greatest steeplechase. (London, Stanley Paul, 1969)
Smyly, Patricia. Encyclopaedia of steeplechasing. (London, Robert Hale, 1979)
Snowy, J. The Stanley of the turf. (London, Chapman & Hall, 1896)
Surtees, Robert Smith. Plain or ringlets? (London, Bradbury & Evans, 1860)
Surtees, Robert Smith. Mr. Sponge's sporting tour. (London, 1852)
Taine, Hippolyte. Notes on England. (London, Strahan, 1872)
Thompson, Phil. On the turf: the origins of horse-racing in the North West. (Bebington, Quarry Publications, 1991)
Tocqueville, Alexis de. Journeys to England and Ireland; edited by J.P. Mayer. (London, Faber and Faber, 1958)
Touzeau, James. The rise and progress of Liverpool from 1551 to 1835. (Liverpool, Liverpool Booksellers Company, 1910)
Tyrrel, John. Chasing around Britain. (Swindon, Crowood, 1990)
Vamplew, Wray. The turf: a social and economic history of horse racing. (Harmondsworth, Allen Lane, 1976)
Victoria History of the County of Lancaster. Vol. 3. (London, Constable, 1907)
Walker, P.N. The Liverpool Competition: a study of the development of cricket on Merseyside. (Birkenhead, Countyvise, 1988)
Wallace, James. A general and descriptive history of the ancient and present state of the town of Liverpool. (Liverpool, R. Phillips, 1795)
Walsh, John Henry ('Stonehenge'). Manual of British rural sports. 2nd ed. (London, Routledge, 1856)
Watson, Peter (ed.). The world's greatest steeplechase. (S.l., Ladbroke Grand National Ltd., 1982)
Wearing, J.P. The London stage: a calendar of plays and players. 3 series, covering 1900-1909, 1910-1919 and 1920-1924. (Metuchen, NJ, Scarecrow Press, 1981, 1982 and 1984)
Weeton, Ellen. Miss Weeton: journal of a governess, 1807-1811; edited by Edward Hall. (London, Oxford University Press, 1936)
Welcome, John. The sporting empress. (London, Michael Joseph, 1975)
Welcome, John. The sporting world of R.S. Surtees. (Oxford, Oxford University Press, 1982)
Whale, Derek M. Lost villages of Liverpool. Parts 1-2. (Prescot, T. Stephenson & Sons, 1984)
Wilkinson, Dyke. A wasted life. (London, Grant Richards, 1902)
Willoughby de Broke, *Lord* [and others]. Steeplechasing. (London, Seeley Service, 1954) *The Lonsdale Library*, vol. XXXII.
Wilton, Thomas Egerton, *Earl of*. On the sports and pursuits of the English, as bearing upon their national character. (London, Harrison, 1868)
Winskill, Peter Turner. The temperance movement and its workers. (London, Blackie, 1893)

Yates, Arthur. Arthur Yates, trainer and gentleman rider: an autobiography. (London, Grant Richards, 1924)

3. Newspapers and Periodicals

All the Year Round
Annals of Sporting and Fancy Gazette
Army List
Army Service Corps Journal
Baily's Magazine of Sports and Pastimes
Bell's Life in London and Sporting Chronicle
Dexter's Turf Times
The Field Quarterly Magazine and Review
Gentleman's Magazine
Gore's Directory of Liverpool and its environs
Gore's General Advertiser
Greyhound Stud Book
Household Words
Illustrated London News
Lancashire Life
Liverpool and Merseyside Illustrated afterwards the *Illustrated Liverpool News Liverpool Commercial Chronicle* afterwards the *Liverpool Chronicle*
Liverpool Courier
Liverpool Daily Post
Liverpool Echo
Liverpool Evening Express
Liverpool Mercury
Liverpool Review
Liverpool Standard
Liverpool Times
Notes and Queries
Perry's Bankrupt and Insolvent Gazette
Porcupine
Racing Calendar
Sporting Magazine
Sporting Review
Sportsman's Magazine
The Stage
Steeple Chase Calendar
Sunday Telegraph
Sunday Times
The Times
Williamson's Liverpool Advertiser

4. Maps

1786. The county palatine of Lancaster, surveyed by W. Yates, engraved by T. Billings. 1: 63,360.
1830. A map of the county palatine of Lancaster divided into hundreds and parishes; from an actual survey made in the years 1828 and 1829 by G. Hennett. H. Teesdale & Co. 1: 85,000.
1849-50. Ordnance Survey 6" survey. 1st edition. Lancashire, sheets 91 and 99.

The Steeple-Chase: note on values

All monetary sums in the text are expressed as contemporary figures. Obviously the purchasing power of the pound has changed over time, and converting these sums into their present day values is a difficult task over which there is room for considerable disagreement amongst economic historians.

For the twentieth century a number of time series have been created, largely based on the retail price index and the pre-war cost of living index. *Whitaker's Almanack* gives the following figures as the comparable purchasing power of £1 in 1997:

Year	Value	Year	Value
1914	56.25	1950	17.50
1920	22.50	1960	12.50
1930	35.00	1970	8.51
1938	35.80	1980	2.36
1946	21.28	1990	1.25

A slightly different set of figures is given by Oksana Newman and Allan Foster in their book *The value of a pound* (1995), which takes 1993 as the base year:

Year	Value	Year	Value
1900	35.87	1950	13.70
1914	31.33	1960	9.24
1920	13.91	1970	6.47
1930	18.82	1980	2.06
1938	19.65	1990	1.18
1946	15.42		

Before 1900 there is less data available from which to make these calculations, and it becomes harder to make a direct comparison, not least because there are more regional variations. The following figures, giving the comparable purchasing power of £1 in November 1998, have been provided by the Bank of England Reference Library. They should be regarded as only approximate:

Year	Value	Year	Value
1890	51.37	1830	40.10
1880	43.26	1820	33.55
1870	41.10	1800	28.84
1860	42.15	1780	56.69
1850	46.97	1770	56.69
1840	35.74		

Picture acknowledgements

The author and publishers are most grateful to George Selwyn for providing the majority of the illustrations for this book, including all the specially-commissioned contemporary shots of Aintree race course and many others from his extensive library.

Grateful acknowledgement is also made to the following for permission to reproduce their copyright photographs and works:

Ordnance Survey

British Sporting Art Trust

Liverpool Central Libraries

The Trustees of the National Museums and Galleries on Merseyside

Bodleian Library, University of Oxford

Sid Lawley

Rouch Willmott Thoroughbred Library

Press Association

Illustrated London News

Liverpool Daily Post & Echo

Whilst every effort has been made to trace the copyright holders of all the illustrations produced in this book, this has not been possible in every case. The publishers will be pleased to rectify any omissions in future printings.

Index

Index